D1724012

Genders and Sexualities in the Social Sciences

Series Editors: **Victoria Robinson**, University of Sheffield, UK and **Diane Richardson**, University of Newcastle, UK

Editorial Board: **Raewyn Connell**, University of Sydney, Australia, **Kathy Davis**, Utrecht University, the Netherlands, **Stevi Jackson**, University of York, UK, **Michael Kimmel**, State University of New York, Stony Brook, USA, **Kimiko Kimoto**, Hitotsubashi University, Japan, **Jasbir Puar**, Rutgers University, USA, **Steven Seidman**, State University of New York, Albany, USA, **Carol Smart**, University of Manchester, UK, **Liz Stanley**, University of Edinburgh, UK, **Gill Valentine**, University of Leeds, UK, **Jeffrey Weeks**, South Bank University, UK, **Kath Woodward**, The Open University, UK

Titles include:

Yvette Taylor, Sally Hines and Mark E. Casey (*editors*)
THEORIZING INTERSECTIONALITY AND SEXUALITY

Thomas Thurnell-Read and Mark Casey (*editors*)
MEN, MASCULINITIES, TRAVEL AND TOURISM

S. Hines and Y. Taylor (*editors*)
SEXUALITIES: PAST REFLECTIONS, FUTURE DIRECTIONS

Yvette Taylor, Michelle Addison (*editors*)
QUEER PRESENCES AND ABSENCES

Kath Woodward
SEX POWER AND THE GAMES

Genders and Sexualities in the Social Sciences
Series Standing Order ISBN 978–0–230–27254–5 hardback
978–0–230–27255–2 paperback
(*outside North America only*)

You can receive future titles in this series as they are published by placing a standing order. Please contact your bookseller or, in case of difficulty, write to us at the address below with your name and address, the title of the series and the ISBN quoted above.

Customer Services Department, Macmillan Distribution Ltd, Houndmills, Basingstoke, Hampshire RG21 6XS, England

Lesbian Lives in Soviet and Post-Soviet Russia

Post/Socialism and Gendered Sexualities

Francesca Stella
University of Glasgow

First published 2015 by
PALGRAVE MACMILLAN

Palgrave Macmillan in the UK is an imprint of Macmillan Publishers Limited, registered in England, company number 785998, of Houndmills, Basingstoke, Hampshire RG21 6XS.

Palgrave Macmillan in the US is a division of St Martin's Press LLC, 175 Fifth Avenue, New York, NY 10010.

Palgrave Macmillan is the global academic imprint of the above companies and has companies and representatives throughout the world.

Palgrave® and Macmillan® are registered trademarks in the United States, the United Kingdom, Europe and other countries.

ISBN 978–1–137–32123–7

This book is printed on paper suitable for recycling and made from fully managed and sustained forest sources. Logging, pulping and manufacturing processes are expected to conform to the environmental regulations of the country of origin.

A catalogue record for this book is available from the British Library.

A catalog record for this book is available from the Library of Congress.

Transferred to Digital Printing in 2015

Contents

Acknowledgements

First of all, I would like to thank the women I met in Russia, who shared their experiences and thoughts with me in interviews and general conversation, and often generously helped out in the projects and welcomed me into their homes, introducing me to their friends and family. It has been a privilege to get a glimpse into their lives, and I hope I did justice to their stories in the pages that follow. I have very warm memories of my time in Russia, and over the years I have been lucky to meet friends, activists and academics who remain a source of inspiration: I remember them here with affection and respect. Some people went out of their way to help me, particularly during my first visits to Russia, when I arrived with only a couple of telephone numbers as clues to follow. Activists and regulars at the Moscow Gay and Lesbian Archive, at the organisation *Ia+Ia* and at initiatives variously linked and affiliated with them provided invaluable help. Special thanks to Olgerta Kharitonova for her unfailing support over the years, and for allowing me to disseminate findings through the pages of the lesbian zine *Ostrov*. Ania and Olia, Raia and El'vira put me on the right track in Ul'ianovsk, where I also benefited from the support of staff at the REGION research centre; Masha, Natalia and Sveta translated two conference papers into Russian. This monograph is dedicated to you all.

The monograph is based on empirical data from two separate projects, which were supported by various institutions and funding bodies; I gratefully acknowledge their support. The original research project ('Lesbian Identities and Everyday Spaces in Contemporary Urban Russia', 2003–2008) was funded through a doctoral scholarship from the University of Glasgow, and additional funding for fieldwork was provided by the Carnegie Trust for the Universities of Scotland, the British Association for Slavonic and East European Studies and the Department of Central and East European Studies (CEES), University of Glasgow. The follow-up project ('Female Homosexuality and Actually Existing Socialism: An Oral History Project of Lesbian Relations in Soviet Russia', 2010–2011) was funded by a small grant from the Carnegie Trust for the Universities of Scotland. Valuable time to think, revise and write up the original work as a monograph was provided by an Economic and Social Research Council (ESRC) postdoctoral fellowship ('Queer Lives and Urban Space: From Russia to the New Europe', ES/I038497/1, 2012).

I would also like to thank all those who over the years have shared ideas, advice, coffee, food and office space with me. Singling out people for special mention is difficult and I apologise in advance for (inevitably) missing people out. I am grateful to Rebecca Kay and Moya Flynn, who supervised the doctoral research where it all began, for their perceptive suggestions, for their support and friendship over the years and for teaching me by example. Hilary Pilkington and Matthew Waites provided insightful comments on the doctoral thesis, and Dan Healey suggested valuable clues to follow. Thanks for support and encouragement to staff and fellow students at CEES during my time there, first as a doctoral student and later as a member of staff – particularly to Jon Oldfield, Elwira Grossman and Claire McManus. I spent a year as ESRC Research Fellow at London South Bank University (LSBU) – thanks to Yvette Taylor, my mentor during the fellowship, for her support, and to everyone at the Weeks Centre for Social and Policy Research. Also, thanks to Mark Freeman, Robert Kulpa and Antoine Rogers for welcoming me to London. After my spell in London, I returned to the University of Glasgow, where I have had the pleasure to work with great colleagues and students. Working across the subject areas of sociology and Central and East European studies has challenged and inspired me, and I am privileged to be part of GRAMNet (Glasgow Refugees, Asylum and Migration Network), a wonderful mix of people. Over the years, my students have taught me a lot, kept me on my toes and reminded me what universities are for. Thanks to the two anonymous reviewers for their constructive comments on the book proposal and the final manuscript. Finally, thanks to the editorial team at Palgrave for their patience and support.

Last but not least, I would like to thank all the people whose company and support have been hugely important to me outside of work. Thanks to Suzanne, for her love, humour and patience, and for inspiring me. To my extended family in Italy ('la bela famea'), for always being there for me – particularly to my mum Carla and my dad Italo, my sisters Laura and Giovanna, my brother-in-law Gianluca and my niece Elenina. To my friends in Glasgow, Italy and elsewhere, for sharing good and bad times – a special mention for Claire, Daniela, Lyndell, Maud, Panos and Roberta, and to the Baradei. And to my fellow drummers at Sheboom, for keeping it real and for reminding me what sisterhood means to me.

Copyright acknowledgements

Some parts of this monograph are based on work previously published elsewhere, and they are reproduced here by kind permission of the publishers.

An earlier version of Chapter 3 was published as Stella, F. (2013) 'Lesbian Lives and Real Existing Socialism in late Soviet Russia', in Taylor, Y. and Addison, M. (eds.) *Queer Presences and Absences* (Basingstoke: Palgrave Macmillan).

An earlier version of Chapter 4 was published as Stella, F. (2008) 'Homophobia Begins at Home: Lesbian and Bisexual Women's Experiences of the Parental Household in Urban Russia', in Healey, D. (ed.) 'Queer Issue', *Kultura. Online Russian Cultural Review*, June. Available at http://www.kultura-rus.uni-bremen.de/, last accessed 7 March 2014. (Also published in Russian in the Moscow-based non-for profit lesbian journal *Ostrov* as Stella, F. (2008b) 'Gomofobiia Nachinaetsia Doma', September issue.)

An earlier version of Chapter 6 was published as Stella, F. (2012) 'The Politics of In/Visibility: Carving out Queer Space in Ul'yanovsk', *Europe-Asia Studies*, 64(10), 1822–1846.

1
Introduction: Locating Russian Sexualities

In spite of a burgeoning social sciences literature in sexualities and gay and lesbian/queer studies, most of the existing empirical and theoretical work has focused on English-speaking or Western European countries (Binnie, 2004; Puar, 2007; Rahman, 2010). Research on postcolonial sexualities has highlighted how current theoretical work remains deeply ethnocentric, and is therefore inadequate to account for the lived experiences of queers from the global South (Murray, 1995; Manalansan, 2002, 2003; Boellstorff, 2005; Jackson, 2009a, 2009b). However, comparatively little has been written about sexualities in postsocialist Eastern Europe and the former Soviet Union; yet similar Orientalist (Said, 1978) discourses constructing the region as 'traditional', 'premodern' or 'underdeveloped' have positioned it as the west's 'Other', both during the Cold War and since the demise of communist rule and the onset of the process of European integration (Bonnett, 2004; Stychin, 2003; Kulpa and Mizielińska, 2011).

This book is based on extensive ethnographic research, and focuses on the experiences, practices and identities of non-heterosexual women in Soviet and post-Soviet Russia. This monograph contributes to theoretical and methodological debates on ethnocentrism and the construction of normative subjects and of Oriental 'others', which are widely struggled with within gender and sexuality studies (Kuntsman and Miyake, 2008; Waites and Kollman, 2009; Casey et al., 2010; Taylor et al., 2010). A focus on Russian lesbian and bisexual women provides an 'intersectional location' (Rahman, 2010) that can illuminate and contribute to existing debates, given Russia's geographical position astride the European and Asian continents, its history as the core nation of the Soviet Union and bearer of an alternative model of (socialist) modernity, and its current marginal position in the process of European integration (Neumann,

1996, 1999). The monograph also makes a more specific contribution to the not extensive gay and lesbian/queer studies literature on Russia. Unlike most of the existing monographs on Russian same-sex sexualities (with the exception of Zhuk, 1998 and Sarajeva, 2011), the book focuses solely on women, thereby foregrounding gender as key in shaping their lived experiences.

This introductory chapter outlines the theoretical and methodological underpinnings of the study, providing an introduction to the key themes of the book and outlining the content of the chapters that follow. The introduction revisits the debates that shape the theoretical, methodological and empirical directions of the research, and shows how this monograph engages with and contributes to them. This book was written in Scotland, UK, where I live and work, with a 'global' academic, English-speaking audience in mind. Both my own geographical location and the dominance of 'western'/Anglo-American perspectives within sexualities studies are reflected in my perspective and in the debates I engage with in the monograph. I am mindful of the fact that the dominance of Anglo-American perspectives reflects not only a strong tradition in social sciences disciplines, but also the current status of English as the international academic 'lingua franca', reflecting geopolitical inequalities in global knowledge production. Thus, I hope that, in providing new critical insights into these debates, this book will to some extent contribute to 'de-centre' dominant, western narratives and theories, alongside other work from, or about, Russia and the postsocialist region (Kulpa and Mizielińska, 2011).

The book was also written while keeping in mind that it may be read by a Russian audience. Indeed, earlier versions of chapters 3 and 4 have been published in Russian (Stella, 2008b, 2014). For both Russian and English-speaking readers, my hope is that the book will contribute fresh insights by combining empirically grounded analysis of Russian sexualities with broader theoretical engagements and methodological reflections. When I started researching Russian sexualities, existing literature on the topic was scant: during the Soviet period (1917–1991), sexuality, and homosexuality in particular, remained off-limit topics of enquiry for both Soviet and researchers working within the social sciences and humanities. During the 1990s and early 2000s, scholarly work by Russian social scientists began to be published in Russia, pioneered by the likes of sociologist Igor' Kon (Kon, 1995, 1998; see also Temkina and Zdravomyslova, 2002; Omel'chenko, 1999, 2002a, 2002b; Nartova, 1999, 2004b, 2004c). The publication of this work followed the partial normalisation of homosexuality in Russian society, marked by the decriminalisation of male same-sex relations (1993) and the Ministry of Health's official demedicalisation of homosexuality (1999). Nonetheless, the bulk of the scholarly work on Russian sexualities published up until the mid-2000s, and available while I was doing my research, was published in English by non-Russian researchers based in North America and Western Europe (see Baer, 2002, for a review). In the last few years, the process of normalising same-sex sexualities seems to have been reversed in Russia, as evidenced by the infamous law banning the 'propaganda' of homosexuality to minors, which came into force in the Russian Federation in 2013. Despite a palpable rise in institutionalised homophobia, lack of funding and the continued marginalisation of gender and sexualities studies within academia, Russian sexualities studies have continued to grow and produce valuable work, informed in particular by queer theory (see the edited collections by Sozaev, 2010, and Kondakov, 2014). I have endeavoured to engage, wherever possible, with the very valuable literature on Russia, particularly the work produced by Russian scholars, despite the fact that Russian sources may not be familiar to the imaginary 'global' English-speaking reader, more *au fait* with the work of internationally recognised academic work published in English. In the spirit of 'de-centering' dominant theoretical perspectives, which, as Connell (2007) cogently argues, lays claim to universality but actually speaks from the global North, I endeavour to engage with ideas, intellectual traditions, concepts and empirical knowledge coming from Russia itself.

A note on language and terminology

This study is informed by both queer theory and cross-cultural perspectives on global sexualities, particularly empirical work situated within the disciplines of sociology, anthropology and human geography, and often informed by postcolonial perspectives. It is in their shared attempt to deconstruct dominant western constructs of gender and sexuality, and in their common antiessentialist stance towards normative 'gay' and 'lesbian' subjects that queer and cross-cultural perspectives often converge: as Weston (1993, p. 360) notes, the deconstruction of essentialist (and ethnocentric) notions of homosexuality is central to both anthropological work on non-western and diasporic sexualities and to queer studies.

Impatient of the limitations of identity politics and of 'homonormativity' (Duggan, 2002), queer theory has offered an insightful critique of fixed notions of identity based on binary notions of sexual orientation (heterosexual/homosexual, straight/gay). This critique has foregrounded the exclusionary potential of traditional gay and lesbian identity politics, which have tended to marginalise individuals whose experiences, practices and identifications do not clearly fit into those categories, notably bisexuals, transgenders, transsexuals, intersex and asexuals (Weeks et al., 2003; Seidman, 1996; Scherrer, 2008). The reappropriation of the derogatory term 'queer' as a subversive term of self-identification partly reflects a commitment to develop more pluralistic politics and research agendas. In academic work, it has become common to use 'queer' as a loosely defined category, potentially more inclusive of all non-heteronormative sexualities and genders, and comprising the whole spectrum of lesbian, gay, bisexual, transgender, intersex, queer/questioning and allied (LGBTIQA)[1] sexualities (Kulick, 2000). Queer theory's critique of binary notions of sexuality and gender ('the heterosexual matrix', Butler, 1990/1999) opened up new ways of thinking about sexuality, gender and their intersections and ties in, at some level, with debates within cross-cultural studies. A vast body of literature has shown that seemingly 'objective' labels, such as 'heterosexual/homosexual', or 'gay/lesbian' are culturally specific, and deeply rooted in western constructs of sexuality, itself a relatively recent invention (Foucault, 1978/1998). Research on non-western sexualities has shown how, while sexual practices may be fairly constant the world over, they are understood and conceptualised differently in different socio-cultural contexts (Weston, 1993; Lewin and Leap, 2002; Boellstorff, 2005).

The deconstructivist stance of queer theory, and its emphasis on difference, has also informed much of the existing literature on Russia, particularly the work published in English by non-Russian scholars (for an overview see Baer, 2002). Russian scholars, too, however, have used 'western' sexualities as a term of comparison, particularly when debating the legacy of state socialism on contemporary sexual practices and subjectivities (Temkina and Zdravomyslova, 2002; Kon, 1995). Debates about Russia's similarity and alterity vis-à-vis the 'west' have, to a large extent, focused on issues of language, history and representation. For example, in his pioneering monograph on Soviet homosexualities, historian Dan Healey talks about the subjects of his research as 'sexual dissidents', on the grounds that the terms 'gay' and 'lesbian' would be anachronistic: there is little evidence that they were widely used by Soviet queers, under a socio-political system which harshly stigmatised same-sex desire and forestalled independent social movements (Healey, 2001). However, I will argue in this monograph that some of this work has overemphasised Russian exceptionalism, partly because it has not given adequate consideration to issues of language, categorisation and cultural translation. For example, in her monograph *Queer in Russia*, which focused on the emergence of a community in search of a shared identity in 1990s Russia, sociologist Laurie Essig argues that Russian queers do not identify on the basis of their sexual practices, and rejects fixed binary notions of sexuality and gender.[2] In collectively referring to her study's participants as queer, Essig explicitly intends to mark them as different from 'western' gays and lesbians:

> This is a record, perhaps a fantasy, of a world of multiple desires and flexible identities that was not yet colonised by Western notions of sex and its meanings. I will leave it to future scholars to decide whether that world has disappeared forever. I look forward to their stories about queerness in Russia.
>
> (Essig, 1999, p. 174)

'Queer', however, is a problematic translation here: Essig's informants' usage of *goluboi* ('queer' man, lit. 'light blue') and *rozovaia* ('queer' woman, literary 'pink') maps on to binary notions of sexual orientation and gender identities; collective terms used in 'queer' circles, such as *tema* (literally 'the theme') or *nashi* (literally 'our people'), are neutral and do not have the same connotations as queer, a derogatory term in English which was reclaimed by queer politics[3] (Baer, 2002; Stella, 2010). More importantly, while intended as a positive marker of Russian 'difference', the term 'queer' does not satisfactorily get around issues of representation, or fulfil queer theory's demand for making visible complexity and fluidity (Garber, 2003; Puar, 2007). As Puar points out, queerness, having currently acquired a paradigmatic status in academic parlance, like 'gay' and 'lesbian' before it, may 'collapse into liberationist paradigms', and claim to speak on behalf of a distant 'other' which is in reality silenced and homogenised by the label 'queer'. Indeed, uncritical uses of queer terminology may paradoxically reify both 'Russian' and 'western' sexualities in the process.

Issues around language, translation and representation are widely struggled with in sexualities studies, and they are addressed here by adopting the following terminology. I use the gendered term 'lesbian' in the title to collectively refer to the women who took part in the research in order to emphasise gender as a key aspect of their experiences. 'Lesbian', however, should always be read as if between scare quotes, since it does not encompass the variety of women's identifications: elsewhere in the book I talk about non-heterosexual, or (more rarely) lesbian and bisexual women. Transgender issues are not explored in the monograph because sexuality (rather than gender identity) was the focus of my empirical research, and gender identity consequently remained marginal to my analysis, although the topic would deserve more attention in the Russian context.[4]

I deliberately avoid collectively naming the subjects of the research as queer, since this label has been used in previous work to mark Russian sexualities as exceptional vis-à-vis the 'west'. The preference for 'lesbian' over 'queer' is empirically grounded: unlike *kvir* (a relatively new word in Russian, modelled on the English term 'queer' but with slightly different nuances, which had a limited circulation in Russia at the time when fieldwork took place[5]), terms like lesbian (*lesbiianka*), bisexual (*biseksual'ka*), 'ex-heterosexual' (*byvshaya geteroseksual'ka*), straight (*natural'ka*, literally 'natural') were commonly used by women both in naturally occurring conversation and during interviews. Thus, throughout the text, the gender-neutral queer is used to refer to spaces and social networks which included both non-heterosexual men and women, as opposed to the gendered terms 'lesbian'/non-heterosexual women. I have strived to retain in the text and in the translated quotes the variety of terms used in everyday conversation, such as lesbian (*lesbiianka*), bisexual (*biseksual'ka*), straight (*natural'ka*, literally 'natural'), ex-heterosexual (*byvshaia geteroseksual'ka*) and more colloquial terms such as *nasha* (literally 'ours'), *takaia* (literally 'like that'), *rozovaia* (literally 'pink'), *tema* (literally 'the theme', a non-gendered collective term for non-heterosexuals). Throughout the text, I include the Russian original terms in brackets, to mark the discrepancy between the Russian and the English translation and to signal diverse subjectivities, and the ambiguities with which terms of identifications are sometimes inhabited.[6] I also preserve other Russian terms, not related to sexuality, such as *tusovka* (an informal social network); this is intended to sensitise the reader to the fact that languages represent and construct heterogeneous conceptual worlds and different social realities (Müller, 2007; Besemeres and Wierzbicka, 2007). The practice of preserving terms in the original language is common in anthropological and cross-cultural research, and it is described by Boellstorff as a cultural 'dubbing':

> In dubbing culture, two elements are held together in productive tension without the expectation that they will resolve into one – just as

it is known from the outset that the speakers' lips will never be in synch with the spoken words in a dubbed film. 'Dubbing culture' is queer: with dubbing there can never be a faithful translation.

(Boellstorff, 2005, p. 5)

This reflection on language and terminology is intended to engender a double dislocation: of the Russian terms and concepts which are examined in the monograph, and of the terminology I use, which is 'wrenched out of its familiar shape to accommodate not only similarity but also alterity' (Hermans, 2003, p. 286). Indeed, 'culture dubbing', as proposed by Boellstorff (2005), is a type of translation aware of its inevitable limitations and contingency. Through 'culture dubbing', I aim to stake a middle ground between the need to destabilise the normative lesbian subject, implicitly grounded in 'western' realities, and the urge to avoid overemphasising Russian difference. Indeed, the notion of 'western sexualities' should also be fractured and problematised, a point I will return to in the conclusion, and for this reason the reader should keep in mind that the term 'west' should always be read as if it were between scare quotes in the text.

Methodology, methods and geotemporal scales

The studies on which the monograph is based were designed to foreground complexity and avoid reifying 'Russian sexualities'. This is an issue that is widely discussed in language-based area studies, and it is in an area studies department that the research on which the monograph is based was undertaken. Research focused on postsocialist Eastern Europe and the former Soviet Union has been critiqued for producing accounts which essentialise national cultures, and reify the phenomena under investigation into discrete categories such as 'the Soviet mindset', or 'Balkan mentalities' (for a critique see Hann, Humphrey and Verdery, 2002, p. 9). As Kuus (2007) notes, there is a tendency to reify identities, understood as a cultural layer superimposed on subjects such as nations, states and societies. These points tie in with critiques of methodological nationalism, a perspective which equates society with the boundaries of the nation-state, and implicitly conceptualises it as the primary unit of analysis in social sciences research (Beck and Szainer, 2006; Chernilo, 2011). Methodological nationalism has been widely critiqued within transnationalism and globalisation studies on the grounds that social life is not contained within the boundaries of national societies (see e.g. Amelina et al., 2012).

The monograph proposes critical regionalism and the use of different geographical scales as a way to avoid reifying 'Russian lesbians' as exceptional vis-à-vis the 'west', and to foreground complexity. Different geographical scales (the nation, urban localities, the body) are examined, and the book considers how sexuality and generation intersect in women's experiences, thus capturing variations across space and time.

The monograph integrates data sets from two separate but related projects. The book originates in an ethnographic project, based on multisited fieldwork[7] conducted in the capital Moscow and in Ul'ianovsk, a regional administrative centre with a population of 650,000 in the middle Volga region. The project followed two intertwined lines of enquiry: first, it explored the ways in which non-heterosexual women negotiated their sexual selves across different 'everyday' settings, based on their experiences of the parental home, the workplace and the street, and looked into how women managed to collectively appropriate certain spaces, sometimes very public ones, as 'lesbian/queer'. A second line of enquiry considered how women's subjectivities were shaped by broader socio-political and cultural transformations in post-Soviet Russia, including shifting discourses about sexuality. In the ethnographic tradition, fieldwork involved collecting different types of data, which were analysed in triangulation. I collected semi-structured, in-depth interviews with 61 women,[8] aged 18 to 56; 34 of them were from Moscow and 27 were from Ul'ianovsk; interviews were conducted in Russian and tape-recorded with the informed consent of the research participants, and focused on the following themes: family relations and social networks; women's negotiation of their sexuality in different environments; relationships and identifications; and attitudes towards, and participation in, 'lesbian' space, including community initiatives, informal networks and commercial venues. As well as conducting semi-structured interviews, I recorded detailed fieldwork notes of the community events and social gatherings I attended, and carried out seven expert interviews with Moscow-based community activists and individuals working on commercial projects targeting a 'lesbian' audience; I also collected sources from the Russian mainstream and gay and lesbian media. I have discussed in detail elsewhere how I conducted the research, and how I addressed issues around positionality, accountability, power relations and representation during and after fieldwork (Stella, 2008a, 2010). While I recognise the importance of reflexivity as an integral part of ethnographic research, which situates the knowledge produced by my research, I refer the reader to these accounts, rather than rehearsing them once more here. I understand ethnography as interpretative, and do not lay any claims to absolute knowledge or objective authority. The use of multiple research methods in ethnographic research 'reflects an attempt to secure an in-depth and all-round understanding of the phenomenon in question' (Denzin and Lincoln, 2005, p. 5); the quality of ethnographic research is enhanced by considering multiple perspectives which challenge and refine the ethnographer's interpretations and arguments (Coffey and Atkinson, 1996). In order to produce a nuanced, multifaceted representation of 'lesbian' life in Russia, data were analysed in triangulation; I have strived to bring into conversation different data sets and perspectives in written accounts of the research. Additionally, a multifaceted account is produced through the use of multisited fieldwork, an approach which was intended to qualify understandings of 'global' and 'national' by exploring how macrotheoretical concepts and structures play out in specific locales, and to explore the complex connections established across these locales (Marcus, 1995; Amelina et al., 2012). The two fieldwork locations, Moscow and Ul'ianvosk, represent strikingly different urban settings, in terms of size, living standards and the presence or absence of a gay scene. The capital Moscow has a population of over ten million, and it is the most affluent and cosmopolitan among Russian cities; its high living standards reflect its ability to successfully restructure its economy after the demise of state socialism, its ability to attract global capital and its integration into the global economy (Brade and Rudolph, 2004). The rise of Muscovites' average spending power has boosted the growth of a vibrant leisure industry (Kolossov and O'Loughlin, 2004), including a relatively established gay scene, while the capital also hosts various national and international non-governmental organisations (NGOs), including the most established Russian LGBT organisations (Nemtsev, 2007). Ul'ianovsk, a provincial centre with a population of 700,000 in the Middle Volga Region, used to be an important manufacturing centre during the Soviet period; however, the city has struggled to recover from the shake-ups of economic transition. The lack of a commercial gay scene and of community organisations reflect Ul'ianovsk's peripheral position on the national and international map, its relatively small size, and its low living standards, which compare negatively with those of other cities in the Volga region, such as Saratov and Kazan (Konitzer-Smirnov, 2003).

The book explicitly aims to fracture essentialist notions of Russian sexualities as the 'other' by attending to generational differences, as well as inter-regional variation, a theme pursued to some extent in the original research project and further explored in a small-scale follow-up study on same-sex relations in Soviet Russia.[9] The study was based on biographical interviews with women involved in same-sex relationships under state socialism and was designed to further explore the generational differences highlighted by the first project. These differences centred around women's abilities to access scene and community spaces (virtually non-existent under state socialism) and information about same-sex desire (heavily censored during the Soviet period), as well as women's intimate practices and experiences of same-sex relations, and their willingness to (dis)identify according to their practices. The follow-up study was based on semi-structured biographical interviews, during which women were invited to talk about their sexual education, sexual experiences and relationships, and sexual subjectivities as they unfolded and evolved during the course of their lives, against the background of other life events. Fieldwork was conducted in Moscow and Saint Petersburg; the 13 participants[10] were recruited through snowball sampling, with the help of community activists and acquaintances. In the process of data analysis, interview data from the oral history study was combined with the interviews with older women collected in the first project; the combined datasets comprised 24 interviews with women born between 1946 and 1969. A narrative approach was used during data analysis: this approach, common in oral history work, is sensitive to language and narrative structures, interviewees' meanings, sense of place and changing sense of self (Riessman, 1993, 2004; Chamberlayne et al., 2000).

The two key foci of enquiry outlined above map on to the monograph's central themes of time (generational sexualities) and space (a multisited analysis of women's negotiations of different 'everyday' spaces in metropolitan Moscow and provincial Ul'ianovsk). These themes are reflected in the organisation of the book. The first part of the book comprises Chapter 2, which charts shifting discourses on same-sex sexualities across Soviet and post-Soviet Russia, and Chapter 3, which explores the experiences and subjectivities of non-heterosexual women socialised during the Soviet period. In the second part of the book, Chapter 4 explores women's experiences of the home, Chapter 5 focuses on their negotiations of the workplace and the street, and Chapter 6 examines how urban space is appropriated as 'lesbian/queer' space in Moscow and Ul'ianovsk.

Intersectional or queer? Identities, subjectivities, performances

Having outlined above some of the key methodological and theoretical underpinnings of my research, I delve further into methodological issues, as discussed in recent debates within sexualities studies. Recent interventions have largely centred on intersectional perspectives (Taylor et al., 2010; Lutz et al., 2011) and on queer approaches (Liinason and Kulpa, 2008; Kulpa and Liinason, 2009; Browne and Nash, 2011b), with some authors pointing out the affinities (Rahman, 2010) and others focusing on the tensions between the two (Browne and Nash, 2011a; Fotopoulou, 2012). While arguably grounded in different theoretical and epistemological traditions, both approaches strive towards making visible the multi-layered complexities of lived experiences, and are therefore of relevance here. It has been noted, however, that intersectionality debates in the social sciences have been primarily theoretical rather than methodological (McCall, 2005; Valentine et al., 2010), and that many different methodological approaches coexist somehow uneasily under the 'intersectionality' banner (McCall, 2005). Moreover, it has been argued that intersectional approaches are in danger of producing additive (rather than relational) 'grids' of social divisions, which still fail to include the multiply oppressed, and may become a mere descriptor of interlocking power relations, depoliticising the very concept of intersectionality in the process (Erel et al., 2010). Queer theory, on the other hand, has been influential in highlighting the fluidity and contingency of sexual subjectivities and in contesting the logics of normativity, and has had a profound impact on social sciences research on sexualities (Plummer, 2005; Valocchi, 2005; Richardson et al., 2006; Taylor et al., 2010). Nonetheless, queer approaches have also been critiqued for being too abstract and text-based, and therefore inherently unable to come to terms with the empirical world, to ground themselves in systematic methods of enquiry (Boellstorff, 2011), or to account for the materiality of queer lives (Richardson et al., 2006; Taylor et al., 2010).

I acknowledge the value of both intersectional and queer perspectives as sensitising concepts, which can productively inform methodological debates, and which have indeed generated methodological innovations in the field of sexualities studies (Taylor et al., 2010; Browne and Nash, 2011b). Nonetheless, precisely because both intersectionality and queer are somehow ill-defined, 'buzzwords', it is not terribly helpful, in my view, to talk about intersectional or queer methodologies in abstract terms, detached from a more grounded discussion of the 'nuts and bolts' of doing research, including issues of research design, ethics and methods. Moreover, as others have pointed out in the case of feminist and queer theory, the dichotomous contrast between queer and intersectional methodologies may be overstated, as the two are often combined in empirical work (Jackson, 1999; Richardson et al., 2006). Indeed, as McCall (2005) shows, both queer and intersectional approaches can be traced back to a fundamental concern of feminist methodologies, namely to make visible the difference among women and to problematise the normative subject of feminist politics. In McCall's definition, intersectional methodologies include not only identitarian perspectives, but encompass more broadly 'perspectives that completely reject the separability of analytical and identity categories' (*ibid.*).[11] My point is not that queer methodologies can be subsumed into intersectional ones or vice versa, but that intersectional and queer approaches can be productively integrated in research methodologies. In my research, discussions about translation, language and subjectivities are inspired by queer perspectives, while the exploration of sexuality and generation draws on intersectional approaches.

The contrast between queer and intersectional methodology is based on understandings of the first as inherently anti-identitarian and deconstructionist, and focused on discourses and subject positions, and of intersectionality as mostly associated with 'theoretical paradigms based in identity categories' (McCall, 2005, p.1771). Foucauldian and queer critiques of identity pertain to its definition as a property of the self existing outside the domain of the social and before discourse (Foucault, 1978/1998; Butler, 1990/1999); yet in social sciences research principled anti-identitarian stances may be attacking a straw man, as nuanced theorisations of identity/identifications as social, relational and fluid also exist, and are worth drawing on (Goffman, 1959/1990a; Hall, 1996; Brubaker and Cooper, 2000; Jenkins, 2004). Unlike Foucault's and Butler's theorisations, which have been critiqued for leaving little room for agency, Hall (1996) points out that identity is a lynchpin for understanding the interplay of agency and structure in the social world: 'it seems to be in the attempt to rearticulate the relationship between subject and discursive practices that questions of identity recur' (Hall, 1996, p. 2). Hall also usefully integrates notions of subject positions, subjectivities and identities, pointing out that each of them performs different conceptual work:

I use identity to refer to the meeting point, the point of suture, between on the one hand the discourse and practices which attempt to 'interpellate', speak to us or hail us into place as the social subjects of particular discourses, and on the other hand, the processes which produce subjectivities, which construct us as subjects which can be 'spoken'. Identities are thus points of temporary attachment to the subject positions which discursive practices construct for us.

(Hall, 1996, pp. 5–6)

In Hall's definition, identity is underpinned by the notion of an agentic, reflexive subject. I subscribe to this understanding of the subject, of which Foucault and Butler are deeply suspicious, since they see it as anchored in notions of the subject as autonomous and substantive, and as and pre-existing discourse (Foucault, 1978/1998; Butler, 1990/1999, 1993).

This understanding of the subject translates into how women's negotiations of their sexual selves, which is a prominent theme in the book, is approached conceptually and methodologically. A substantial body of literature within human geography and sociology has productively explored how sexuality is negotiated across space (Valentine, 1993, 1995, 1996; Adkins, 1995, 2000; Taylor, 2007). This work widely references Judith Butler's theory of performativity, which has been rightly credited with inspiring innovative work on sexuality and space. Nonetheless, it has also been noted that translating Butler's textual approach to empirical work has proved difficult, not least because she has theorised 'a subject abstracted from personal lived experiences, as well as from its historical and geographical embeddedness', ill-suited to empirical social sciences research concerned with issues of intentionality, agency and reflexivity (Nelson, 1999, p. 131; Brickell, 2003, 2005; Jackson and Scott, 2010a). Indeed, while Butler is commonly misunderstood as arguing that subjects actively 'do' gender by enacting gendered performances, a closer reading of her early work reveals an understanding of performativity as a process of repetition which invokes the subject, rather than as a performance enacted by an agentic subject (Hall, 1996; Brickell, 2003, 2005). Butler argues that gender

is not a noun, but neither it is a set of free-floating attributes, for we have seen that the substantive effect of gender is performatively produced and compelled by the regulatory practices of gender coherence. Hence, within the inherited discourse of the metaphysics of substance, gender proves to be performative – that is, constituting the identity it is purported to be. In this sense, gender is always a doing, though not a doing by a subject who might be said to preexist the deed. [...]. There is no gender identity behind the expression of gender; that identity is performatively constituted by the very '"expressions' that are said to be its results.

(Butler, 1990/1999, p. 33)

I take on board some of Butler's insights, particularly around how the discursive production of gendered subjects is informed by heterosexuality (the 'heterosexual matrix'), and about the naturalisation of specific constructs of sexuality and gender through stylised repetition. However, in framing the empirical discussion of women's negotiations of their sexuality, I draw on Goffman's conceptualisation of performances as presentation of the self (Goffman, 1959/1990a), as well as (to a lesser extent) on Butler's performativity.

Goffman notes that social actors partaking in a social interaction are engaged in certain practices in order to avoid embarrassment, and conceptualises the presentation of the self in social interaction as performance, using a dramaturgical metaphor. Goffman emphasises that social actors are involved in a process of impression management, and that individual actors' ability to leave an impression is based on two kinds of activity: the expression they *give* (involving mainly verbal symbols, on which the actor has great control) and the expression that they *give off* (other, non-verbal clues which other can read as symptomatic of the actor). Performances are enacted in particular contexts or settings, which comprise a frontstage, where performers are being watched by an audience, and a backstage, a hidden space where they are not under the scrutiny of a wider audience (although they may still be in the presence of other social actors performing alongside them, as part of a 'team'). Goffman's subject is never transcendental or asocial, since he understands the self as comprising both the subject's perceptions and internal states as being shaped by social norms and, most of all, by and through social interaction. Goffman's notion of performance presupposes an agentic, reflexive subject; thus, the subject exercises agency in social interaction, which involves managing impressions made on other participants in a social encounter; nonetheless, agency is never unmediated, as performances (and the self itself) are negotiated in specific contexts (settings) and with other social actors. The latter include audiences ('those performed to'), other performers, and those who 'neither perform in the show nor observe it', but who nonetheless may shape the performance more indirectly and remotely. Moreover, performers may be participants in a collective (team) performance, where their role and individual performance is largely prescribed through their membership in a team (e.g. work collective, family), or orchestrated by a director because of the performer's subordinate position within the team. Importantly, for Goffman, social interaction is premised on a shared understanding of a communicative situation between all social actors involved, which can be sustained, renegotiated or disrupted; thus, some facts, if 'attention to them is drawn during the performance, would discredit, disrupt or make useless the impression that the performance fosters', with potentially negative consequences for the performer(s) (Goffman, 1959/1990a, p. 141).

I also draw on Goffman's notion of stigma, or 'the phenomenon whereby an individual with an attribute deeply discredited by his/her society is rejected as a result of the attribute' (Goffman, 1963/1990b, p. 6). Stigma results from a slippage between widely held, normative expectations (in Goffman's definition, *virtual identity*) and the discovery of an attribute the individual possesses which contradicts these expectations (*actual identity*). The negative reaction of others to the individual upon this discovery casts the individual as deviant and the others as normal, thus reinforcing widely held social norms and beliefs. Plummer (1975) draws on Goffman (1963/1990b) to discuss stigma as pertaining to sexuality, including same-sex sexuality, and points out that sexual stigma is enmeshed in, and specific to, specific socio-cultural contexts. The stigmatisation of same-sex sexualities creates specific interaction problems for individuals involved in same-sex practices, and is reflected in how they manage information related to their discredited sexuality. Thus, concealing or playing down this discredited sexuality is, according to Plummer, a fundamental part of their ability to cope with stigma. These are common strategies of information management, enabled by a variety of factors: same-sex sexuality, unlike other discredited social attributes, is not necessarily 'written on the body' and can be hidden; sexuality is widely considered a private matter in industrialised societies; and social actors operate in different settings and are able, to some extent, to compartmentalise their performances. Thus, the visibility of same-sex sexualities is not necessarily a consequence of an individual's 'coming out' (declaration); disclosure can also be enacted by others as a result of discovery (catching someone in the act), denunciation (exposure and public shaming by a third party) or recognition (stereotypical symmetry, or identifying someone as gay on the basis of certain cues commonly associated with homosexuality, see Plummer, 1975).

This broad conceptual framework will be used to frame the analysis of women's negotiations of their sexuality across different everyday settings (the home, the workplace, the street). Thus, the book aims to bring into conversation more generic conceptualisations of situated performances and impression management with prevalent understandings of concealment/disclosure of same-sex sexualities in terms of 'coming out of the closet' (Sedgwick, 1990; Seidman el al., 1999; Seidman, 2004; Brown, 2000), and engage with critiques of the coming out narrative as an ethnocentric project which reinscribes western sexualities as 'the normative measure of sameness and difference' (Manderson and Jolly, 1997, p. 22).

Time: Generational sexualities

The first part of this monograph explores generational differences in women's experiences and identifications and locates them within the specific socio-cultural contexts of socialist/postsocialist Russia. Debates about queer sexualities and temporalities have involved a consideration of both micro-level perspectives concerned with the life course of individual queers and intergenerational perspectives (Taylor, 2010; Cronin and King, 2010; Binnie and Klesse, 2013), and macro-level perspectives aimed at historicising narratives of queer globalisation (Halberstam, 2005; Jackson, 2009a; Kulpa and Mizielińska, 2011). These two perspectives are discussed in distinct bodies of literature which rarely overlap. The monograph aims to bring into conversation macro-level perspectives (explored in Chapter 2, charting shifting discourses on sexuality, gender and citizenship across Soviet and post-Soviet Russia) with micro-level ones (explored empirically in Chapter 3, which focuses on the Soviet past as experienced by the women who came of age and had same-sex relations under state socialism). While most theorising on queer geotemporalities has thus far focused on capitalist modernities (Jackson, 2009a), the empirical exploration of understandings and lived experiences of sexuality produced by socialist modernity can contribute new insights to these debates, and once again contribute to debunk western-centric perspectives. Empirical work on Russia and Eastern Europe can shed light on the workings of a particular model of state socialism grounded in Marxist-Leninist ideology, which, with significant national variations, was adopted across the region after World War II (WWII). The term 'state socialism' is used here to refer to a political and economic system which was intended as either a transition stage towards the development of fully fledged communism, or as an end in itself. Under state socialism, the means of production were mainly owned by the state, which played a key role in both economic life, through central planning, and the accumulation of capital for the purpose of rapid industrialisation and modernisation, and in political life, through the establishment of a single party system.

Work on generational sexualities has drawn on biographical methods, concerned with the exploration of the interplay between individual biography, history and 'the problems of a social structure in which biography and history intersect' (Mills, 1959/1970, p. 247). Empirical work within LGBT and queer studies shows that biographical narratives are not just accounts of individual non-heterosexuals' lives, as these narratives are shaped in fundamental ways by 'the ideas and values of the historical period in which they are embedded' (Rosenfeld, 2002, p. 160), while queer subjectivities in old age are influenced by earlier life experiences (Kennedy Lapovsky and Davis, 1993; Plummer, 1995; Stein, 1997; Rosenfeld, 2002, 2009). Some of this work has drawn on the notion of generational cohorts to explore the interplay between discourses, identity narratives (e.g. the 'coming out' story), 'identity careers' and subjectivities (Rosenfeld, 2002, 2009; Stein, 1997; Hammack and Cohler, 2009; Plummer, 1995, 2010). Age cohorts can be identified through shared critical life events (e.g. having lived through WWII, the 'sexual revolution' of the 1960s) which shape a generation's formative years, and generate shared collective memories (Haavio-Mannila, Kontula and Rotkirch, 2002; Rotkirch, 2004; Plummer, 2010). Research on generational same-sex sexualities raises a number of conceptual issues with which the first part of the monograph engages.

Firstly, recent interventions have highlighted the excessive emphasis on sexual identities, either self-proclaimed or ascribed, in much extant research on generational sexualities (for a critique see Heaphy, 2007; King and Cronin, 2010; see also Kulick, 2000). An example of the primacy given to sexual identities is Rosenfeld's (2002, 2009) work on older gay men and lesbians in the US; Rosenfeld identifies the rise of the gay liberation movement and of lesbian feminism in the late 1960s as a pivotal discursive shift from homosexuality as deviance to homosexuality as a positive social identity. Gay liberation is thus identified as a defining moment in her interviewees' 'identity careers' towards a positive identification as gay or lesbian. An emphasis on the emergence of gay liberation and other 'new' social movements, such as second wave feminism as a generational watershed of sorts is common in much US and UK literature on generational sexualities (Plummer, 1995; Stein, 1997); however, this reference point is not relevant to the study of

Soviet Russia, where neither gay liberation nor second wave feminism emerged, for reasons highlighted in Chapter 2. Moreover, in affording so much analytical and explanatory purchase to sexual identities, sexuality is reduced to self-proclaimed or ascribed identities, obscuring how the regulation of gendered sexualities (the 'heterosexual matrix', Butler, 1990/1999) is deeply intertwined with the social construction of normative femininities (and masculinities), and how the latter are mediated through social institutions such as marriage and the nuclear family (Rich, 1980; McKinnon, 1992; Jackson, 1999). Thus, the focus of Chapter 3 is not exclusively on women's subjectivities and identifications, but also women's intimate practices, as the chapter explores how the Soviet 'working mother' gender contract structured women's aspirations and their negotiation of sexual and romantic relationships (Ashwin, 2000; Temkina and Zdvravomyslova, 2002).

Secondly, in relation to the critique of a prevalent focus on identities, King and Cronin (2010) argue for the importance of applying the insights of queer theory to the study of older lesbians, gays and bisexuals in order to challenge the notion of sexual identities as fixed, stable and binary. A related point is that sexual subjectivities change over the life course, not just in childhood and adolescence but also throughout adulthood: in her work on older gay men and lesbians from the Los Angeles area, Rosenfeld (2002) acknowledges changing identifications, and conceptualises them as 'identity careers'. An approach relying on binary notions of sexuality as either gay or straight ignores the fluidity of sexual desires and identifications, while failing to acknowledge bisexuality as more than a transitional stage in the process of reaching sexual maturity and/or 'coming out' as gay or lesbian (for a critique Rust, 1993, 2000). Such approaches are underpinned by the assumption that sexual identity formation is a process taking place in early life, and leading to a stable heterosexual or homosexual identity during adulthood. This assumption has often led researchers to bracket queers' experiences of heterosexual relations, marriage and parenthood, or to read them as attempts to 'pass' or to conform to heteronorm, as a case of 'false consciousness' and 'double life', or as a stage on the path towards the development of an 'authentic', stable gay or lesbian identity (Hammack and Cohler, 2009; Rosenfeld, 2002, 2009). It has been argued that in 'western' societies 'double life', where same-sex relations were lived in secret and in parallel with the formation of heteronormative relations and kinship, has been more typically the experience of older, pre-gay liberation generations (Seidman, 2004; Cronin and King, 2010); the gradual 'normalisation' of same-sex relations has made this experience less common for younger generations. Yet research recently conducted in the UK shows that some individuals adopt a non-heterosexual identity in later life, or remain involved in bisexual practices throughout their life (Cronin and King, 2010; Taylor, 2009); to some extent, these experiences cut across generational cohorts. It is important to point this out because some of the literature on Russian same-sex sexualities has emphasised the coexistence of same-sex practices with heterosexual relations and marriage as evidence of the exceptional and 'queer' fluidity of Soviet/Russian sexualities vis-à-vis 'western' binary constructs of sexuality as either 'gay' or 'straight' (Tuller, 1996; Essig, 1999; Baer, 2009). While essentialising polarisations between 'east' and 'west' is unhelpful, it is important to understand lived experiences of same-sex relations within specific socio-historical frameworks. A focus on how women reconcile sexual desires and personal aspirations with normative social pressures may be better able to capture the complexities of lived experiences and subjectivities, while not dismissing experiences of heterosexual coupledom and parenthood as a case of 'false consciousness'. As Engebretsen (2009, p. 3) argues in her article on relationship strategies among *lala* (lesbian) women in contemporary China, such a focus also requires 'a rethinking of the notions and meanings of agency [and] power', and of approaches to historicise the global diversity of same-sex sexualities.

Having outlined key points of contestation in debates on generational sexualities and queer temporalities, I briefly sketch the contents of chapters 2 and 3. Chapter 2 provides a macro-level, socio-historical contextual background, and serves as a frame of reference for the empirical chapters to follow, particularly for the benefit of readers not familiar with the Russian context. The chapter draws on secondary literature, and maps work on Russian same-sex sexualities on to broader shifts in the gender order and in dominant discourses on sex and sexuality in Soviet and post-Soviet Russia. It charts Soviet socio-legal regulation of same-sex desire, implemented through the criminalisation of consensual relationships between men, the pathologisation of lesbianism, and the stigmatising silence surrounding same-sex sexualities in the public domain (Healey, 2001; Engelstein, 1993, 1995; Kon, 1995, 1998). The regulation of same-sex desire is framed within a broader discussion of intimate life and of the key features of the gender order under state socialism. The Soviet gender order was premised on the 'working mother' gender contract, the nuclear family as the founding unit of Soviet society and monogamous heterosexuality harnessed to the reproductive needs of the socialist state (Ashwin, 2000; Buckley, 1989). It is widely acknowledged that wide-ranging attempts to reform the Soviet system, followed by the dissolution of the Soviet Union, the demise of state socialism in 1991 and the birth of the newly independent Russian Federation marked the onset of deep and radical transformations in Russian society. These were reflected in the pluralisation of discourses on sex and sexuality, resulting in a 'sexual revolution' of sorts (Kon, 1995; Rotkirch, 2004) and eventually in the decriminalisation and demedicalisation of same-sex sexualities in the 1990s. Nonetheless, in post-Soviet Russia sexual citizenship never extended to legal recognition and protection for non-heterosexual citizens by state institutions: throughout the 1990s and early 2000s it remained confined to freedom of consumption, expression and association. These freedoms, however, have become increasingly restricted since the mid-2000s, amidst moral panics about sexual liberalisation and declining birth rates, and the backlash against the new visibility of same-sex desire. The focus of the chapter is change resulting from largely endogenous socio-economic and political transformations associated with the demise of state socialism, rather than the influence of global sexual politics and culture, which are only very marginally explored here.

Chapter 3 focuses on the lived experiences and subjectivities of those women in my sample who belong to the 'last Soviet generation' (Yurchak, 2006; Byford, 2009), or the generational cohort of women born between the early 1950s and the early 1970s and who came of age between the 1970s and the mid-1980s, a timespan here referred to as 'late Soviet period' or 'late socialism'. The categorisation of women in my sample into two distinct generational cohorts may seem inconsistent with the overall methodology of the monograph, and I acknowledge it is in part arbitrary. Nonetheless, this division is based on empirical findings from the original ethnographic study, which revealed marked generational differences between the 'last Soviet generation' and the 'generation of transition', who came of age during Gorbachev's perestroika (1987–1991), or after the breakup of the Soviet Union and the demise of state socialism in Russia (for a more detailed discussion, see Chapter 2). The chapter adds new empirical insights to existing literature on Soviet Russia, which has mainly focused on mechanisms presiding to the socio-legal regulation of same-sex sexualities, or on the environments of the clinic and the prison camp, where same-sex sexualities were symbolically confined. While most existing literature foregrounds the repressive role of the Soviet state (Healey, 2001; Essig, 1999; Engelstein, 1995), the chapter argues that the extent to which the Soviet medical establishment attempted to 'cure' women of their desires should be reassessed vis-à-vis the role of other, more informal mechanisms of surveillance and of the materialities of Soviet state socialism in shaping women's lived experiences, particularly the Soviet gender order (Connell, 1987; Ashwin, 2000). The chapter also queries narratives of Russian exceptionalism by showing that women's reluctance to identify according to their sexual practices may reflect generational differences, and different narratives of social identity available to Soviet and post-Soviet women. Collectively, chapters 2 and 3 contribute to broader debates about sexuality and (post-)socialist modernity, queer geotemporalities and critical regionalism, which will be explored in detail in the conclusions. One of the key contributions of the monograph is its recuperation of postsocialism as a critical standpoint and supraregional framework of analysis. I argue that postsocialism can be a useful concept to provincialise dominant theoretical perspectives within sexualities studies, which are implicitly based on a hidden western-centric geography. Unlike postcolonialism, which has been immensely popular in research and theoretical work on non-western societies, postsocialism is yet to become an established part of the theoretical toolkit of global gender and sexualities studies.

Space: 'Time/space' strategies, urban locations and 'the global closet'

The second part of the book shifts the level of analysis from time, explored through generational differences, to space, examined through non-heterosexual women's negotiations of their sexualities in 'everyday' settings and strategies collectively deployed to carve out 'lesbian/queer' space. The focus here is on the 'time/space strategies' (Valentine, 1993a) deployed by women in negotiating different environments, or, to use Goffman's terminology (1959/1990a, 1963/1990b), on their practices of impression management in their everyday presentation of the self.

Issues of self-management and disclosure for non-heterosexuals are widely conceptualised in the literature through the metaphor of the closet/coming out. Notions of visibility/invisibility and private/public are central to widespread understandings of the closet as a metaphor for the symbolic erasure and forced concealment of non-normative sexualities; in Sedgwick's definition, the closet is 'the defining structure for gay oppression this century' (Sedgwick, 1990; see also Brown, 2000; Brown and Browne, 2011). Nonetheless, the notion of visibility as empowering, on which this definition of the closet is premised, and the ability of the closet/coming out paradigm to account for the complexities of non-heterosexuals' negotiations of their sexuality, are widely contested. Writing about the US context, Seidman et al. (1999, p. 12) have argued that, while American society remains 'organised by the institution of heterosexuality', many Americans live 'beyond the closet', as they are able to (selectively) integrate their sexual self into a variety of social contexts and interactions, and their lives are no longer organised around the idea of a 'double life' (Chauncey, 1994). While the literature foregrounds the role of gay liberation in popularising the concept of the closet (Brown, 2000), Seidman et al. (1999, p. 14) caution against its use in social research as a 'taken for granted, ahistorical ground of gay life'. Indeed, while the closet has been theorised as a global form of oppression, empirical research has shown that the coming out narrative, originating in Anglo-American societies, does not resonate with the experiences and understandings of queers in other societies (Jolly, 1997; Manalansan, 1997, 2003; Decena, 2011). Moreover, Brown (2000) has argued for the need to spatialise the metaphoric closet and explore its materiality: indeed, empirical research has shown that visibility may be a privilege not readily available to working-class lesbian women (Taylor, 2007), or migrant working-class Filipino gay men (Manalansan, 2003).

The monograph argues for the need to reassess and reconceptualise the 'closet/coming out' paradigm. While the closet metaphor is a useful tool to analyse how the construction of space as private/public is used to uphold heteronormativity (Sedgwick, 1990), Goffmanian notions of non-heterosexuals as performers who are called to manage self-impressions and 'fronts' during social interaction may usefully be integrated into debates on the closet to give more prominence to issue of agency. Indeed, while the closet and coming out are value-laden and culturally specific concepts (Jolly, 2001; Provencher, 2007), 'coming out' is not necessarily an empowering act, as its subversive potential is conditional on space and place, and does not adequately account for agency.

The monograph's empirical exploration of women's practices of disclosure and experiences of different urban locations and settings problematises ahistorical, aspatial notions of the closet, and the notion of 'coming out' as individual choice, detached from any consideration about the specific rules governing interactions in a particular socio-spatial context. To this end, the monograph explores practices of disclosure (or not), and perceptions of dis/comfort and safety/danger in different settings, namely the home (Chapter 4), the workplace and the street (Chapter 5). Moreover, chapters 5 and 6 examine the ambiguous visibility involved in women's collective appropriation and use of public and semi-public urban locales as 'lesbian/queer'. Although this appropriation is often deliberately sheltered from the gaze of the uninitiated (Sarajeva, 2011; Stella, 2012), the discreet use of very public space contrasts with the emphasis in Anglo-American literature on the visibility of cosmopolitan queer space (Binnie and Skeggs, 2004) and on nonheterosexual women's limited ability to inhabit public space, widely understood as the preserve of men (Valentine, 1995; Casey, 2004; Taylor, 2007).

A second theme running through chapters 4, 5 and 6 is how differently women experience metropolitan Moscow and provincial Ul'ianovsk, particularly in terms of their ability to safely negotiate their sexuality and to carve out 'lesbian' space in public and semi-public settings. This comparison contributes to debates about 'queer cosmopolitanism' (Binnie and Skeggs, 2004) and the city in queer imagination (Weston, 1995; Rooke, 2007), which have hitherto mostly focused on metropolitan areas (however, see Valentine, 1995, and Moran and Skeggs, 2004, for a comparison between different urban settings).

Chapter 4 focuses on women's experiences and navigations of home, considering both the parental home for women still living with their family of origin, and the relations established between the parental home and the home of choice for women who had established an independent home. The chapter explores the complex emotional connotations of 'home', variously experienced as a place of comfort, authenticity and ontological security and as a place of scrutiny, discomfort and violence (Weston, 1991; Weeks, Heaphy and Donovan, 2001; Valentine et al., 2003; Taylor, 2009). The first part of the chapter explores women's strategies of identity negotiation within the parental home; it looks at 'coming out' both as an individual and a collective process, and explores how disclosure impacts on family relations. The chapter goes on to examine experiences of everyday homophobia in the family home, and shows that these are rooted in culturally specific expectations about femininity and 'healthy' transition into adulthood, particularly in the notion of motherhood as a key marker of 'proper' adult womanhood. Finally, the chapter explores how normative notions of family, coupledom and adulthood continue to influence women's negotiations of their identities and relationships within kinship networks.

Chapter 5 continues the exploration of women's practices and strategies for negotiating 'everyday' space, focusing on the workplace and the street, and drawing more explicitly on Goffman's dramaturgical model and notions of presentation of the self, front and backstage, and expressions given and given off (Goffman, 1959/1990a). The chapter begins with a detailed discussion of women's negotiations of their sexuality at work, where acknowledgement of their sexuality (either through women's disclosure, or through co-workers discovery, exposure or recognition, see Plummer, 1975) was rare. Concerns about the potential outcomes of disclosure, as well as the desire to maintain professional boundaries and protect one's privacy meant that women often chose to remain invisible as a lesbian or bisexual, by hiding behind co-workers' tacit assumption of heterosexuality. The chapter then goes on to discuss women's negotiation of the public street, examining issues around comfort, personal safety and anonymity, and highlighting the importance of place by exploring differences between cosmopolitan Moscow and provincial Ul'ianovsk. The street emerged as a paradoxical space, which harboured risks of verbal and physical violence but was also used by informal 'lesbian/queer' networks in both cities to meet and socialise. Finally, drawing on the empirical exploration of women's practices of disclosure developed in both Chapter 4 and Chapter 5, the chapter also engages critically with the closet (Sedgwick, 1990; Brown, 2000; Seidman, 2004) as a concept invoked to account for women's agency in negotiating their sexuality, and as rooted in rigid binary notions of private and public, and visibility and invisibility.

Chapter 6 explores the strategies collectively used by women-only and mixed *tusovki* to carve out 'lesbian/queer' space in the urban landscape. I consider how metropolitan/provincial location shapes the configuration and appropriation of urban space as queer, comparing metropolitan Moscow to provincial Ul'ianovsk, but mainly focusing on Ul'ianovsk, a city with no institutionalised queer space. Indeed, most of the literature on urban queer space, whether focused on Russian or on 'western' cities, has privileged metropolitan locations as hubs of consumer culture, largely neglecting the experiences of queers who live in locales which lack institutionalised and visible gay scenes. Thus, the chapter deploys a holistic notion of queer space, not limited to the commercial scene and to community organisation, but encompassing more transient and precarious appropriations of urban space as queer. Besides mapping queer space in Moscow and Ul'ianovsk, the chapter also considers the social practices of 'lesbian/queer' *tusovki* meeting on the street, and explores the strategies through which public and semi-public locations, such as street corners and mainstream bars and clubs, are collectively appropriated. Finally, re-engaging with debates about the closet and the empowering and transformative potential of in/visibility outlined in Chapter 5, I consider whether the Ul'ianovsk *tusovka*'s appropriation of urban space can be seen as subversive and political, even if this appropriation is neither overt nor visible.

2
Same-Sex Sexualities and the Soviet/Post-Soviet Gender Orders

The chapter offers a contextual socio-historical background to the empirical chapters that follow, by charting shifting discourses on sex and sexualities across Soviet and post-Soviet Russia. More specifically, I consider the normativities they produced and their implications for non-heterosexual citizens.

Gender-specific aspects will be highlighted by framing discourses on sexuality within the Soviet and post-Soviet gender orders, as theorised by sociologists' work on Russia (Zdravomyslova and Temkina, 2007a, 2007b, 2007c; see also Ashwin, 2000, and Rotkirch and Temkina, 2007). This work draws on Connell's theorisation of the gender order (Connell, 1987, 2006), defined as the prevalent social organisation of gender relations within a society. Connell contrasts gender orders and gender regimes, where the latter refers to the localised pattern of gender relations within specific social institutions or organisations (school, the family), and which may reproduce or diverge from the broader gender order (Connell, 1987, 2006). Zdravomyslova and Temkina (2007a) define the Soviet gender order as *etacratic*, or state-centred, because under state socialism the Party-state[1] exercised a great deal of control over citizens' private and public lives through its near-monopoly on socialised means of production and on political life. They argue that the post-Soviet gender order was much more pluralistic because, after the demise of state socialism, it was shaped by a greater variety of social actors (Zdravomyslova and Temkina, 2007b, 2007c; Rotkirch and Temkina, 2007).

Dominant discourses on sexuality and sexual morality are deeply intertwined with the existing gender order (Connell, 1987). Theorisations of sexual citizenship[2] have pointed out that notions of citizenship are grounded in normative assumptions about gender and sexuality, which institutionalise male privilege as well as heterosexuality as the unquestioned norm (Evans, 1993; Richardson, 2000; Bell and Binnie, 2000). Thus, sexual citizenship bridges the private and the public sphere, and refers to all types of exclusions/inclusions that various 'sexual communities' experience, ranging from political, social, cultural and economic participation (Richardson, 1998, 2000). It has been noted that, even in societies which have decriminalised and demedicalised same-sex relations, the boundaries of sexual citizenship are policed through heterosexist constructs of private and public spheres (Richardson, 2000, p. 77), and therefore they entail 'different mobilizations and spatializations of minority sexual citizenship in relation to "mainstream society" ' (McGhee, 2004, p. 358). While drawing on these insights, I maintain that the notion of sexual citizenship is not entirely adequate to discuss same-sex sexualities in Russia, particularly Soviet Russia. First of all, Soviet state socialism was underpinned by notions of citizenship that are very different from those operating in western capitalist societies. As Alexopoulos (2006) shows, following Marshall's (1977) distinction between civic, political and social citizenship, only social citizenship rights were both granted by law and protected through extensive welfare provision in Soviet Russia[3]; the exercise of civic and political rights, however, was severely restricted under the rule of the Party-state. Secondly, throughout the Soviet period non-heterosexuals were formally excluded from the citizenry, as same-sex sexualities were criminalised and medicalised, and actively constructed by the Soviet state as non-legitimate and deviant. I will therefore draw on the notion of sexual citizenship only when discussing post-Soviet Russia, to explore the emergence of new opportunities for representation, association and consumption for non-heterosexuals post-1991.

The chapter charts shifting discourses on sexualities, framing them within macro-level changes in the Soviet/post-Soviet gender orders, and focusing on the regulation of same-sex sexualities. While the demise of state socialism in 1991 represented a crucial turning point, this chapter stresses continuities as well as changes between Soviet and post-Soviet Russia.

The Soviet gender order and institutionalised homophobia

As in other modernising societies, discourses of sexuality that aimed to control the health and growth of the population emerged in Tsarist Russia during the late nineteenth century (Engelstein, 1992; Healey, 1993, 2001). The medical and legal regulation of same-sex desire, and the appearance of categories of male and female homosexual, was part of a broader repertoire of medical and legal discourses which penetrated into the Russian empire through the influence of Western European industrialised societies (*ibid.*).

The October Revolution (1917) and the foundation of the Soviet socialist state radically transformed Russian society, and saw the emergence of new discourses on sexuality and gender. While Tsarist Russia had been a rural country, with an overwhelmingly peasant population and a limited industrial base, the Soviet government engineered a large-scale process of industrialisation, urbanisation and bureaucratisation of everyday life, as part of an ideologically driven plan to modernise the country. As Hoffmann (2003) notes, Soviet state socialism was a quintessentially modernising project, of which women's emancipation and the transformation of family and intimate life were an integral part. During the 1920s, the newly formed Soviet state promoted legislation which aimed to free Soviet women from the yoke of the patriarchal family, including legal recognition of *de facto* marriages, abortion, divorce, maternity leave and alimony; these provisions were among the most progressive in the industrial world at the time (Ashwin, 2000; Buckley, 1989). Liberalisation also characterised attitudes towards sexual matters, as offences against public morality, including male same-sex relations and prostitution, were decriminalised (Engelstein, 1995; Buckley, 1989; Healey, 1993). Moreover, sexual matters, largely considered the domain of morality and religion in Tsarist Russia, were reframed as a scientific concern, to be dealt with by medical and health professionals (Healey, 2009).

By the 1930s, however, the utopian optimism and social experimentation which had characterised the early years of the new regime came to an end. According to Hoffmann (2003, p. 7), the Stalinist period (1928–1953) was crucial in consolidating the key features of Soviet modernity, through the introduction of the command economy, rapid industrialisation, the collectivisation of agriculture, and the consolidation of a heavily centralised political and administrative system. The Stalinist period also signalled a return to more conservative gender and family policies, which institutionalised a distinctive Soviet gender order. The latter was rooted in biologising notions of femininity and masculinity as polar opposites, and endorsed the nuclear heterosexual family as the founding unit of Soviet society (Zdravomyslova and Temkina, 2007a; Ashwin, 2000).

While the family had previously been viewed with suspicion, as a bourgeois institution, the Soviet regime now emphasised the social function of the 'new' Soviet family. The latter was to serve the needs of the socialist state, rather than being championed as a private commitment or source of personal fulfilment. Indeed, the primary loyalty of Soviet citizens was to the collective and the state, rather than to the private sphere of personal relations embodied by the pre-revolutionary family (Ashwin, 2000; Shlapentokh, 1989; Kharkhordin, 1999). In spite of the Soviet state's formal commitment to gender equality and the emancipation of women, citizens' rights and duties to the state continued to be defined on the basis of their gender. Women's roles in Soviet society were defined by the 'working mother' gender contract: they were expected to contribute to the building of state socialism both through paid employment and through childbearing and domestic labour. In return for the fulfilling of her duties, the state protected the working mother by providing a vast array of maternity benefits and welfare provisions, which allowed her to comply with her maternal role without having to give up paid employment (Ashwin, 2000; Issoupova, 2000; Baraulina, 2002), and emancipated her from financial dependence on men.

The 'working mother' gender contract was a distinctive feature of state socialism in the Soviet Union and in other parts of the communist Soviet bloc: all citizens, irrespective of their gender, were mobilised into the workforce, and this resulted in much higher employment rates for women than in the capitalist west (Einhorn, 1993). In some respects, this bolstered women's status in Soviet society: the right to work and free education, as well as access to extensive welfare, was guaranteed to all, and women's participation in the public sphere of work and politics was encouraged and protected by the state. However, male privilege in the public sphere was largely preserved, as male citizens were assigned the roles of soldiers (defenders of the Motherland) and workers (builders of socialism) (Kukhterin, 2000; Goscilo and Lanoux, 2006), while women, by virtue of their 'naturally' caring role, were tasked with the double burden of housework and paid employment. Domestic work was mostly considered to be the responsibility of 'working mothers', and was rarely equally shared in Soviet households; thus, Soviet women carried the double burden of paid employment and unpaid domestic labour (Ashwin, 2000). On the other hand, men were largely marginalised in the private sphere of family life, as the paternalistic Soviet state emasculated men 'as head of household by eroding their roles as primary providers in their families' (Johnson and Robinson, 2007, p. 28; Issoupova, 2000).

Reproduction and childbearing were considered women's most precious contribution to society, and portrayed as the 'natural calling' of each woman. While during the 1920s Bolshevik feminists such as Aleksandra Kollantai had tried to assert women's right to sexual pleasure outside the realm of reproduction and marriage, Stalinist policies explicitly harnessed female sexuality to reproduction, reinforcing the double standards that assume an 'active' and 'unbridled' male sexual drive and a 'passive' and 'restrained' female sexuality. Throughout the Soviet period normative femininities were strongly associated with motherhood, and state policies remained staunchly pronatalist. While the notion of reproduction as women's responsibility towards the nation is not unique to Soviet Russia (Yuval-Davis, 1997), the persistent emphasis on reproduction as a duty to the state, rather than as a matter of private choice, arguably is. The need for an extensive workforce to modernise the newly born Soviet Union, to make up for the huge population loss caused by WWII and later to further economic growth under an economic system that was very labour intensive meant that the 'cult of Soviet motherhood' was not just a matter of mobilisation in time of national crisis, but remained a lasting feature of the Soviet gender order (Hoffmann, 2003; Buckley, 1989; Field, 2000).

The Soviet government's recriminalisation of male homosexuality (1934) broadly coincided with the campaign to strengthen the heterosexual nuclear family, and can be seen as part of a broader effort to harness sexuality to reproduction and emphasise the value of the nuclear family's role as the founding unit of Soviet society. Both male and female same-sex sexualities transgressed the Soviet gender order, and were stigmatised as deviant and perverted; however, much like in other parts of the capitalist industrialised world, the regulation of same-sex desire in Soviet Russia was differentiated along gender lines (West and Green, 1997). Only same-sex relations between men were criminalised, and punishable with up to five years in a prison camp; the anti-sodomy law, introduced in 1934, remained in place until 1993, unlike in other socialist states, where similar legislation was repealed much earlier (Long, 1999). Male homosexuality was also condemned as a vice that had no place in Soviet society, and was consistently associated with the moral corruption and the influence of bourgeois western societies (Healey, 2001). Although criminalisation concerned only male sexuality, both male and female homosexuality were defined in similar terms as a perverted attraction to persons of the same sex in medical discourse. Initially, the medical profession overlooked female homosexuality and considered it a deviance that could be corrected by pressures to conform to 'compulsory motherhood'; however, from the late 1950s, the resurgence of Soviet sexology also marked a renewed interest in lesbianism, which was to be cured through forced hospitalisation, the use of psychiatric drugs and psychological therapy (Healey, 2001, p. 244; Gessen, 1994). While men having sex with men could potentially incur harsher punishment, they also enjoyed greater sexual licence in some respects, as male sexuality was less strictly tied to reproductive and family roles (Healey, 2001).

Intimacy, sexuality and real existing socialism

Countering common narratives of Soviet Russia as a monolithic, totalitarian society, ruled with an iron fist by the Soviet Party-state, many scholars have shown that the latter did not achieve a complete 'top-down' control of Soviet citizens. The state-centric gender order was preserved throughout the Soviet period; however, a limited liberalisation of gender policies occurred after Stalin's death in 1955 (Zdravomyslova and Temkina, 2007a; Rotkirch and Temkina, 2007). Moreover, despite the socialist state's scope to intrude into citizens' private lives through its control of economic assets and political life, to some extent intimate life was 're-privatised' in the late Soviet period. Throughout the early Soviet period, marked by the upheavals of forced industrialisation, collectivisation and urbanisation, in urban areas communal living in workers' hostels or shared flats (*kommunalki*) had been the norm. The 1960s, however, marked the start of mass housing construction, designed to give to each family its own apartment (Attwood, 2010): although this goal was not met and severe housing shortages continued, flats in high-rise blocks became the most widespread form of housing in Soviet cities.

Moreover, for many Soviet citizens, the private sphere and the realm of family and intimate relations came to be perceived as a site of authenticity, and a refuge from the intrusive Soviet state (Shlapentokh, 1989; Einhorn, 1993; Oswald and Voronkov, 2004). Besides the private sphere, which was never completely safe from the interference of state bureaucracy, Oswald and Voronkov (2004) distinguish two public spheres. The first 'official-public' sphere was the domain of the Party-state and officialdom, strongly regulated from above and policed through strict censorship; this sphere did not allow for the emergence of autonomous political subjects or social movements independent of state structures, and was characterised by a high level of conformism to the official party line. The second 'private-public' sphere encompassed spontaneous collective activities and spheres of communication, comprising personal networks and subcultural *milieus*. The 'private-public' sphere, however, did not amount to a platform where citizens could freely come together to articulate common interests and become political subjects: this articulation was actively discouraged, censored and punished by the Party-state, largely preventing the emergence of an autonomous civil society and independent political subjects.[4] The 'private-public' sphere escaped the rigid control of Soviet authorities, but retained an informal character, and remained outside the margins of the public sphere proper. It was only within informal environments, such as dissident and subcultural circles and personal social networks, that issues around intimate citizenship could be expressed and articulated, although they did not acquire any public visibility (Zdravomyslova, 2003).

As Rotkirch notes, by the 1960s sexual behaviour among the Soviet urban population was beginning to change along the same patterns as those of other industrialised countries. The key features of this 'sexual revolution' in the 1960s and 1970s were earlier sexual debuts, greater numbers of sexual partners over the life course, increasing rates of premarital sex and extramarital affairs, and higher divorce rates (Rotkirch, 2004, p. 94; Kon, 1995). While most western capitalist societies at the time experienced a liberalisation and pluralisation of representation of sex and sexuality, in Soviet Russia changes in sexual behaviour were barely reflected in the public sphere, as sexuality continued to be a legitimate topic of discussion only when linked to marriage and reproduction. A neglect of the sexed body and a negative attitude towards non-reproductive sex and sexual pleasure (even within the realm of married coupledom) were pervasive features of the Soviet gender order (Zdravomyslova, 2001; Kon, 1995).

Giddens (1992) sees the emergence of 'plastic sexuality', or sexuality disconnected from its ties to procreation and kinship, as a key moment in the transformation of intimacy in western societies, linked to the emergence of more pluralist and reflexive discourses on sex and sexuality. This was linked not only to the wider availability of more reliable contraception, disentangling women's sexuality from reproduction, but also to the rise of social movements, such as second wave feminism and gay liberation, which contributed to the pluralisation and politicisation of discourse about sexuality. In Soviet Russia, however, the disconnection between sexuality, reproduction and kinship did not occur in the public sphere. The Party-state's monopoly over the public sphere did not allow for the politicisation of sexuality 'from below', and the notion that 'the personal is political' did not resonate in a society where the private sphere was widely experienced as a refuge from state intrusion and from the hypocrisy of the 'official-public' sphere. Thus, public discussion on family planning and sexual intimacy remained constrained even in the late Soviet era (Popov, Visser and Ketting, 1993; Temkina and Zdravomyslova, 2002; Zdravomyslova, 2001), and discussion of sex in the public domain – 'whether educational, entertaining, pornographic or philosophical' (Rotkirch, 2004, p.

93) – remained severely limited, given the Party-state's control over the public sphere and the acknowledgement of sexual intercourse as legitimate only as part of married life.

Moreover, reliable birth control remained largely unavailable, both as a result of state pronatalist policies and as a side effect of the 'shortage economy', which made contraceptives difficult to come by or unreliable (Popov, Visser and Ketting, 1993; Popov and David, 1999; Rivkin-Fish, 1999). In the absence of alternatives, abortion, which was legal and universally available, was widely used as a means of birth control, even though it was actively discouraged by health practitioners. It is widely acknowledged that in Russia the 'sexual revolution' took place in two phases: the late Soviet period was characterised by a liberalisation of sexual practices; however, this was combined with a 'lack of institutional reflexivity towards these practices' (Rotkirch, 2004; Zdravomyslova, 2001). The second phase of the 'sexual revolution', the pluralisation of discourses about sex and sexuality, did not take place until the late 1980s/early 1990s, in parallel with the relaxation of media censorship under Gorbachev and the demise of state socialism (*ibid.*).

The discursive reinforcement of the 'natural' link between sexuality, reproduction and the nuclear family was facilitated by the state's monopoly over the means of production and the allocation of employment and welfare, which gave it a great deal of control over citizens' living arrangements and intimate lives (Zdravomyslova, 2003; Kharkhordin, 1995, 1999; Shlapentokh, 1989; Oswald and Voronkov, 2004). Support for the nuclear family was upheld through welfare allocation and in the state-controlled media, while there was very little recognition for alternative models of family and intimate relations (Temkina and Zdravomyslova, 2002; Klugman and Motivans, 2001). Early marriage and childbearing were almost universal and although, like elsewhere, the number of single-parent families grew steadily from the 1960s, late Soviet Russia was characterised by relatively low levels of cohabitation and childbearing outside of marriage by European standards (Klugman and Motivans, 2001, p. 9). Nonetheless, beyond this appearance of conformity and neglect of bodily pleasures, there was a marked discrepancy between official discourses and everyday practices. This is well documented in the work of Anna Rotkirch (2000, 2002, 2004), based on autobiographical accounts of Russian men and women's sexual lives collected in the 1990s, and in Elena Zdavomyslova's research on the café Saigon *tusovka*, which touches on sexual practices in dissident and countercultural circles (Zdravomyslova, 2003).

The regulation and invisibility of same-sex desire

In the late Soviet period same-sex practices continued to be heavily stigmatised and censored. Despite the liberalisation in Soviet criminal legislation that followed Stalin's death, the repeal of the law criminalising male homosexuality was not on the cards. On the contrary, conviction rates for men having sex with men increased from the 1960s onwards, and the law continued to be enforced until it was finally repealed in 1993 (Healey, 2001). Many more men were charged but not prosecuted or convicted, and the police monitored homosexuals by maintaining 'pink lists' of suspected homosexuals (Gessen, 1994, p. 21; Kon, 1998, p. 314). Although lesbianism was never criminalised, both male and female homosexuality were strictly censored in the public sphere as one of the bourgeois vices that officially did not exist in Soviet society. Both female and male same-sex desire were symbolically confined to the prison camp, an environment where they could find expression and be tolerated as a surrogate of heterosexual relations and justified by the need to satisfy one's sexual urges in an 'unnaturally' same-sex environment. This created a strong association between homosexuality, social deviance and criminality in the eyes of the Soviet population (Zhuk, 1998; Kuntsman, 2009).

In late Soviet Russia, medical research on sex and sexuality established a neat divide between 'normal' sexuality, which was considered problem-free by virtue of its 'naturality', and barely in need of professional attention, and 'deviant' sexuality, which was considered both perverted and anti-social. The discipline of sexology, known as sexopathology in the Soviet context, classified homosexuality as a sexual perversion (Kon, 1997, p. 226). The use of forced psychiatric treatment on both men and women is documented, although it was more often directed at women, since male homosexuality was punishable by law (Gessen, 1994, p. 17). Women who were diagnosed as lesbians could be hospitalised and treated with psychiatric drugs; after being discharged, they were registered as mentally ill and were subjected to periodic examinations and sometimes to further psychiatric treatment, although by the late 1980s periodic medical checks were easier to evade (Healey, 2001, p. 244; Gessen, 1994, pp. 17–18). Moreover, as patients suffering from a mental illness, they could also be denied access to certain professions and to a driver's licence (*ibid.*).

As already noted, beyond reproduction, sexuality was considered a strictly private matter; overt references to sex and erotica were considered dubious and morally reprehensible, and were heavily censored by Soviet authorities. Discussion of same-sex desire, however, was even more constrained: both male homosexuality and lesbianism became taboo not only for Soviet media, but also in academic and professional circles, where even subjects such as same-sex relations in ancient Greece were considered improper and compromising (Kon, 1997, p. 225). While male sexuality was more publicly condemned as a crime, lesbianism remained much more hidden from public view, a fact that seemed to have contributed to low societal awareness of same-sex relations among women throughout the Soviet period (Clark, 1997; Gessen, 1997).

There is some evidence that in late Soviet Russia subcultural queer spaces and forms of solidarity existed in urban areas; however, these remained confined to the 'private-public sphere', and retained a distinctively clandestine character. Same-sex relations remained largely invisible, and their legitimacy was not articulated in the public sphere through gay and lesbian identity politics until the mid-1980s; in this respect, as Heller notes, 'gay and lesbian identities have no formal history of existence in [*Soviet*] Russia as in the West' (Heller, 2007, p. 197; see also Essig, 1999; Healey, 2001). Male homosexual street subcultures continued to exist in the biggest Russian cities throughout the Soviet period. Places for male homosexual encounters included cruising areas around certain public squares and gardens, as well as cafés: in Moscow these included the square adjacent the Bol'shoi theatre, a well-known cruising area, and by the late 1980s the nearby café Sadko, which was frequented by a mixed clientele but informally known as a 'gay' (*goluboi*) café (Essig, 1999, p. 84). There is also anecdotal evidence that in the late Soviet period, 'lesbian' networks gathered in private flats, or on the margins of relatively more visible and established male homosexual street subcultures (Zven'eva, 2007; Kozlovskii, 1986; Essig, 1999). However, unlike in 'western' capitalist societies, in Soviet Russia this did not lead to the development of a urban consumer culture, intertwined with the emerging gay and lesbian movement (D'Emilio, 1983; Castells, 1983; Chasin, 2000). This was linked to limited leisure infrastructures and opportunities for consumption in the Soviet command economy, as well as to the characteristics of the Soviet political system. It was only in the 1980s that informal politicised gay and lesbian groups began to emerge, although their existence is only patchily documented.[5] Nonetheless, the existence of sites of contestation indicates that, although the Soviet gender order was strongly heteronormative, by the 1980s it allowed for a limited articulation of solidarities based on a shared sexuality.

The post-Soviet gender order and the 'second sexual revolution'

The breakup of the Soviet Union and ensuing demise of state socialism was both preceded and followed by deep and broad-sweeping political, economic and socio-cultural transformations, first and foremost the transition to market capitalism and the privatisation of state assets, the transition to a pluralistic political system and the establishment of a constitutional democracy, and the process of nation-building for the newly independent Russian Federation.

These sweeping changes also affected gender policies and relations in Russian society. The Soviet gender order was monopolised by the Party-state and constructed around a single legitimate, ideologically approved gender contract (the 'working mother'). This existed alongside 'non-legitimate' gender contracts, encompassing practices and lifestyles which were heavily stigmatised and sanctioned (such as prostitution or homosexuality), and 'everyday' gender contracts, a pragmatic accommodation which involved outwardly 'fitting in' with the officially sanctioned gender contract but privately taking part in practices not acknowledged or contemplated by it (e.g. extramarital affairs), without straying into illegitimate, heavily stigmatised practices (Zdravomyslova and Temkina, 2007a, 2007c).

Beginning from the late 1980s, a shift occurred, from a Soviet etacratic gender order to a more pluralistic one. In addition to the old 'working mother' contract, newly legitimised contracts include the 'career-oriented woman' (a woman who focused on her professional career, rather than on family, and who may choose to remain childless/single), the 'housewife' (the stay-at-home wife of a male breadwinner) and the 'sponsored contract' (a transactional relationship where the woman is sponsored by a wealthy lover, and where sex is exchanged for gifts or other economic benefits). Despite the pluralisation of legitimate gender contracts, practices, values and norms grounded in the Soviet past remained highly influential (Zdravomyslova and Temkina, 2007b). The 'working mother' gender contract, in which women contribute to the family unity as independent earners and as main carers, remained the reality for most Russian women, dictated by the economic need to feed their family (either as part of a dual income family or as a single mother). However, in the post-Soviet period, being a 'working mother' is no longer an obligation to the state, and the state plays a lesser role in supporting women to fulfil their dual role as workers and mothers. State support through extensive welfare provision was replaced in post-Soviet Russia by the partial privatisation of welfare in the context of economic restructuring and widespread poverty, thus putting additional pressure on women to fulfil their roles as independent earners (Zdravomyslova and Temkina, 2007b).

Moreover, given the Soviet state's formal, but largely unfulfilled commitment to gender equality through 'emancipation from above', the idea of gender equality became widely discredited through its association with the Soviet past (Kay, 2000; Zdravomyslova et al., 2007d). Particularly in the 1990s, a common refrain was that the Soviet system had distorted men and women's 'natural' gender roles by 'emasculating' men (by reducing their authority in the private sphere of the family) and 'masculinising' women (by granting them access to 'male' occupations and diverting their energies from their 'natural' calling as mothers and carers). The corollary of this idea was that market capitalism, supported by the (neo)liberal state, would return Russian men and women to their 'natural' roles. Thus, in the post-Soviet period essentialist notions of femininity and masculinity as rigidly defined opposites grounded in biology were reinforced (Kay, 2000, 2006; Zdravomyslova et al., 2007). Despite the pluralisation of legitimate gender contracts, the new socio-political and economic system did not necessarily bring greater gender equality.

Transformations in the gender order were also reflected in a growing pluralisation of discourses on sexuality. According to both Rotkirch (2004) and Kon (1995), the liberalisation of the public sphere and the emergence of more pluralistic and open discussion of sex and sexuality in the media and popular culture amounted to a second 'sexual revolution' of sorts. The progressive loosening of state censorship over the media, which was started in the late 1980s by Gorbachev's reforms, led to a veritable burgeoning of representations of sexuality in the media; this phenomenon became even more conspicuous in the 1990s, with the introduction of market-oriented reforms, as sex and sexually explicit images became a marketable commodity and pornography and erotica a new line of business. Russian citizens' eager interest in a theme that was once heavily censored is evidence of the widespread desire to reclaim the sexed body, once the exclusive discursive domain of Soviet officialdom, as a private and individual realm, whose sensual needs and pleasures are valued in their own right (Omel'chenko, 1999, 2000). The articulation of pluralist discourses on sex and sexuality reflected more closely the everyday practices of Russian citizens, unlike in the Soviet period, where the existence of diverse, non-procreative sexual practices outside the boundaries of the married couple was hypocritically denied (Zdravomyslova, 2003). Liberals generally welcomed this pluralisation as potentially leading to a greater rationalisation of sex and sexuality (e.g. family planning, sex education, sexual health) (Zdravomyslova and Temkina, 2007a). Nonetheless, from the mid-2000s conservative discourses, reflecting very palpable anxieties about the graphic representations of sex and sexuality in the media and changing sexual norms, have become more prominent than liberal ones, and have increasingly framed sexuality as a social problem. Concerns about the influence of western popular culture on the sexualisation of Russian media, and widespread opposition to sex education in schools and family planning have long been voiced by nationalist parties from the right and the left, and by religious groups. Since the late 2000s, however, they have also found favour in mainstream party politics and with the ruling governments (Rivkin-Fish, 2006; Stella, 2007, 2013b). Russia's demographic decline has been used as an argument to support pronatalist policies to boost the national birth rate, and to restrict free access to abortion in 2003 and again 2011 (Rivkin-Fish, 2006, 2010; Henrich Böell Foundation Moscow, 2012).

Recent policy interventions to solve the demographic crisis have focused on financial support to families (initially named 'mother's capital', later 'family capital') as a way to increase the birth rate (Borodzina et al., 2011, 2013). This rhetoric bears striking resemblance to Soviet discourses, which framed motherhood as an essential part of a woman's life and as a 'social mission' (Kay, 2000, pp. 65–71; Henrich Böell Foundation Moscow, 2012; Borodzina et al., 2011, 2013). However, in post-Soviet Russia the state has relinquished its monopoly over economic, political and social life, and therefore its power to harness female sexuality into reproduction. Thus, in post-Soviet Russia motherhood is framed as a private choice rather than a duty to the state; nonetheless, the notion of motherhood as an essential part of a woman's life has not lost its compulsive moral force (Baraulina, 2002).

Sexual citizens at last? New queer visibility and moral panics

Changes in policy and legislation reflecting a liberalisation of the public sphere have been crucial in redefining the boundaries of sexual citizenship for non-heterosexuals since the demise of state socialism. In April 1993, as part of a wide-ranging legal reform, the article of the Criminal Code criminalising male homosexuality was repealed, following in the way of other ex-Soviet Republics. The new Penal Code, introduced in 1997, equalised the age of consent, as well as punishment for heterosexual and homosexual rape (Kon, 1998, pp. 318–319; LeGendre, 1998, pp. 20–21). Moreover, in 1999 the Ministry of Health eliminated homosexuality from its new classification of mental illnesses (Alekseev, 2002). Decriminalisation and demedicalisation were implemented from above, rather than resulting from public debates and consultations; indeed, according to sociologist Igor' Kon (1997), decriminalisation was pushed through because it was a precondition for Russia's membership of the Council of Europe. No affirmative legislation explicitly recognising sexuality as ground for discrimination was introduced following decriminalisation, and support for LGBT rights across the political spectrum has been non-existent.

Although informal queer spaces and politicised groups had already begun to emerge during the 1980s, decriminalisation paved the way for greater opportunities for consumption and association. During the 1990s commercial clubs and bars targeting a queer clientele began to open in the bigger Russian cities, some of which have since developed a vibrant gay scene. Russian LGBT media, which consisted of self-produced Xeroxed newsletters and literary magazines in the early 1990s (Essig, 1999), also developed significantly, and some of them became commercially successful: by the mid-2000s they included a number of popular gay and lesbian websites[6] and a few gay/lesbian lifestyle magazines,[7] as well as *samizdat* publications produced on a non-commercial basis. The new visibility of same-sex sexualities was not confined to queer subcultural spaces and LGBT media: representations of same-sex relations became common in mainstream media and popular culture over the 1990s. This process initially concerned mainly male homosexuality, but since the late 1990s images of lesbianism also became common, following the success and lasting popularity of Russian pop and rock acts such as Tatu, Zemfira, Nochnye Snaipery, Butch and Mara (Gurova, 2003; Nartova, 2004a; Heller, 2007). Some of these acts enjoyed enormous mainstream success, particularly among young people; the fact that they addressed, more or less explicitly, a novel and previously taboo theme such as lesbianism is generally acknowledged to be one of the reasons for their popularity (Titova, 2002; Grachev, 2002; Kabanova, 2003; Golovin, 2003; Paton-Walsh, 2003). These bands also acquired a massive following in lesbian/queer circles (see Chapter 6), as the Russian gay and lesbian media were keen to appropriate their frontwomen as 'lesbian' icons. All these 'lesbian' acts, however, retained a certain sexual indeterminacy: Zemfira and others hinted or ambiguously played with a lesbian image, but they did not explicitly identify with them, evading questions about their own sexuality and disavowing the 'lesbian' subtext of their songs and performances in interviews (Stella, 2008a). Drawing on Clark's insight, lesbian visibility in Russian popular culture can be seen as largely driven by market mechanisms, and therefore premised on sexual indeterminacy, in order to entice and entertain mainstream (and presumed heterosexual) audiences and a queer niche market simultaneously; while 'allow[ing] a space for lesbian identification', they 'must necessarily deny the representation of lesbian identity politics' (Clark, 1993, p. 132).

Following decriminalisation, sexual citizenship in post-Soviet Russia has largely been confined to rights to sexual expression and consumption, but does not extend to the political sphere of civic rights and liberties. The Russian context has some similarities with societies where, despite formal decriminalisation, same-sex sexualities continues to be policed through a heterosexist private/public divide, and limited liberalisation for a long time concerned only consumption and popular culture (for a discussion of the UK in the 1980s and 1990s see Evans, 1993; Richardson, 1998, 2000; McGhee, 2004). The limited liberalisation of the 1990s was followed by a backlash against the visibility of same-sex sexualities, couched in moralistic terms and reflecting moral panics about sexual liberalisation and its detrimental effect on the country's demographic crisis, and the pernicious influences of 'western individualism' and lifestyles on Russian young people.

Previous invisibility contributed to the perception of homosexuality as a new phenomenon: indeed, since the 1990s homosexuality has commonly been referred to in the Russian media as a 'nontraditional sexual orientation' (*netraditsiionnaia orientatsiia*), a term which is meant to be neutral but conveys the idea of a phenomenon alien to Russian traditions. The new visibility of same-sex sexualities in the public sphere has long been a source of anxiety, and has been particularly contentious if associated to political claims or politicised groups.

Since the 1990s, several Russian grassroots groups and organisations have been repeatedly denied official registration, although no law officially forbids the registration of LGBT organisations (LeGendre, 1998; Nemtsev, 2007). More recently, the yearly ban on attempts to organise a Pride march in Moscow (2006-present) has been a graphic reminder of how contentious the visible presence of same-sex sexuality in public remains (Stella, 2013b). Moscow Pride also illustrates how sexuality has become increasingly politicised, both from above and from below. New LGBT organisations such as GayRussia, formed in the mid-2000s, have been keen to adopt identity politics grounded in claims to recognition, visibility and equal rights (Stella, 2013b; Kondakov, 2013). On the other hand, campaigns to promote 'traditional' Russian family values and gender roles, supported by an unholy alliance between prominent members of the political elite and the Russian Orthodox Church, have increasingly portrayed same-sex sexualities as a 'western' lifestyle, alien to Russian traditions and contributing to Russia's demographic crisis. The backlash against the new visibility of homosexuality has culminated in the 2013 law against the 'propaganda' of 'non-traditional' sexuality to minors, which severely restricts the representation of same-sex sexualities in education, the media, and any sphere where the material is potentially accessible to minors (Wilkinson, 2013). The law is part of a broader legislative and policy initiatives aimed at defending Russian traditional values and protecting minors against pernicious influences. It is also indicative of a more general crackdown on civil liberties over the last few years, particularly freedom of expression and association, and of a stifling of pluralism in the political sphere in Russia. The empirical material discussed in this monograph was mostly collected in 2004–2005, before the backlash against the 'new' visibility of same-sex relations began to escalate in the late 2000s. Nonetheless, since the demise of state socialism, same-sex sexualities have been largely tolerated if discreet and confined to the private sphere, and on condition that sexual subjects do not become political subjects.

Generational sexualities and representations of same-sex desire

As the previous sections have shown, regulation of same-sex desire is enforced not only through criminalisation and medicalisation, but also through the enforced silence and invisibility surrounding same-sex sexualities. This symbolic erasure stigmatises same-sex sexualities, even as restrictions to the public discussion of sexual matters apply more widely, and other non-normative sexualities may also be constructed as deviant (Kon, 1995). Symbolic erasure was more strongly enforced under the etacratic Soviet gender order, where the public sphere was dominated by official ideology and therefore was less pluralistic. I draw here on interview material to show how shifting discourses on gender and sexuality are reflected in access to representations of same-sex sexualities for women from the 'last Soviet generation' and the 'generation of transition'.[8]

Noticeable differences emerged between the two generations, in terms of both ease of access and types of sources available. Younger women came across representations of lesbianism and bisexuality during their formative years and through a variety of sources, including newspaper and magazine articles, TV and radio programmes, films and specialised literature. Inna (Moscow, b. 1980) recalled watching a TV programme on lesbianism at the age of 13, and later telling her mum how she had seen 'such a great programme about lesbians! *(laughs)*'. Similarly, Maia (Ul'ianovsk, b. 1984) happened upon the American film *Colour of Night* (1994), featuring a lesbian subplot, when watching TV aged ten, and Zulia (Ul'ianovsk, b. 1980) remembered watching a pornographic film featuring a lesbian sex scene with her friends as a teenager. The wide range of representations of lesbianism mentioned by younger women in interviews range from fictional to pornographic, from scientific to politicised; sources of information ranged from mainstream press to LGBT information bulletins, and their availability reflects the pluralisation of discourses on same-sex desire and sexuality started in the late 1980s. Not all representations of lesbianism were perceived as affirmative and positive, or necessarily engendered a sense of identification; nonetheless, they constituted a semiotic and narrative repertoire which women could tap into to make sense of their experiences and desires, and even to fashion a 'queer self' (Holliday, 2001). This contrasts with the accounts of women from the previous generation, who had a much more limited access to a narrower range of representations of same-sex sexualities in their formative years. Older women often remembered very vividly the occasion when they first heard of the existence of same-sex relations, and medicalised notions of same-sex desire as pathological or deviant were prevalent in their recollections. Iana recalled how, at the age of 12, she first became aware of the word 'lesbian' and its meaning:

> She [*the girl she had a crush on*] was very cute, very interesting, and in general I just considered it absolutely normal [to show an interest in her], but [...] obviously I was giving her too much attention, as it happens, I wanted to talk to her all the time, I kept looking at her. And so it happened that one girl even asked me if I was a lesbian. I did not even know the word, and once I was back in Moscow I looked it up in the dictionary. [...] There was at the time a Soviet encyclopaedic dictionary, and it said that lesbianism is a perverted attraction between two women. Perverted... Well, of course I noticed

the word 'perverted', but the most important thing for me was that
it existed in nature. So I came to this as a bookworm [*laughs*]!

(Iana, Moscow, born 1966)

Other interviews also indicate that pathologising notions of lesbianism
circulated widely through reference work and books available to a non-
specialist readership, although a minority also had had access to more
affirming representations of same-sex desire through literary work by
the likes of Sappho, Proust or Colette. State censorship regularly purged
or banned work and media outputs which made explicit reference to
homosexuality, sex and erotica, as the latter were considered 'ideologically harmful' topics (Yurchak, 2006, pp. 214–215). Work by the
abovementioned authors may have escaped censorship because they
belonged to the accepted highbrow literary canon, although they were
likely to be the preserve of the educated urban intelligentsia. It should
be noted, however, that other women, like Iana, first heard the word 'lesbian' from peers or relatives. This suggests that same-sex relations may
have been an 'open secret' (Sedgwick, 1990) rather than being a topic
passed under complete silence, of which unsuspecting Soviet citizens
had no awareness whatsoever (Kon, 1995, 1997). Exposure to representations of same-sex desire was not just a matter of age, but also of
geographic location, social networks and socio-economic background,
as chapters 4, 5 and 6 show. Nonetheless, the relative in/visibility of
same-sex desire, and the presence/absence of narratives of social identity
grounded in a shared sexuality shaped very profoundly the experiences
of women from different generations, and the ways in which they articulated their subjectivities over time, as illustrated in the chapters to
follow.

Conclusions

The chapter has framed the regulation of same-sex sexualities within
shifting discourses on sexuality and sexual morality, and located the
latter within the Soviet/post-Soviet gender orders.

The particular model of state socialism which developed in the
Soviet Union shaped a distinctive gender order, which institutionalised
heteronormativity through the criminalisation and medicalisation of
same-sex desire and channelled women's sexuality into reproduction
through the notion of motherhood as an essential duty to the state.
Throughout the Soviet period, public discussion and information on

sex and sexuality was severely censored, as the individual pursuit of bodily pleasures was considered at odds with the collectivist ethos of Marxist-Leninist ideology. Public representations of sexuality were legitimate only if related to family intimacy and reproduction: this naturalised heterosexuality as linked to the imperatives of procreation, while 'deviant' same-sex sexualities were othered not only through medicalisation and criminalisation, but also through their symbolic erasure from the public sphere. A public 'reverse discourse' (Foucault, 1978/1998) did not emerge in Soviet Russia until the late 1980s: spaces for political opposition and countercultural movement were severely constrained by the Party-state. At the same time, limited opportunities for consumption and the non-commercial character of the leisure infrastructure were not fertile ground for the emergence of a queer consumer culture.

The demise of state socialism and the deep economic and sociopolitical transformations that preceded and followed it shaped a new, more pluralistic gender order, fashioned not only by state institutions but also by the market and by a variety of social actors. The new gender order did not necessarily usher in greater gender equality, but was accompanied by a second 'sexual revolution', and resulted in a more open and frank discussion of sex and sexuality in the public sphere. This, together with the decriminalisation and demedicalisation of homosexuality in the 1990s, opened up new opportunities for self-expression, association and consumption for non-heterosexual citizens. Nonetheless, the visible presence of same-sex sexualities in public remained contentious, particularly if associated with political claims. The public arena continues to be regulated by a heterosexist private/public divide, and in recent years there has been a noticeable backlash against the new visibility of homosexuality. Shifting discourses on sex and sexuality are reflected in the experiences and subjectivities of women from different generations.

3
Lesbian Relationships in Late Soviet Russia

This chapter contributes to debates about queer existence under real existing socialism, and particularly about the space for individual and collective agency under a political and economic system which was arguably able to exercise particularly strong forms of coercive and disciplinary power over the private lives of its citizens. It has been persuasively argued that the constraining effect of homonormative ideals was stronger in communist regimes than in western societies, where similar medical and legal discourses aimed at regulating 'deviant' sexualities also existed (Kon, 1997; Healey, 2001; Liśkova, 2013). Nonetheless, a question that remains largely unanswered is the extent to which 'disciplinary drives' controlled by the Party-state and inspired by collectivist ideology shaped lived experiences under state socialism, and the extent to which they allowed 'for agency, reflexivity and change' (Liśkova, 2013, pp. 14–15). Drawing on an analysis of original interview material, this chapter explores the lived experiences and subjectivities of Russian women involved in same-sex relations, or experiencing same-sex attraction, in the late Soviet period.

Existing work on Soviet same-sex sexualities has almost exclusively focused on mechanisms of regulation of same-sex desire mediated through the 'expert gaze' of the medical and legal professions.[1] Much of the literature draws on a Foucauldian framework, and seeks to understand how modes of biopower mediated through the law, medicine and education, and theorised by Foucault as a constituent feature of modern liberal capitalist societies (Foucault, 1978/1998), were articulated under state socialism in Soviet Russia (Engelstein, 1993, 1995; Healey, 2001). Existing research is mostly based on archival and documentary sources, such as police records, court documents, medical literature and memoirs of Gulag prisoners (Healey, 2001; Kuntsman, 2009; Zhuk, 1998). Thus, the literature has tended to privilege the perspective of professionals or witnesses, and to focus very heavily on the environments of the clinic and the prison camp, where homosexuality was symbolically confined by the Soviet state. While offering very valuable insights, existing literature offers only tentative and partial answers to many questions about the lives of Soviet queers: for example, how did non-heterosexuals live in 'ordinary' contexts (i.e. outside of the clinic and the prison camp) under real existing socialism? What made their lives so invisible? How did they negotiate their relationships?

Revisiting the Soviet past is important because Russian understandings of sexuality have been portrayed in existing literature as radically different from 'western' ones. Russian exceptionalism vis-à-vis 'the west' has often been linked to the country's 'totalitarian' Soviet past, particularly in literature produced by foreign researchers in the 1990s. For example, Essig (1999) has argued that Russian sexualities are inherently more fluid that western ones and are not premised on binary notions of sexuality as either heterosexual or homosexual. Essig substantiates her argument by referring to the high incidence of bisexual and transgender practices in the Moscow queer communities she studied. She also notes the wide use among Russians of euphemistic and ambiguous terms such as *goluboi, rozovaia, tema* and *nashi* (Essig, 1999, pp. x–ix and p. 197, n. 28), potentially more fluid categories than 'gay' or 'straight'.

The chapter shifts the focus from the macro-level of the 'expert gaze' to the micro-level of non-heterosexual women's everyday practices and experiences. It also foregrounds women's agency in the day-to-day negotiation of their intimate life, in an attempt to produce a more nuanced account of the Soviet past, and fracture polarised, essentialist notions of 'western' and 'Russian' sexualities. The first section discusses the role of medical professionals as well as the role of more pervasive and subtle mechanisms of everyday surveillance and shaming which contributed to make same-sex relations between women invisible in Soviet Russia. The second section analyses women's negotiations of their intimate relations and shows how the Soviet gender order shaped in fundamental ways women's relationships, everyday experiences and subjectivities. The final section links women's shifting subjectivities to their shared experience of isolation and their involvement in 'lesbian' social networks later in life, as same-sex sexualities became more visible in Russia over the 1980s and 1990s.

Biopower and same-sex desire in Soviet Russia

As noted above, existing literature on 'lesbian' existence in Soviet society has largely focused on the role of the medical establishment in policing and stigmatising 'deviant' behaviour (Healey, 2001; Essig, 1999; Gessen, 1994). Indeed, in Soviet Russia the only legitimate discourse about same-sex desire between women was produced by medical experts, and the notion of lesbianism as a pathology or deviance seems to have persisted among medical practitioners after the demise of state socialism and the official de-medicalisation of homosexuality. Essig (1999) and Gessen (1994) emphasise the pathologising character of Soviet medical discourses, and the potential consequences for women involved in same-sex relations in Soviet Russia. Both relate cases of women who had been reported to medical practitioners (usually by family members) and subjected to forced psychiatric treatment during the 1980s. According to Gessen (1994), a common experience for women reported to medics was being committed to a psychiatric hospital to undergo treatment. Once the treatment was deemed complete, the label of mental illness stuck, as women were expected to register with a psychiatric clinic for periodic checks and could be banned from certain professions and from obtaining a driving licence. Essig (1999) also highlights the importance of medical discourse in policing sexual morality in Soviet Russia, and stresses that female same-sex desire was considered as a disease to be 'cured', through either psychiatric treatment or gender reassignment surgery.[2]

Findings from this study, however, indicate that, alongside the 'expert' medical gaze, other more ordinary mechanisms of social control and scrutiny may have been as important in constructing same-sex desire as deviant. Moreover, forced psychiatric treatment may not have been a universally accepted practice among medical practitioners. None of the women I interviewed underwent forced psychiatric treatment because of their sexuality; there were, however, cases of women who, while being treated for other conditions, made medical practitioners aware of their attraction to women. Liuba (Moscow, born 1962) went to see a psychiatrist in 1987 when she was going through a period of depression, and disclosed her experience of being rejected by a woman she was in love with. As a result, Liuba was referred to a sexopathologist who did not administer treatment to cure her of her attraction to women, although the possibility of heterosexual 're-education' was suggested:

I went to a psychiatrist first [...]. She referred me to a sexopathologist. She took me to the Psychiatric Institute. I remember there was a laboratory there, with the sign 'sexopathology'...
And they never tried to cure you?
No, absolutely not. As I understand it, they treated me for depression. [...]. The worst thing is that they never gave you any information. It's impossible that sexopathologists didn't know about lesbians. They didn't say anything. Apart from nonsense such as 'show an interest in men'. In the same vein, they mentioned that they had this guy [presumably a patient] who liked men, and they supposedly re-educated him, and he started showing an interest in women.

Liuba's referral to a sexopathologist, and the attempts to 're-educate' another patient clearly signal that same-sex desire was seen as abnormal and pathological by medical practitioners. Nonetheless, no attempt was made in Liuba's case to forcibly 'cure' her of her lesbianism.

The experiences of another interviewee, Sofiia (Saint Petersburg, born 1953), also suggest that psychiatric treatment may not have been a universally accepted practice among medical practitioners. While working as a policewoman in a small town in the Urals in the late 1970s, Sofiia was called to deal with the case of a 17-year-old girl who had served a prison sentence in an all-women institution. The teenager had returned to live with her mother, along with a girlfriend, and they had started to live 'like husband and wife'. Worried about the situation, her mother had taken her to a psychiatrist, who ruled out medical treatment as ineffective in changing an individual's sexuality.

I went to see a psychiatrist because the girl's mother became very anxious about her; she took her to a psychiatrist and told her exactly what was happening. And the psychiatrist told her, 'I can prescribe some medication, but they won't be any use' [...] And when I understood that this cannot be cured, I started to ask the psychiatrist more questions, supposedly about that girl, but in reality I was asking about myself. She told me that you have to accept it for what it is, and added that until the age of 25 an individual's identity is still not rigidly defined, [*sexual*] orientation can change before the age of 25.

Like Liuba's consultant, the psychiatrist from Sofiia's hometown in the Urals adopted a hands-off approach and did not forcibly cure the young offender. Unlike in Liuba's case, however, the psychiatrist did not suggest the possibility of 'heterosexual reeducation', arguing instead that human sexuality is not something that can be artificially 'corrected' (*neispravimo*). Thus, treating lesbianism with psychiatric drugs may not have been a universally accepted practice. These discrepancies suggest that official medical guidelines may have changed over time, or that there may have been dissenting voices among medical practitioners; nonetheless, Liuba's and Sofia's stories also show that the notion of same-sex attraction as a deviance from 'natural' heterosexuality was upheld by medical practitioners even when the possibility of psychiatric treatment was denied. Essig (1999, pp. 228–229) emphasises the importance of medical discourse in policing the borders of sexual morality in Soviet Russia, arguing that 'threat of the Cure' operated mainly on a symbolic level to deter women from engaging in 'deviant' sexual practices:

> The possibility of being diagnosed as sexually/mentally ill and the resulting forcible interment in a Soviet psychiatric institution worked primarily at a symbolic level. The Cure [...] circulated as a threat. The diagnosis/cure symbolised removal from normal society into illness, perversion, and disease. It kept women on the *straight* and narrow.[3] Even women who enacted same-sex desire generally also enacted – or at least play-acted – heterosexual desire. Many lesboerotic women married men and/or had children, sure signs of 'health'. If a woman stepped too far out of line, the threat of the Cure could force her to return to the family of man.
>
> (Essig, 1999, pp. 28–29)

Medical knowledge no doubt played a key role in upholding the notion of same-sex desire as abnormal and deviant through the authority of 'objective' science; nonetheless, interviews show that pressures to conform to heteronorm were embedded in women's gender socialisation and manifested themselves in much more ordinary situations. Moreover, punishment (symbolic or otherwise) for engaging in 'deviant' sexual practices could come from social institutions other than the medical establishment, as in the case of Iulia (Saint Petersburg, born 1966), a working-class woman who had moved from Tatarstan to Saint Petersburg as a teenager to train as a tiler and plasterer. While working on construction sites and living in hostel accommodation with her workers' collective on the outskirts of Saint Petersburg, Iulia, then aged 20, was caught being intimate with another girl in the hostel's dorms. The pair was duly reported to the workers collective's comrades' court.

> We had what was called a hostel 'commandant', who could enter the room without knocking, to say for example 'be quiet' and the like. They caught us... They caught me with a girl, and they even had a comrades' court [*tovarishcheskii sud*] [...] We used to have criminal courts and comrades' courts: the workers' collective gathered and listed the offences committed by the person on trial, and the other comrades from the collective decided, for example, to deprive the worker of their salary, or some production prize, or voucher, or another popular option was to shun them [*boikotirovat'*]. This meant not talking to the convicted person for a while, ignoring them. We had a comrades' court and they decided to ignore us. And they told us that they would bring the case to the *Komsomol*[4] if we didn't stop this nonsense [*zanimat'sia erundoi*]. Everyone knew about us, but again the word 'lesbian' was never uttered, this was referred to as bad behaviour. [...] Morally corrupt behaviour [*moral'noe razlozheniie*]: members of the *Komsomol* do not behave like that.

Comrades' courts were nonprofessional tribunals staffed by volunteers (usually selected members of housing and work collectives); established to try minor offences, they were revived under the 1959 reform of Soviet law, which was intended to prevent the worst excesses of Stalinism and to involve ordinary Soviet citizens in the running of the justice system. They had the specific function of performing a persuasive and morally edifying role rather than a coercive function, although they also had the power to impose small fines and to recommend 'eviction from an apartment, temporary demotion to a lower-paying job, [...] dismissal or physical labour tasks for a small period' (Berman and Spindler, 1963, pp. 842–843; Gorlizki, 1998). Although comrades' courts were not explicitly tasked to deal with matters of personal relationships, these were understood to fall under the broad definition of 'antisocial behaviour' which did not constitute a criminal liability but was considered to be against accepted social norms. Thus, in actual fact Comrades' courts were called to deliberate on matters of sexual morality, such as extramarital affairs and sexual promiscuity (*ibid.*). Indeed, Iulia and her girlfriend had to stand a trial of sorts for 'morally corrupted behaviour' (*moral'noe razlozheniie*) unbecoming to a member of the *Komsomol*. Sexual morals, rather than sexual deviance, were invoked during the trial: as Iulia explained, the word 'lesbian' was never uttered, and no reference was made to pathologising notions of homosexuality. Nonetheless, punishment by public shaming was clearly intended to pressure the two young women to conform to heteronorm and to acceptable expressions of female sexuality. The outcome of the couple's exposure and shunning was exactly as intended, as Iulia's girlfriend succumbed to the pressure and ended the relationship.

Iulia's story also illustrates that the policing of sexual morals was not exclusively performed by experts and officials called upon to uphold accepted standards of 'Soviet' morality (medical practitioners, members of the Comrades' Court, the *Komsomol*). Indeed, Iulia's trial and punishment also involved the participation of her co-workers and even of Iulia's mother, who was notified of Iulia's conduct by letter, and asked to influence her behaviour, despite living miles away. Thus, while much existing literature has emphasised the role played by Soviet institutions, such as the punitive psychiatry and the legal system in regulating sexual and gender dissent, an exploration of women's lived experiences outside of the contexts of the clinic and the prison camp foregrounds the role of much more mundane and subtle disciplining mechanisms operating in the private and semi-private spheres. This includes the scrutiny by family members, peers and co-workers of 'excessive' interest shown in women, as in the instance related by Tania (Moscow, born 1969). Tania first learned about the existence of same-sex relations from her grandmother, who was concerned about the nature of her close friendship with another girl called Ol'ga:

> I remember that I was ill and bed-ridden, and Olia came to visit. And my grandmother also visited. My grandmother suddenly became suspicious, and started to ask why we were always together [*tak mnogo obshchaemsia*]. She began to talk to Ol'ga in the room next door. I can't remember what she said, but Ol'ga ran away in tears. And my grandmother told me, 'I think she wants something from you. You know, there is such a thing as love between women'.

Tania's relationship with Ol'ga was simply a friendship, and she was surprised at the time by her grandmother's reaction; the latter, however, shows that anxieties over same-sex relations as abnormal were part of family socialisation into normative femininity. It should also be pointed out that the notion of deviant femininity was not exclusively associated with same-sex sexualities, or with sexualised behaviour. Throughout the Soviet period, pronatalist policies and the 'working mother' gender contract reinforced the notion of marriage and the nuclear family as the golden standard, while a strong stigma was associated with remaining unmarried and childless, particularly for women.

Indeed, as the next section will show, Soviet conventional notions of marriage and the nuclear family shaped women's intimate practices and the ways in which they negotiated their same-sex relations in fundamental ways. Developing Healey's (2001)'s insight about the importance of the Soviet gender order in shaping 'lesbian' existence under real existing socialism, I argue that 'compulsory heterosexuality' (Rich, 1980), understood as hegemonic discursive practices endorsing heterosexual romance, marriage and the nuclear family as the 'natural' norm, was key in de-legitimising same-sex relations and in making them invisible.

Intimacy, same-sex relations and the working mother

Interviews with women from 'the last Soviet generation' reveal commonalities in their experiences and strategies to negotiate intimate relationships. Firstly, they experienced same-sex desire and/or relationships in isolation from 'lesbian' social networks. They also operated in a wider social context where same-sex relations were not only stigmatised but also invisible, a theme that will be explored in more detail in the next section. Secondly, lesbian affairs where one or both partners were married, or involved in a parallel heterosexual relationship, were common; thus, the notion of marriage and motherhood as unavoidable and as markers of 'respectable' womanhood feature prominently in older women's narratives, whether they had actually been married and become mothers or not. Recalling one of her first visits at a Moscow social club catering for older lesbians, Anna (born 1963, Moscow) spoke about a sense of recognition among the women present, as most of them shared the experience of marriage and parenthood:

> When I was at B.'s club, where they offer psychological support, there were perhaps twenty women, and when the psychologist asked, who had children, all did, who got married, almost everyone. We all got married.

Among the older women who took part in my research, the experiences of marriage and motherhood were indeed common, although not universal, in contrast to the profile of younger women. This is consistent with findings from previous research: Essig (1999) noted that most of the women involved in her research project had been, or were still, in a heterosexual marriage, an observation echoed in Rotkirch's article on lesbian relations in the late Soviet period (Rotkirch, 2002). This is likely to reflect the centrality of marriage and the heterosexual, nuclear family to the 'working mother' gender contract and the prevalence of marriage over other forms of partnership and cohabitation in Soviet Russia (Kaz'mina and Pushkareva, 2004, pp. 211–213). Demographic data shows that marriage was an almost unavoidable feature of Soviet life: according to the 1989 census, only 3.7 per cent of the male adult population and 3.5 per cent of the female population had never been in an officially registered union; although divorce rates were also very high by Western European standards, it was also very common for people to remarry, sometimes several times (Kaz'mina and Pushkareva, 2004, pp. 211–213; Bogdanova and Shchukina, 2003). Not only symbolic status, but also specific material benefits accrued to marriage and parenthood: for example, centralised mechanisms of housing allocation prioritised married couples with children, reflecting the institutional endorsement of the nuclear family (Attwood, 2010).

Older women often contrasted their 'lesbian' present to their 'heterosexual' past, where same-sex desire was hidden behind the semblance of a 'normal' heterosexual family life, or not explicitly articulated as 'lesbian' (see also Essig, 1999; Rotkirch, 2002; Tuller, 1996). It is tempting to read the widespread experience of heterosexual relations and marriage as a case of false consciousness, double life and compliance to dominant models of femininity. Nonetheless, women's accounts challenge such a straightforward interpretation, showing instead that their everyday practices subtly 'challenged pressures towards hetero-conformity', although the women involved in these practices may not necessarily reject, or aim to subvert, the 'working mother' gender contract that upheld heteronorm (Engebretsen, 2009, p. 3). Heterosexual marriages were sometimes short-lived, and motivated by practical reasons such as finding a living space and obtaining a residence permit: for example, Liza (born 1960s, Ul'ianovsk) moved to Leningrad as a young woman and got married to a heterosexual man she met through a lesbian friend; the purpose of the marriage was to obtain a residence permit[5] [*propiska*] and be able to remain in the city. Her husband knew about her lesbianism and, although they lived together, their relationship was not sexual; when she moved away from Saint Petersburg, she voluntarily gave up any rights she had on her ex-husband's flat.[6] In other cases, reasons for getting married were more complex, and ranged from a desire to have children to a real emotional attachment to one's husband, particularly for women who had identified as heterosexual in earlier parts of their lives and talked about their heterosexual relationships as meaningful and grounded in genuine feelings of love and attraction. Even when well aware of their attraction to women, women did have agency in negotiating the terms of their heterosexual relationships and motherhood, as Katia's experiences (Moscow, born 1956) of her engagement and marriage indicate:

> [*After the end of a relationship with another woman*] I fell for one of my [*female*] teachers, I lost my mind, I almost quit college, I was jealous of her and thought that somehow I had to put my life in order [*ustraivat' zhizn'*]. My first fiancé died, he was a film director, he was a very good person. It was difficult for me to imagine a married life with him, but he was a very good person [...]. Then I started saying that, well, I will get married anyway to the first man who comes by [*pervogo vstrechnogo*]. I just wanted a child. Of course I was just plucking up courage by saying that I would get married to any man. I chose myself a suitable, promising [*perspektivnyi*] person. I mean, suitable because we had common interests. And promising in the sense that he would not just sit and watch TV, but he would try and make something out of his life. This is how things turned out. I didn't particularly hide from my husband my crushes [*on women*], but he was ok with it [*on normal'no k etomu otnosilsia*].
> *Did he know about them from the very beginning?*
> Yes, and so did my closest friends. [...] But the fact that he knew was not a bad thing. At least our relationship was clear.

Katia retrospectively talked about her marriage as a choice taken in order to settle down and to have a child. Like other ever-married women, she spoke about marriage as a fact of life and an inevitable rite of passage to adult womanhood; however, she also emphasised that she had sought a companion who would make a good husband and father. After her marriage, Katia had a daughter and maintained a good relationship with her husband, who (unusually) was aware of her lesbian affairs from the beginning of their relationship and did not see them as threatening. Katia continued to be romantically and sexually involved with women after getting married: however, she saw her loyalties and responsibilities as lying mainly with her family, and her lesbian affairs could only be accommodated on the margins of family life. Only after her daughter moved out and her elderly mother died did Katia feel freer to pursue more actively her lesbian love interests. Other women who had been married talked about how they jostled same-sex relations with heterosexual marriage and motherhood and how the two were not incompatible, as long as romance did not interfere with family duties and responsibilities. The realities of marriage and heterosexual family life were not universally experienced as unproblematic, and some women were quick to point out the oppressive and constraining aspects of their living arrangements. Anna (born 1963, Moscow), for example, enjoyed a degree of freedom and independence in her marriage, but found the experience of living a 'double life' crippling and unsettling on a personal level; moreover, even after her daughter had moved out, she did not have the heart to end her 20-year marriage, both for fear of hurting her devoted husband and because she was unable to imagine a different life for herself. Nonetheless, women's retrospective accounts emphasised that they had agency in negotiating intimate relationships and ways to become a mother, both within and outside of wedlock. Some women deliberately chose to have children out of wedlock in order to avoid the trappings of heterosexual marriage. Iulia (Saint Petersburg, 1966) had mainly been involved with women and realised in her mid-20s that she wanted a child. She conceived her son with a male friend, with the mutual agreement that he would not be involved in the child's upbringing:

I befriended men, and they made friends with me. So I spoke to a friend and told him I wanted a child. And he...We had a verbal agreement: 'If you are not going to burden me with a child...', I mean, we made a deal. That he was not present and would never be. He had his travels...He had plans, he wanted to go abroad and not come back, he was a sailor in the merchant navy, and he did not want any burdens. I promised that I would not blackmail him. We made a deal, and I gave birth.

Like Iulia, Tamara (born 1952, Moscow) had a strong desire to have children; as a young woman she had sexual relations with both women and men, but found the realisation that she could form meaningful emotional attachments only with women very painful, as she expected she would be unable to have children. She accidentally became pregnant with her first child in her mid-20s and decided to give birth and raise the child on her own, with the help and support of her mother. Tamara later met a married man who was willing to conceive and parent 'from a distance' two more children with her, but she continued to be romantically involved mainly with women.

Same-sex relations where one or both partners were married, or involved in a parallel heterosexual relationship, were common, and same-sex relations mostly remained hidden behind the semblance of a 'normal' heterosexual family life. Indeed, marriage and motherhood were sometimes strategically used as a 'front' to avoid associations with stigmatised 'deviant' femininities. Tania (Moscow, born 1969) thus recalled the marriage of the girlfriend she had been involved with as a teenager:

> At the time, our relationship reached a deadlock, at least I could not see how to make it work again. Anything could happen, beginning from Ol'ga's marriage. We met on Friday, and on Monday I was told that there was one Alesha, who was meeting her after work. I could not understand what was going on. [...]. She got married. And then, after 22 days, she managed to get rid of her husband [*laughs*]. She ticked in the box for the future, so to say. I don't judge her for this. I asked her, I pestered her about this, I said: explain to me at least one thing, why, what pushed you to get married in such a rush?!? She told me that people could see through our relationship and so on. But I didn't get an answer that made sense.

For Tania's girlfriend, getting married was a way to divert suspicions regarding the real nature of her relationship with Tania and to reaffirm a 'respectable' femininity. Although marriage was rarely pursued with this aim alone in mind, other women mentioned that their status as mothers, wives, widows or divorcees could be used to keep suspicion of being sexually 'deviant' at bay and to mask their lesbian relationships as friendships. The invisibility of same-sex relations, however, did not only result from women's strategy to negotiate a 'respectable' femininity, but also from the fact that cohabitation with a female partner during the Soviet period was an extremely rare occurrence for the women interviewed, and often was not even contemplated as an option for very practical reasons, as Tamara (born 1952, Moscow) explains:

> During the Soviet period the majority of the women I dated eventually got married and lived a heterosexual life, I mean, same-sex relations had no prospects. For two women, well, you could of course live, sort of, together, but at the time there were huge problems with housing, and it was difficult to explain to your parents why your girlfriend was staying. There was no way around it, lesbian couples simply had nowhere to live.

Under the political economy of state socialism, Soviet citizens had limited control over their living arrangements: as private ownership was virtually non-existent, publicly owned housing was allocated to most citizens through local councils or the workplace. A chronic housing shortage, compounded by the preferential allocation of housing to married couples with children, meant that single unmarried individuals, and often single-parent families too, were expected to live with their family of origin, or in *kommunalki* (shared flats), or in hostel accommodation (Attwood, 2010; Di Maio, 1974). Tamara herself, as a single mother with four children who had relationships mainly with women, lived with her mother until the latter's death. Thus, during the Soviet period, living with another woman was rarely an option, or involved fortuitous and temporary living arrangements, such as sharing a room in a student or workers' hostel or in a *kommunalka*. The high symbolic and material capital that accrued to the nuclear family, and to marriage and motherhood as obligatory rites of passage into adult womanhood, resulted in severe constraints on the possibility of lasting same-sex relationships. Women like Tamara, who had mostly been involved in same-sex relations, talked about dating mainly 'straight' women, who would eventually get married and lead a heterosexual life.

At the same time, heteronormative ideals about couple relations and parenthood shaped the experiences and expectations of women involved in same-sex relations. Lack of long-term prospects of sharing a home with a female partner and starting a 'proper' family contributed to the widespread perception of same-sex relations as unviable. In women's retrospective accounts of the Soviet past, same-sex relations compared unfavourably to heterosexual coupledom, which was seen as offering better prospects to settle down and to receive social approval by conforming to the key markers of respectable femininity and adult womanhood – getting married, moving out of the family home and starting a family. Larisa (born 1951, Saint Petersburg) had her first lesbian relationship in her early 20s with a woman she met at work; although Larisa was living on her own after the death of her mother, her girlfriend Marina continued to live with her parents for fear that moving in with Larisa would reveal the real nature of their relationship. Marina, pressurised by her family, eventually decided to get married in order to start a family. The affair continued for some time, but eventually Larisa and Marina decided to end their relationship so as not to wreck Marina's marriage, although they remained friends. Larisa herself eventually got married 'out of calculation' (in her own words), in order to start a 'normal' family herself, although she continued to have lesbian affairs throughout her marriage. Aglaia (born 1957, Saint Petersburg) similarly split up with her first girlfriend when the latter decided to get married, a decision Aglaia understood and supported at the time because, as she explained, 'with a man you can start a family'. Similarly, never-married, childless women experienced their marginalisation not only as stemming from the pathologisation of same-sex relationship, but more importantly as a consequence of what was outwardly perceived as their 'failure' to conform to normative femininity. The realisation that marriage and parenthood were incompatible with their desire and disposition to have relationships exclusively with women was experienced as a loss by many of the women who remained single and childless. Sofiia (born 1953, Saint Petersburg) never wanted to get married and start a conventional family, and had relationships exclusively with women. She experienced same-sex relations as short-lived and casual, and the realisation that her partners saw relations with women as unviable in the long term, ending the relationship in order to get back to married life, or start a heterosexual relationship, led to a period of depression:

> I did not want to get married, I did not want children at the time, I looked at women only as objects of sexual desire, that is how I felt during this period. And I thought that I was born a moral freak [*moral'nyi urod*], why am I like this?! It was a really painful time for me, when I did not want to go on living.

The fact that marriage and heterosexual relationships were commonplace among Soviet queers has been interpreted as evidence of the exceptional fluidity of Russian sexual practices and identities vis-à-vis binary 'western' constructs of sexuality as either heterosexual or homosexual (Essig, 1999; Tuller, 1996; Heller, 2007; Baer, 2009). This interpretation, however, is arguably symptomatic of the excessive explanatory power accorded to sexual identities in much scholarship on sexuality (Kulick, 2000), and risks essentialising Russian sexualities as 'exceptional' and exotic. As noted in Chapter 1, however, research on same-sexualities conducted in the US and UK, shows that intertwined narratives of hetero/homosexual pasts and presents, and evidence of the fluidity of sexual practices and subjectivities, are not unique to Soviet Russia (Rosenfeld, 2002, 2009; Taylor, 2009).

I propose, instead, that the particular configuration of 'compulsory heterosexuality' inscribed in the 'working mother' gender contract, by upholding heterosexual romance, marriage and the nuclear family as the 'natural' and socially desirable norm, made same-sex relations both invisible and unviable in Soviet Russia. Indeed, the analysis of older women's intimate practices shows that the notion of marriage and motherhood as key markers of adult womanhood shaped in fundamental ways their subjectivities and relationship strategies.

Queer *tusovki*, shared narratives and changing subjectivities

Much of the literature on Soviet same-sex sexualities, particularly work published in English by non-Russian scholars, has emphasised the radical difference between western and Russian sexualities. The point that Russian queers do not identify on the basis of their sexual practices, and resist fixed notions of identity such as 'gay' and 'lesbian' is particularly emphasised by Essig, an American sociologist who conducted research in Moscow in the 1990s (Essig, 1999). Essig's monograph *Queer in Russia* has been particularly influential, as the first and for a long time only research monograph on same-sex sexualities in post-Soviet Russia available to an international, English-reading audience, although similar views also echo in other scholarly and journalistic accounts of 'queer' life in Russia (Tuller, 1996; Baer, 2009). Essig (1999, p. 174) describes the 'queer' Russia she explored in the1990s as 'a world of multiple desires and flexible identities that was not yet colonised by Western notions of sex and its meaning', and identifies this fluidity as a peculiarity of Russian sexual culture, predicting that Russians would continue to resist binary notions of identity rooted in western culture, since Russia has a 'long cultural tradition of' not assuming 'coherent and stable identities' (*ibid.*). Essig argues that the fluidity of Russians' sexual subjectivities and practices is an inherent characteristic of Russian culture, unwittingly essentialising both Russia and 'the west' in the process.

Findings from other empirical studies conducted in the late 1990s and early 2000s in Russia, including my own, contradict Essig's argument about the fluidity of sexual subjectivities and practices as evidence of Russian exceptionalism (Nartova, 1999, 2004c; Omel'chenko, 2002a, 2002b; Zelenina, 2006; Stella, 2010; Sarajeva, 2011). Empirical evidence points to the fact that, by the late 1990s, women involved in non-heterosexual relations did identify on the basis of their sexual practices, albeit inhabiting categories of identity such as 'lesbian' or 'bisexual' with a degree of ambiguity (Stella, 2010; see also Nartova, 2004c; Zelenina, 2006). I argue that a generational perspective can offer more nuanced explanations for the discrepancy between women's identifications and their intimate practices, noted by Essig and others researching Russian same-sex sexualities across the 1980s and early 1990s.

As noted previously, older women involved in my research often contrasted their 'heterosexual' past to their 'lesbian' present; reluctance to identify according to their same-sex practices can be linked both to the notion of shifting sexual subjectivities and identifications over the life course (Rosenfeld, 2002, 2009; Plummer, 2010) and to the fact that more pluralistic discourses about same-sex sexualities, including terms such as 'lesbian' as a reclaimed term and positive narrative of social identity, only became available to them later in life. The complexity of the meanings associated to different sexual and intimate practices, and the ways in which subjectivities and identifications may change over the life course is nicely captured by Kira (born 1956, Saint Petersburg), a widow with three marriages behind her and two adult children. Looking back, Kira juxtaposes her 'heterosexual' family life and previous bisexual practices with her 'lesbian' present, when she is exclusively dating women and is very involved in the organisation of informal lesbian gatherings:

> I like the word 'lesbian' – perhaps I don't fully have the right to call myself a lesbian, although I do it all the time. Because I lived a heterosexual life, I mean, in essence I am bisexual. The fact that there are no men in my life at the moment, and that perhaps there may not be [*in future*] does not mean that I have become a lesbian. I have always been bisexual, and perhaps I am still one. Everyone considers [*a bisexual*] a woman who sleeps with both men and women at the same time. It is not necessarily like that, you can love a woman, you can love a man, and not necessarily mix the two. [...] They [*women from her 'lesbian' social network*] challenged me here, 'You have not been "on the theme" [*v teme*] for very long', I say, it depends on how you look at this. How do you start counting how long I have been 'on the theme'? From 2005–06 [*when she started socialising in 'lesbian' circles*], or from twenty years ago, when I met my first woman? Who can say? Each one will answer in their own way.

Women with a 'heterosexual past', like Kira, may struggle to reconcile their practices and subjectivities with neat categories of sexual identity. However, women with limited or no experiences of heterosexual relations were also somehow reluctant to identify according to their sexual practices. They often contrasted their present, in which their practices were articulated as 'lesbian' or 'bisexual', to a past where same-sex desires and relationships remained hidden and were not articulated in terms of sexual identity. Aleksandra (born 1946, Moscow), who, as a young woman, had relations with both men and women, and was briefly married in her late 20s, started to have relations exclusively with women after the end of her marriage. Despite her long-term same-sex relationship, she linked her reluctance to identify as a lesbian in the past to her experience of isolation and lack of contact with other non-heterosexuals:

My permanent [*postoiannaia*] sexual life with women started rather late. Soon after the separation from my husband, at 27–28. With my partner we've been living together for more than 30 years. We never talked about this, we never talked about being lesbians. We just loved each other and started living together, that's all. At the time our social circle was heterosexual, our friends were heterosexual. And then, little by little, some gay men appeared around us, then others. And our friends, our social network, began to change. In general, most of our closest friends are now gays and lesbians. And all the more now. And only later, by degrees, I got to the understanding that I am a lesbian.

Aleksandra's experiences suggest that sexual subjectivities and identifications reflect women's engagement not only in same-sex sexual practices, but also in socio-cultural ones: as Plummer (1995) argues, sexual identities are relational, and feed upon communities and shared narratives. The latter were, by and large, unavailable to older women during the Soviet period: they mostly experienced same-sex desire and/or relationships in isolation from 'lesbian' social networks, and operated in a wider social context, where same-sex relations were not only stigmatised but also invisible. Tania's memories echo Aleksandra as she (born 1969, Moscow) recalls how, when she was involved in her first same-sex relationship in the late 1980s, neither she nor her partner identified on the basis of their sexual practices because they had no contact with other non-heterosexual women:

We didn't have any contacts with lesbians. We didn't have any of that. I remember that I never pronounced this word [*lesbian*] about myself. I mean, I didn't think anything. I understood that I loved the person, and this person happened to be a woman. We had no organisations; we had no bars, no cafes, nothing like that. [...] I knew, I had read about the fact that these women, who love women, exist. But I didn't rank myself as one of them. Perhaps I was a bit, let's say, dishonest to myself. I didn't think over the fact that I had a particular [*sexual*] orientation. [...] I was in love with the person. For me this was more, how can I say this, other, social... In society there are certain attributes you have to conform to. I never thought about this, that I had to conform to something.

As Tania points out, widespread isolation and lack of contact with others involved in same-sex relationships, and the very informal and hidden character of queer subcultures in Soviet Russia, resulted in the lack of shared social practices and narratives of identity (Plummer, 1995). Thus, sexual subjectivities were more fluid than in 'the west' because 'homonorm' (Duggan, 2002) failed to crystallise in Soviet Russia.

Like Aleksandra and Tania, all the women from the 'last Soviet generation' who took part in my research lived in isolation and did not have any contact with, or access to, queer or 'lesbian' social networks until at least the early 1990s, when the relaxation of media censorship made it possible for informal 'queer' groups to acquire some degree of visibility. Although there is evidence that such networks existed in Soviet cities, only one of the older women who took part in the research had belonged to a queer *tusovka* in her youth. Liza (Ul'ianovsk, born 1960s) moved from her native Ul'ianovsk to Leningrad (today's Saint Petersburg) at the age of 17 as a working student, and pursued her humanities education while also working various unskilled jobs. In the passage below, Liza talks about how she met members of the Saint Petersburg queer *tusovka* 'absolutely by chance', and found out that its members socialised on the central Nevskii Prospekt, near the shopping mall Gostinnyi Dvor and the nearby park at Ekaterinskii Sad. This chance encounter gave her the confidence to make a pass on Tamara, the girl she had been in love with for two years:

> She [*Tamara, the young woman she had a crush on*] was already sexually experienced, I did not have a clue. She always said that women cannot have sexual relations. [...] Then I met the Saint Petersburg *tusovka* absolutely by chance. [...] I was always looking for an excuse to nestle up to her, when we were on the bus I always wished it was thronged. She seemed to respond, but we never talked openly. I courted her for two years. Then I found out about sex between women, in theory at least, when I met Masha and Ksiusha.[7] They put me on the right track... [*laughs*] [...] Ksiusha singled me out. She stared at me... well, it's a long story. We were sitting on the same train, and she started telling me that she had a girlfriend, and she was in love with her. It was a shock for me, and I asked her how it ended, and she said that they got married. Then I met her girlfriend and we became friends.

This was a momentous encounter for Liza: after making Masha and Ksiusha's acquaintance, she initiated a sexual relationship with Tamara, while also actively socialising with the Saint Petersburg queer *tusovka*.

Following the breakup of her relationship with Tamara, Liza moved to the city of Alma-Ata[8]; through her contacts in Leningrad, she was able to locate the city's predominantly male queer *tusovka*, which similarly socialised in the city centre, near the Youth Theatre. As Liza's experience shows, the hidden and clandestine character of queer networks meant they could only be located through personal contacts and, for this reason, were very difficult to access. Indeed, most interviewees from the 'last Soviet generation' had been completely oblivious to the existence of these networks as young women. For those, like Tamara (born 1952, Moscow), who had been vaguely aware of them, their clandestine character prompted associations with the criminal underworld and sexual promiscuity, engendering dis-identifications, particularly among women belonging to the educated intelligentsia:

> There was a lesbian mafia, where all sorts of criminal activities were going on, where people were blackmailed. Perhaps [*name of an acquaintance*] may be able to tell you about this. [...] Because she belonged to those circles, she knows them as an insider. But I was from polite society [*iz prilichnogo obshchestva*], I studied in a prestigious institution, and later I worked at this very educational institution. She [*later*] helped me through her criminal environment, because I was isolated and closeted [*v podpole*]. [...] They gathered at the so-called *pleshki*.[9] The Moscow *pleshka* was located at Kitai-Gorod, at the time it was called Nogin Square, this is where people met, it was a single *pleshka* for men and women. There was another well-known place, across from the Bol'shoi Theatre, which was mainly a cruising area for men. But I never went to these places, I was afraid of them, for me that was not associated with homosexuality [*gomoseksual'nost'*], but with criminality, deviance, I was afraid of them.

Tamara's associations between queer *tusovki* and criminality or deviance, and her reluctance to become part of this world, suggests that in Soviet cities queer *tusovki* had classed connotations, and were associated with working-class and bohemian subcultures.[10] This is confirmed by autobiographical material recently published in Russia, such as the memoir of singer-songwriter Ol'ga Krauze (Krauze, 2009), who was part of the same Saint Petersburg *tusovka* as Liza.

Only beginning from the late 1980s – with the gradual relaxation of censorship which allowed for the pluralisation of discourses on sex and sexuality, and the emergence of the first commercial and community spaces – did women from the 'last Soviet generation' began to be aware of 'lesbian/queer' spaces and informal networks. It was often through information found in the press, on TV and (later) the internet that interviewees started to socialise in 'lesbian' circles, or to form personal networks, which included other non-heterosexual women. For women like Zhanna (born 1962, Moscow), personal dating ads were not only a means to find a partner, but also a way to be introduced to 'lesbian' networks and to end their isolation:

> There was this silly personal ads paper. It had a section called 'She plus she'. I wrote a personal ad and got it published. And I got lots of letters. More than a hundred. I made a selection. If there were grammar mistakes, I just replied 'no'. I tried to reply to everyone, I wrote, 'sorry'. I met four or five of the women who replied to my ad. I understood that there was a *tusovka*. One of these women took me there.

Women dated the appearance of the first newspaper articles discussing homosexuality and of the first personal dating ads to the relaxation of censorship inaugurated by Gorbachev in the late 1980s, and to *perestroika*, understood as the period of economic restructuring and political transition spanning from the Gorbachev leadership until the late 1990s. The internet, which became widely available in urban Russia from the late 1990s, also resulted in the creation of virtual queer communities and enhanced opportunities to contact 'lesbian' networks for those women who had access to personal technology (see Chapter 6). This contact was initiated at different points in time, and at different stages in women's lives, depending on individual circumstances, and women had different levels of involvement in 'lesbian' networks. At the time when the research was conducted, all the older women who took part in the study had some level of contact with community spaces and informal lesbian networks. For many, making contact with social networks which hinged on the articulation of same-sex desire as a shared narrative of identity was a turning point in their 'identity careers' (Rosenfeld, 2002, 2009), and many did identify as lesbian or bisexual, although often with some degree of ambivalence.

Conclusions

By focusing on the lived experiences of women involved in same-sex relations, rather than on expert discourses aimed at regulating and disciplining same-sex desire, the chapter has contributed new empirical and conceptual insights to extant work on Soviet homosexualities.

While most previous literature has emphasised the role of punitive medicine in enforcing heteronorm and disciplining same-sex desire, the chapter has shown that forced psychiatric treatment of lesbianism may not have been a universally accepted practice in Soviet Russia. Instead, findings point to the importance of more subtle, 'everyday' mechanisms of surveillance, stigmatisation and shaming, inscribed into the Soviet 'working mother' gender order and the political economy of state socialism, and aimed at harnessing women's sexuality to reproduction.

These mechanisms shaped women's experiences of same-sex relations as non-exclusive and often taking place alongside heterosexual marriage and parenthood. Nonetheless, interview material also shows that women exercised agency in negotiating their intimate relations and family life. Indeed, as Zdravomyslova (2003) points out, during the late Soviet period the discrepancy between officially sanctioned sexual morality, reflected in the public sphere, and the actual intimate practices of the Soviet population, became increasingly apparent. Disciplinary mechanisms also contributed to making same-sex relations invisible, foreclosing opportunities for association and the emergence of shared stories and identity narratives coalescing around a shared sexuality. This accounts for a reluctance to identify on the basis of same-sex practices, as noted by some researchers in the 1990s. It has been argued that the indeterminacy of sexual identifications among Russian queers reflects peculiar national understandings of sexuality as fluid, which differ deeply from binary 'western' notions of gay/straight, male/female (Essig, 1999). I have argued instead that Russian exceptionalism vis-à-vis 'the west' has been overstated, and that changes in women's subjectivities can be illuminated by a generational perspective, as their 'identity careers' (Rosenfeld, 2002) to a large extent map on to shifting discourses on sex and sexuality in late Soviet/post-Soviet Russia, and to new opportunities for association and consumption.

The above discussion about 'lesbian' relationships and subjectivities in Soviet Russia highlights the plurality of queer geotemporalities, and chimes with critiques of the global influence of 'western' constructs of sexuality as a driver of change in non-western contexts. Theorisations of the 'modern' homosexual are widely acknowledged to be based on the experiences of 'western' societies (Foucault, 1978/1998), and typically posit a strong link between capitalism, individualisation and the crystallisation of gay and lesbian identities (D'Emilio, 1983). Yet the topic of sexuality and socialist modernities is still underexplored in the literature. Further empirical explorations of queer lives under state socialism across the former 'Soviet bloc' and beyond can challenge western-centric assumptions in sexualities studies, as well as soften and complicate essentialist accounts of 'Russian' and 'western' sexualities. Moreover, while the global proliferation of queer identities and cultures is widely seen as a process emanating from 'the west', a focus on endogenous transformations within societies 'in transition' can challenge the assumption that global influences radically transformed local sexualities or created entirely 'new' sexual cultures, and reveal continuities as well as discontinuities with the socialist past.

4
Family Matters: Negotiating 'Home'

This chapter shifts the focus of analysis from time (the intersection between generation and sexuality) to space (the way in which women negotiated their sexuality across different places and locations), a theme which also runs through the following two chapters.[1] Chapter 4 focuses on the private space of 'home', while chapters 5 and 6 deal with women's negotiations of public or semi-private spaces (the workplace, the street and places where 'lesbian' or 'queer' *tusovki* socialise).

Interview data indicates that 'home' was perceived by non-heterosexual women both as an intimate, comfortable space and as a place where everyday homophobia was most commonly experienced. Indeed, particularly for young women still living in the parental home, home was the place where they felt most vulnerable and exposed, and social relations within the home were also the most uncomfortable to negotiate; on the other hand, interviewees generally downplayed experiences of discrimination and marginalisation in public and semi-public places, where one's sexuality could be more easily bracketed or hidden behind a public 'front'.

This chapter focuses on women's negotiation of home as a physical space and as a site of social relations, rather than on family. Focusing on home rather than family opens up the field of enquiry to include material aspects of family life, and to account for the different ways in which people 'do' family, kinship and personal relations (Widerberg, 2010; Morgan, 2011). An abstract focus on family as an institution would fail to account for the specific living conditions prevalent in urban Russia, a context which was often referred to during interviews and needs to be spelled out here.

Firstly, in post-Soviet urban Russia, young people's access to an independent living space continues to be restricted by the endemic scarcity and overcrowding of housing, a legacy of the Soviet shortage economy.[2] The most common form of housing in urban areas remains flats in housing blocks several storeys high, where living conditions are often cramped and afford little privacy.[3] Lack of privacy and limited prospects to leave the parental home clearly affected the lives of younger women, the majority of whom still lived with their family of origin, whether because in full-time education or because they were unable to afford to live independently. However, unlike in Ul'ianovsk, in Moscow a significant number of younger women were incomers and lived independently in shared flats or university accommodation; moreover, there was no straightforward link between adulthood and independent living, as some women in their 30s and 40s had moved back in with relatives, either out of economic necessity or because they were caring for older family members. Indeed, owing to very unstable socio-economic conditions and to the scaling down of welfare provision, in post-Soviet Russia the support of kinship networks has often been crucial to the survival strategies of poorer households (Rimashevskaia, 2003; Pavlovskaia, 2004).

A second reason why a focus on home rather than family is deemed productive here is that it allows an exploration of the parental home, as well as of women's experiences of leaving the family nest and establishing an independent household. Literature on same-sex families usually makes a firm distinction between families of origin – where LGBT youth is typically subjected to scrutiny and homophobic prejudice – and 'families of choice', 'alternative' family formations based on affective ties and creative household arrangements not based on blood relations (Weston, 1991; Weeks, Heaphy and Donovan, 2001). However, 'parental homes' and 'homes of choice' are not isolated entities, but are connected by both personal and symbolic ties (Morgan, Patiniotis and Holdsworth, 2005, p. 98; Buck and Scott, 1993; Bertone and Pallotta-Chiarolli, 2014). A focus on home better teases out the connections between the two, without overstating the separateness of heterosexual and non-heterosexual kinship.

This chapter explores the complex emotional connotations which make 'home' both a place of comfort and discomfort. It explores women's experiences of the parental home as a site of gender socialisation, and how women negotiate their sexuality within the parental home; more briefly, the chapter also explores women's transition to an independent home, and how their relationships with family members are affected by their sexuality, even after they leave the parental home.

Family matters

The private sphere of the home is associated in both the popular imagination and academic writing with a safe haven, or a space of ontological security and authenticity (Duncan, 1996; Moran and Skeggs, 2004; Valentine, Skelton and Butler, 2003). Indeed, the word 'home' typically conveys feelings of comfort and authenticity: to 'feel at home' is to feel safe, at ease, in a familiar, intimate place where there is no need to hide behind a 'public persona', where one can 'be oneself' (Rapport and Dawson, 1998). However, much like work on domestic violence (Stanko, 1985), research on LGBT youth's experiences of the parental home has contributed to expose the 'myth of the safe home'. Indeed, for many LGBT young people the parental home is the environment where they are socialised into normative heterosexuality and normative gender roles, and it is often experienced as a place of surveillance, discomfort and closetedness, where children, particularly as dependents, can become vulnerable to marginalisation and violence (Takács, 2006; Valentine, Skelton and Butler, 2003; Dunne et al., 2002; Prendergast et al., 2002). Within the enclosed space of the home, children are subjected to the 'family gaze', which Morgan defines as 'the way in which family members constitute other family members or relationships through the deployment of the gaze' (Morgan, 2011, p. 93).

Most of the women who took part in my study experienced the parental home ambivalently. The parental home was associated with emotional security and comfort, and with loving family relationships; yet at the same time it was often experienced as a site of scrutiny and control, where disclosing one's sexual orientation could have negative consequences. For younger women, who are often still financially dependent on their parents, coming out could ultimately compromise their independence within the family home.

Women whose sexuality was disclosed or uncovered in the home (either through their intentional coming out or accidentally; see Plummer, 1975) experienced a variety of immediate reactions from family members, ranging from damning, to mixed, to accepting. A situation of family conflict, however, was a rather common consequence of coming out, being outed, or being suspected to be gay. In the most extreme cases, disclosure resulted in being taken to a psychologist, being locked in the parental home, being subjected to emotional blackmail, being physically assaulted or voluntarily leaving the family home. For Dasha, conflict in the parental home led to a period of homelessness.

I ran away from home a few times, this happened in XXX [*her home-town*] and in XXX [*the city where she moved to, and where she lived with her grandmother*]. It was pretty tough, I mean, independence was hard to obtain. At the time I didn't have any qualifications, so I had to work as a cleaner and as a letter carrier. But I stood up for myself. [...] The first time I was 17. It was really horrible, I had to starve, but in the end I got the best of them. [...] In the end my parents said: 'Come back, do what you want, we won't hassle you.' The first time, when I left home at 17, it was because my dad hit me. I had brain concussion, for this reason I left. I think this is unacceptable [...] In [*her grandmother's city*] I left home when I met a butch girl [*who became her girlfriend*] and my parents started to object, I left home for five months. I had to leave the music school and say goodbye to this career, because it was tough, I didn't have anything to eat, I was hungry and cold, my fingers didn't bend and I could not play and exercise. I had to leave, and I still regret it.

(Dasha, Moscow)

As Dasha's experience shows, affirming one's identity and independence in a situation of family conflict can come at a very high price for young women. Far from representing a 'merely cultural' (Butler, 1997) form of oppression, homophobia within the parental home can have very real consequences for the lives of young women, affecting not only their emotional wellbeing, but also their material circumstances. Although conflict was a fairly common outcome, not all women experienced this to the same degree. Some family members were more accepting of homosexuality, although acceptance was often tempered with reservation and a sense of loss:

She [*her mum*] came home, this was when I was still living in XXX [*her hometown, a city in the south of Russia where she was living with her parents*], and she was crying. I say, 'Mum, why are you crying?'; she says: 'I fell out with the woman from the canteen [*bufetchitsa*]'. 'What happened?' 'She said that you love a woman'. 'And what did you say?' 'I said, this is my daughter, and I will always love her the way she is'. It was as if a burden fell off my shoulders. I didn't have to tell her, she told me openly that she accepts it.

(Ira, Moscow)

Ira's mother, who had already had inklings about her daughter's sexuality, clearly signalled her unconditional love for her, a gesture that came as a huge relief for Ira. However, her mother was also deeply upset by the news: as Ira pointed out later in the interview, she was not just hurt by her acquaintance's judgemental attitude, but also concerned that her daughter won't be able to have children and start a 'proper' family. Ira's story highlights two crucial issues in young women's negotiations of the parental home: first, heterosexuality was both assumed and expected in the parental home; secondly, family members' expectations were deeply rooted in normative notions of femininity and of women's 'natural' roles as wives and mothers. Because these expectations were deeply ingrained, disclosure (voluntary or accidental) in the family home often caused tensions. In many cases these tensions were eventually overcome; however, resolving conflict often took time, as both young women and their family members had to come to terms with their sexuality. Instances in which family members did not see same-sex attraction as inherently problematic were much rarer.

> Although, when my mum and I had our first discussion about this... She asked, well, all these men want to marry you, and you keep turning them down, you're so difficult. I told my mum that I love Iana, and that, as they say, I am not interested in men. 'Well then, the most important thing is that you are happy.' Thus we settled the matter.
>
> (Oksana, Moscow)

Oksana's experience was fairly unusual among my respondents, in that she felt safe enough to 'come out' to her mother of her own accord, and that her mother acknowledged her sexuality. Indeed, because of the high stakes involved, women did not always consider disclosing their sexuality to family members a safe or viable option.

Strategies for negotiating sexuality in the parental home

For young women, disclosure in the parental home was a very sensitive issue, given the high stakes involved. Disclosing one's sexuality was not always a matter of personal choice: indeed, many women were not open about their sexuality in the parental home, or their sexual identity remained ambiguous by virtue of a complicit 'don't ask, don't tell' family protocol. Disclosure was for many a case of being found out, or being second guessed, in homes which often afforded little privacy. Women related cases when family members became aware of their sexuality by reading their private correspondence, by observing their androgynous looks, 'strange' friends and lack of interest in dating boys, by catching them being intimate with another female, or by being informed by solicitous friends and neighbours. Negotiating one's sexual identity in the parental home involved varying degrees of openness for different women, depending on one's personality, family relations and circumstances. Most young women deployed various strategies of dissimulation, often playing on family members' assumptions that they were 'naturally' heterosexual. The expectation that disclosing their sexuality was unsafe, as it represented a potential source of conflict and distress, was widespread, and often based on awareness of intolerance of sexual 'otherness' in the family environment. Fear of being outed was often a source of anxiety, particularly for those women who were acutely aware of family members' negative views of same-sex relations. Maia had a difficult relationship with her mother, who showed both concern for her daughter and fear of her sexuality:

> My mum has a very negative attitude to this [*homosexuality*], she doesn't know. She understands, but doesn't want to believe it. She is waiting for me to say that I have a girlfriend, but she doesn't want to hear it. She finds the very idea unpleasant. For her, this is the worst thing that a person can do, it's worse than drug addiction. For her, they [*gay people*] are not persons. She said that if she learns something [*about her*], she will disown me and kick me out.
> *How do you know she'll do that?*
> She often talks to me about this. Because I am 20 and I only hang out with girls, and because of my looks [*very androgynous*]. And when she asks me questions, or tells me about things she's heard, she would always tell me that she doesn't like it. And she takes it out on me. When she abuses lesbians, I defend them, and this upsets her. And it gives me away.
> *You stand up for gay people, but don't tell her about yourself?*
> Yes. I don't tell her because I don't want to lose my mum. Only for this reason.
>
> (Maia, Ul'ianovsk)

In spite of hints and suspicions, Maia's sexuality remained ambiguously suspended between her mother's insight and their common fear of spelling out the obvious. For Maia, still living with her parents, confirming her mother's inklings could trigger domestic warfare, compromising their relationship. This option was therefore ruled out as too risky, both materially and emotionally. Maia was torn between conflicting loyalties:

first, her need to affirm her identity and defend lesbians in general; and second, her love for her mother. Maia interpreted her mother's anxiety and her demand that she go to see a psychologist as misplaced maternal concern. Awareness of negative attitudes to homosexuality in the parental home prompted a cautious and guarded behaviour. For some women, this meant not discussing or hiding their sexuality altogether in the parental home, a process which often continued after they had moved out. For others, it meant 'coming out' to their families only after they had moved out, or had achieved some degree of independence within the parental home. Still others deferred the exploration of their sexuality to a period when they had secured an independent living space, an event often associated with moving to another city for either study or work, particularly among Moscow respondents. In Alia's experience, exploring her sexuality was conditional upon moving out of the parental home:

> I had my first girlfriend when I was 21. I was already at college [*in Moscow*], I lived in a student hall [*obshchezhitiie*], separately from my parents [...]. It was 1993 [...]. We met at the beginning of my first year [*at college*], but I called her only a year later. At the time, this was not out of character for me. I was so stressed out, I had left my parents' home for the first time – a serviceman's household, in a small military town [*in the Moscow Region*], where I had finished school. I couldn't see anything apart from these obstacles, I didn't have a social life. I wanted to stand on my feet and quietly finish my first year, get used to my new environment. So that they would not kick me out, they would not know about me, of course I was afraid that there may be consequences. I wanted to establish myself in this new place. When I finished my first year and I started to feel freer, I called this girl. I thought that I would have to explain for an hour who I was, a whole year had gone by. But she recognised me straight away, she was glad to hear from me, and we arranged to meet up.
>
> (Alia, Moscow)

Alia's strategy is based on previous negative experiences in the family home: when her mother found out about her crush on another girl by sneakily reading her mail, she threatened to disown Alia and leave her without her family's material support if she did not change her ways. The decision not to disclose one's sexual identity to family members, however, did not only stem from fear of losing material support, or from women's unwillingness to disrupt family peace. Concerns about putting a strain on family relations, or about becoming emotionally estranged from loved ones were also prominent. Moreover, young women living in the parental home did not necessarily regard themselves as dependents occupying a subordinate position: support was often mutual, and resources and responsibilities were shared. Particularly when living with older, sick or vulnerable family members, interviewees were concerned that their 'coming out' may prove unnecessarily stressful, or painful for their relatives, and did not see any particular gain in revealing their sexuality. While very open about her sexuality to friends and acquaintances of both sexes, Lara, a woman in her early 20s who worked as a lawyer and lived with her family of origin at the time of the interview, was positive that she did not want her family to know:

I had a hard time when some girls called at home; there was never anything between us but they liked me, and perhaps they thought they were in love with me. They called my mum and told her that, you know, your daughter has this [*lesbian*] lifestyle. Well, I tried to demonstrate to my mum that of course that's not true, I have a husband [*although at the time she had divorced him and moved back with her family of origin*], and everything's normal. My mum is a person of very strict principles, she would not get over it [*ne perezhivet*]. She has a weak heart, I don't want to traumatise her, I don't want her, or my granny, to know. If my dad was alive, I think he would understand me. I think it would be a big problem if my family knew.

(Lara, Moscow)

The advantages of 'coming out' to her family were not apparent to Lara: her sense of responsibility and the urge to protect her grandmother and ill mother from an uncomfortable truth predominated. Indeed, coming out was not always perceived as a necessary or empowering act, and authenticity ('being oneself') was not considered paramount in women's decisions on whether to disclose their sexual orientation. These were often based on a complex interplay between emotion, affect and a pragmatic assessment of the benefits and risks involved. Strategies to negotiate the family home rarely involved denial (deliberately 'passing' as heterosexual): it was more common to exploit ambiguities and commonly held assumptions in order to remain invisible as a lesbian or bisexual woman. In this respect, women often remained 'tacit subjects' within the family home, occupying an ambiguous space simultaneously 'in' and 'out' of the closet (Decena, 2011). Silence and dissimulation, however, were not the only strategies deployed to negotiate one's sexuality in the parental home; a few women had come out on their own initiative, most commonly to mothers and siblings, rather than fathers, who were perceived as more aloof from family life, or had not been involved in their child's upbringing at all. Kristina talked about coming out as an act of personal growth, which was necessary to maintain an open and trusting relationship with her family, and compared her experiences with those of her girlfriend Sveta.

> [...] I didn't have the same tension, because my mum had relationships with different men, while Sveta's mum had a family for family's sake [*sem'ia radi sem'i*]. But I had a family for love's sake [*sem'ia radi liub'vi*], and my family values first of all the feelings that you have for a person, perhaps for this reason they accepted Sveta so easily, and it wasn't just my mum, but my gran and grandpa as well, they know everything too. They are quite open, they were simply presented with the facts [*postavili pered faktom*] and they accepted them. [...] From the very beginning, no one informed them, but they were gradually given hints, you have to be skilful at this. [...] It was all built on honesty and openness. I mean, they were always open and honest with me, and I was always the same to them.
>
> (Kristina, Ul'ianovsk)

For Kristina, disclosure was empowering in a context where openness and respect were central to family relations. Even for Kristina, though, coming out was a protracted process of negotiation, which involved patience and emotional intelligence, rather than a dramatic, 'one-off' event, as it is sometimes conceptualised in the literature (for a critique see Seidman et al., 1999). It is a commonly accepted wisdom that coming out to one's family is paramount to non-heterosexual individuals' healthy psychological and emotional development (for a critique see Green, 2002; Seidman et al., 1999); findings from this study, however, suggest that this assumption should be questioned. On balance, openness was not necessarily seen as positive and empowering, and interviewees tended to downplay the values of personal authenticity and affirmation of one's identity commonly associated with the act of coming out (see also Nartova, 2004c; Omel'chenko, 2002b, pp. 497–498). On the other hand, they often emphasised the importance of skilfully navigating the parental home without unnecessarily disrupting family relations, compromising one's independence and causing discomforts and conflict.

Rethinking coming out and homophobia in the parental home

In much sociological literature, coming out of the closet is conceptualised as an individual endeavour: either as a 'speech act' challenging the silence surrounding same-sex desire, or as the personal act of 'privately and publicly coming to terms with a contested social identity' (Seidman et al., 1999, p. 9; Plummer, 1995, pp. 82–84; Brown, 2000). However, as the previous sections and other research show, disclosure is not always tantamount to a voluntary act of 'coming out' or to a personal choice, but may result from unwanted exposure by family members. Thus, Valentine, Skelton and Butler (2003) propose reframing coming out as a collective process of identity negotiation.

A related point is that 'home' extends beyond the physical boundaries of one's abode, as family ties extend beyond the parental home, and do not exist in isolation from other social networks (Moran and Skeggs, 2004, pp. 94–97). Women were aware not only of scrutiny from family members, but also from neighbours and acquaintances. This was especially the case with women who grew up in Ul'ianovsk, and who described time and again the city as a small place 'where everyone knows everyone else'. Lack of anonymity was raised as an issue in Ul'ianovsk, but not in Moscow; this is due not only to Ul'ianovsk's smaller population, but also to the fact that in my Moscow sample there was a high proportion of incomers who had moved to the capital from other cities, whereas women from my Ul'ianovsk sample were mostly local, and had strong ties to their local communities, where 'your neighbour's opinion still counts' (Klavdiia, Ul'ianovsk). Women from Ul'ianovsk were more concerned about the possibility that rumours about their sexuality may spread to the parental home. Being outed by family acquaintances was a very unpleasant experience for Valia:

> They [*her parents*] guessed, and some kind people helped, they told them on my behalf. Some of my enemies. I still don't understand who, but that's what happened, someone told them [*her parents*]. And my mum drove me to a corner with this question, is it true or not. I could not say 'no'. There was no point in denying it.
> *What was their reaction?*
> Very negative. Well, of course unpleasantries [*nepriiatia*], and tears, and my mum went hysterical: 'I gave birth to you and you make me such a gift, I want grandchildren'. I tried to explain to her that if I am in a relationship with a woman it doesn't mean that I won't

have a family, I won't have children. But she said that she would feel ashamed in front of everyone.

(Valia, Ul'ianovsk).

Scrutiny from the wider community affected not only Valia, but members of her family as well. Valia was outed to her family and subjected to her mother's emotional outburst; her mother was concerned not only by her daughter's sexuality, but also by the assumed negative judgement of the wider community, which would make her 'feel ashamed in front of everyone'. As Valentine, Butler and Skelton (2003, p. 484) note, children are the public face of a family, and parents expect to be held responsible by the wider community for their children's upbringing; a lesbian or bisexual daughter may be considered a reflection of bad parenting skills and therefore negatively affect a family's reputation. Thus, homophobia is not only something that affects LGBT children, but also it is a process of marginalisation that can be passed on to others, particularly to family members (Valentine, Butler and Skelton, 2003, p. 493).

This point resonates with Russian sociologist Elena Omel'chenko's study on homophobic prejudice among young people in Ul'ianovsk, based on interviews with both heterosexual youths and young gay men (Omel'chenko, 2002a, 2002b). Omel'chenko questions the usefulness of the concept 'homophobia' in making sense of negative attitudes towards, and fear of, homosexuality. Omel'chenko notes that homophobia is generally defined in medical and psychological literature as an irrational hatred or fear of homosexuality, stemming from prejudice or from fear of being a closeted homosexual. Faithful to the etymology of the word, Omel'chenko suggests a more nuanced definition of homophobia, indicating that 'fear' (phobia) is central to the way her respondents, both heterosexual and non-heterosexual, make sense of their encounters with the sexual 'other'. Following Omel'chenko's argument, family members' reactions, and the way in which they responded to their children's sexuality, may not always be described as homophobic, if homophobia is equated with an emotional reaction leading to violence or verbal abuse, and stemming from an irrational fear of homosexuality. Omel'chenko redefines homophobia as fear for oneself (in Valia's mother's case, fear of not having grandchildren), fear of others' reactions (shame, fear of being judged as a bad parent), and concern for others (fear that her daughter may be going down the wrong path). In the same way, lesbian and bisexual women's decision not to disclose their sexuality at home may not necessarily be prompted by internalised homophobia, if this is defined as self-hatred and the inability to accept one's sexuality. Reluctance to come out may involve fear for oneself (fear of material consequences, of loss of emotional support and of rejection), fear of others' reactions (fear of conflict, violence and rejection), and fears for others (particularly for vulnerable family members) (Omel'chenko, 2002a, pp. 479–500).

An understanding of homophobia as a fear affecting both non-heterosexuals and the people close to them, and rooted in normative, hegemonic constructs of gender and sexuality calls for a reconceptualisation of disclosure as an interactive and collective process, in which family members in particular are actively involved (Plummer, 1975; Valentine, Skelton and Butler, 2003). While coming out has been widely theorised as an individual choice and as an empowering speech act, disclosure (as voluntary coming out or as being outed by others, Plummer, 1975) and impression management (Goffman, 1959/1990) seem more fitting concepts to understand women's identity negotiations in the parental home. Indeed, disclosure may not always result, in the long term, in the open acknowledgement of a family member's homo- or bisexuality. Long-term outcomes were varied: in some cases, women's sexuality was ultimately accepted and acknowledged in the parental home, while in others it remained an underlying source of conflict, surfacing from time to time in the form of emotional blackmail or cutting remarks. In many families, however, the topic was swept under the carpet and seldom ever mentioned again, leaving women's identity shrouded in ambiguity, as in Sasha's case.

> In the same way that we [*she and her parents*] stopped talking to one another, we started again ... But we didn't talk about these issues [*her intimate relations*], we didn't apologise to each other. We didn't broach the subject. Time had simply passed. And now things have turned out in such a way that my parents don't meddle with my life. Who am I going out with? A guy? A girl? It doesn't matter. It's such a sensitive topic, for them and for me. They used to show too much interest. And now we don't talk about it.
>
> (Sasha, Moscow)

For Sasha, silence underlines unresolved conflict and a strain on family relations, and is experienced as hostile and homophobic. Indeed, it wasn't uncommon for family members to block out direct disclosure or subtle hints about an interviewee's sexual orientation. Ignorance can be bliss and help preserve family peace, since 'guessing and knowing are very different things' (Zoia, Ul'ianovsk). On the other hand, family members may struggle or refuse to acknowledge women's sexuality, like Maia's mother, who 'understands, but doesn't want to believe it', and was waiting for her daughter to break the news which she didn't want to hear (Maia, Ul'ianovsk). If we think of identities as relational and as constantly renegotiated in social interaction (Jenkins, 2004), they need not only to be affirmed and made visible, but also to be validated by others.

Sexuality, adulthood and everyday homophobia

In order to make sense of the everyday homophobia experienced in the parental home, it is necessary to explore family members' gendered expectations about young women's development into adults. The parental home is key to children's gendered socialisation as site where naturalised gender norms are passed on to children; moreover, routes out of the parental home and into adulthood are discursively tied to normative notions of sexuality and gender (Moran and Skeggs, 2004; Valentine, Skelton and Butler, 2003; Arnett, 1997). As Arnett (1997) notes, young people's transition to adulthood is constructed by social institutions, and typically revolves around a few rites of passage, namely finishing education, entering the workforce, getting married and becoming a parent. Young women's refusal to go through normative rites of passage was often met with painful disappointment and resistance by family members, particularly by mothers. Ania, aged 27 at the time of the interview, had been under constant pressure from her mother to get married and have children since she was in her early 20s.

> She [*her mum*] saw everything [*she saw Ania kissing her first girlfriend*]. But, funnily enough, she didn't say anything at the time. I learned that she had seen us only after three or four years. It turned out she knew everything, but she didn't say a word. But later, when I grew up, [*her mother started to say*], one way or another, you need to have kids, and I want grandchildren. And she began to talk about it with me all the time. She began to push me, to make scenes [*ustraivat' skandaly*]. She was very aggressive. [...] She tried to interfere [*rasstroit'*] in my relationship. She said, it's a game, and it will all end. [...] Childhood will end sooner or later. When will you change your mind? You are getting older [*u tebia skol'ko uzhe let*]. It's time to think about children. You have to have children, at your age you should have children, and so on and so forth. And you just go on playing games. Perhaps she still doesn't understand that it's not a whim, that it comes

from the head and I was born with this. There is no way you can change it.

(Ania, Ul'ianovsk)

For Ania's mother, a sexual relationship between women could be tolerated if it represented a passing phase; beyond the threshold of adolescence, however, it became a sign of immaturity and reluctance to become a responsible adult. Several other young women pointed out that their same-sex relationships were not taken seriously in the parental home, and were considered nonsense (*erunda, pridur', prikhot'*), a childhood game (*igra, detstvo, detskii sad*), a period of care-free fun (*razvlecheniie, eshche ne nagulialas'*) or teenage rebellion (*bunt, pokazukha*). Same-sex relations were often dismissed by family members as a passing phase in the transition towards more 'serious' and 'proper' heterosexual relationships, with their expected corollary of parenthood and family responsibilities. Women typically experienced pressures from family members to get over their attraction to females, pressures which sometimes continued even after they left home. For example, in spite of the fact that Ania had been living for a year with her girlfriend at the time of the interview, her mother still hoped that she would eventually 'grow out of it', and was convinced that her girlfriend would eventually leave her to settle down with a man and start a (heterosexual) family.

Other young women experienced pressures similar to Ania's, and this suggests that motherhood, more than marriage or heterosexual couple-dom, was regarded as an essential part of adult womanhood. The notion of motherhood as a key rite of passage into adulthood is not unique to Russia: research on lesbian lives conducted in Britain has shown that persistent perceptions of lesbianism and motherhood as antithetical trigger anxieties among family members (Valentine, Butler and Skelton, 2003; Taylor, 2007).[4] The importance attached to motherhood in the Russian context can be linked back to the Soviet 'working mother' gender contract, which institutionalised the notion of reproduction as a duty to the state (see chapters 2 and 3). Although motherhood has been reframed as a private choice, its compulsive moral force as women's 'natural' destiny and as a signifier of normative femininity is not diminished in post-Soviet Russia (Bridger, Kay and Pinnick, 1996; Baraulina, 2002). Non-heterosexual women's perceived inability to become mothers positioned them as incomplete women in the eyes of family members; at the same time, the view that motherhood is an essential part of a woman's life experience was echoed by many young women. Ira, in a committed relationship at the time of the interview, was under pressure from her mother to have children:

Of course, she [*her mother*] knows everything. She knows that we live together, and that we have lesbian friends [*obshchaemsia s takimi zhe*]. But from time to time she asks, 'When are you getting married?' [...] I mean, I didn't have to tell her [*that she is a lesbian*], she told me openly that she accepts this, although periodically she has a fit of hysterics [*ona mne ustraivaet isteriki*]: 'Give me grandchildren!' She thinks that if I give birth this means I am not a lesbian.

(Ira, Moscow)

Ira's mother thought of motherhood as 'naturally' taking place within a heterosexual relationship ('When are you getting married?'); for her the association 'lesbian mother' is simply unimaginable ('She thinks that if I give birth that means I am not a lesbian'). Interestingly, interviewees reported that mothers and close female friends were those more likely to try and talk them into the idea of marriage and parenthood, and worry that they could have unfulfilled or unhappy lives because of their perceived inability to start a family. Same-sex couples' biological inability to conceive a child without external intervention made motherhood inconceivable or 'wrong' in the context of a same-sex relationship. For some parents, motherhood was not necessarily seen as involving marriage or heterosexual cohabitation.[5]

She understands what kind of relationships I have, but she thinks it will all go away. She hopes that one day I will have a child. Because she herself gave birth to me when she was already 38. And, as far as I know, she never had a stable, long-term relationship with anyone. [..] I think she thinks that I'll have fun and then, when I'm approaching forty, I will get married. Or perhaps I won't get married, but I will have a child, and I will be like everyone else.

(Varvara, Moscow)

Varvara's mother, who brought her daughter up as a single mother, contemplated the idea that her daughter too may have children on her own. Lesbian motherhood, however, remained an alien concept to her, as she imagines that motherhood will make Varvara grow out of her lesbian phase ('she thinks it will go away'). Giving birth (rather than starting a heterosexual relationship) is what will make Varvara 'normal' in the eyes of her mother.

Motherhood, rather than heterosexual coupledom, was widely under-stood to be the threshold to adult womanhood. Nonetheless, in many families heterosexual marriage remained the ideal to which young women should aspire to, and heterosexual relationships were consid-ered instrumental in starting a family and having children. Moreover, heterosexual relationships were generally regarded as giving women a more secure financial position, social status and emotional support, and were sometimes contrasted to same-sex unions, perceived as immature, sterile and highly volatile relationships. Although Masha's mother was in some ways accepting of her daughter's sexuality, she also tried to talk her into the idea of dating men:

She says that she guessed, that it's ok, she said that she understands. And she tries not so much to 'cure' me, but she is anxious about it [*napriagaetsia*]. Because my dad, you see, left the family and didn't give me much support. So she thinks that I need to have a man, who can support me, provide for me [*obespechivat'*], love me. That I need a rock to hold on to [*opora*]. She thinks that I won't find this support in a same-sex relationship. And also, she tries to instil in me the idea that I have to go out with guys, get married and so on.

(Masha, Moscow)

Even when women's homo- or bisexuality was met with a degree of understanding, family members' attempts to talk young women into heterosexual coupledom and parenthood continued. In a few instances, these pressures led young women to start heterosexual relations in par-allel with lesbian ones, in order to fulfil family expectations or to be able to present a respectable heterosexual 'front' to the wider commu-nity. Kristina explained how her partner Sveta's previous heterosexual relationship, which almost culminated in a marriage and took place in parallel with lesbian affairs, was chiefly motivated by pressure from her parents:

All her actions were directed towards obliging her parents, I mean, she has a very authoritarian mum, who could not accept this [*her lesbianism*] in any way, nothing else could exist apart from a fam-ily made of the union of a woman and a man. [...] Her mum put pressure on her, she kept telling her that in any case she had to get married and be with a man, you may have to put up with him, sub-mit to him, but you won't dishonour your family, because her family is quite well known in the city [...] And if you get married and give birth ... I mean, she was ready to get divorced afterwards [*after having had a baby*], I mean, her motivation was just this: her parents.

(Kristina, Ul'ianovsk)

Particularly among young women from Ul'ianovsk, heterosexual coupledom and marriage were talked about as a 'safer' choice and as a way to comply with accepted social norms. Zoia, in her mid-20s and living with her parents at the time of the interview, was involved in a long-term same-sex relationship with Elizaveta, a married woman with two children, also in her mid-20s. Zoia was not out to her parents, who nonetheless suspected her relationship with Elizaveta was a sexual one and repeatedly expressed their disappointment that she did not show any inclination to get married and start a family. Zoia had started dating a man with a view to getting married, a decision her parents enthusiastically welcomed and Elizaveta also supported. Zoia explained her plans for the future as follows:

I would say that I am socially bi[*sexual*], but in actual fact I am not. I live in a society where it is acceptable to get married, and for this reason I socially build a relationship with a man, but if things don't work out, I will say that I am a lesbian. I'll reserve a try, and if things don't work out I will turn the page.

(Zoia, Ul'ianovsk)

Zoia and Elizaveta intended to continue their relationship after Zoia's marriage, although they did not know how this could be managed with the husband-to-be, who, unlike Elizaveta's husband, was not aware of Zoia's lesbian relationship.

Moving out and the 'family gaze'

Even after moving out of the parental home, women continued to be subjected to what Morgan (2011) calls the family gaze. The degree of pressure and influence exercised by family members eased after women left the parental home, but it did not cease altogether. For example, even after Sveta and Kristina moved in together, Sveta's mother kept trying to convince them that they both needed to start a 'proper' family by getting married and having children; this would not prevent them, in her view, from keeping their relationship going 'on the side'. Moreover, women's same-sex relationships often received little acknowledgement or recognition from family members. In some instances, this was due to the fact that women's sexuality itself remained an off-limits topic of conversation, and was often shrouded in ambiguity. Sometimes this ambiguity was created by lesbian and bisexual women themselves, who were keen to shelter their intimate life from the family gaze. For example, Liudmila, a woman in her 30s living with her partner in Moscow, at the time of the interview was expecting a visit from her mother, who lived in a different city. Liudmila was planning to hide from view a few objects which may reveal to her mother the 'true' nature of her relationship with her cohabiting partner. In other instances, lack of recognition from family members belied the fact that they struggled to think of same-sex unions as 'adult' relationships or 'real' families, even in the case of women who had lived together for a long time. Iana humorously described her parents' attitude towards her ten-year relationship with her cohabiting partner Oksana:

> It's not a problem for my mum and dad, they just don't pay any attention to it. Girlfriends, girlfriends…what is a girlfriend[6]? My mum just says that she's not interested in the topic. She accepts Oksana, Oksana is her best friend, and in general the best in the family [*laughs*]. Here go Iana and Oksana, two girlfriends who live together. She does not take it in, that it's a woman living with another woman.
>
> (Iana, Moscow)

Even though Iana had talked to her mother about the nature of her relationship in unambiguous terms, Oksana continued to be recognised, not as her partner, but as her 'friend'. Iana perceived her parents' lack of acknowledgement as unproblematic, since her partner was still accepted as a member of the extended family, and was well liked by her parents. Nonetheless, Iana's long-term relationship was couched in terms of friendship by her parents, and, in spite of their long cohabitation, Iana and Oksana were not acknowledged as a couple.

The invisibility of same-sex couples was rooted in the symbolism of 'home' as the site of heterosexual family relations. Indeed, even after women had moved out and established an independent household, family members often continued to measure their relationships by heteronormative standards, and to judge them as 'lacking', incomplete or immature. Lack of recognition for same-sex relations from members their family of origin was compounded, in the eyes of many women, by lack of legitimisation from wider society, where 'family' was celebrated as the founding unit of society, while also discursively constructed in the singular as the heterosexual, nuclear family, composed of a married couple with children. The absence of formal legal status for same-sex couples in Russia was seen as evidence that they are not valued as 'proper' families and continue to be marginalised from mainstream society. Galia, who was living with a long-term partner, commented:

> We bought a flat together, we can live quietly here, and society doesn't meddle in our life. But, as it happens, we have to protect our rights somehow 'on the side' [*cherez levoe ukho*]. I mean, when heterosexuals get married, the state rises to protect this basic unit of society [*iacheika*], while, to defend ourselves, we have to think over issues of testament, property, guardianship of children.
>
> (Galia, Moscow)

The heterosexual, nuclear family was perceived to have a monopoly on the moral values associated with 'family'. Although their relationships remained invisible and excluded from the symbolism of 'family', many women in long-term relationships reclaimed and subverted this symbolism by referring to them as 'our family', or 'our same-sex marriage'.

Lack of recognition for same-sex relationships had repercussions on women's experiences of leaving the parental home. Not infrequently, upon moving out, emotional, practical and financial support from family members were conditional upon approval of young women's 'lifestyle' choices. For example, Ul'iana, a woman in her mid-20s who had a very close relationship with her parents and had always been open to them about her sexuality, recalled that her parents offered no material help when she moved in with her girlfriend. When they went through a difficult period in their relationship, they offered no emotional support, and after a very painful breakup they seemed relieved that their daughter was now free to start a 'proper' (heterosexual) relationship:

> I told you earlier that if I lived with a man, things would be a lot easier, and my parents would help, and we'd have a place to live, and perhaps we'd have children, in short, we'd have everything. But they don't want to help [*two*] women, they think it's just a whim [*pridur'*].
>
> (Ul'iana, Moscow)

Thus, the family gaze continued to affect women's relationships even after they moved out of the family home, as lack of acknowledgement from family members contributed to make same-sex relations invisible.

Not all families of origin showed open disapproval of women's same-sex relations, or withdrew material and emotional support. The parental home often remained an important source of support and a reference point, and support was often mutual. Even in the presence of conflict, ties with the parental home were rarely severed altogether, and the parental home itself sometimes provided a shelter in times of need: some women temporarily moved back to the parental home, in some instances with their partner. Nonetheless, sexuality shaped the relations between the parental home and the home of choice, and remained a source of conflict and awkwardness. The parental home continued to be experienced as an ambiguous space: on the one hand, it symbolised security, support and emotional closeness, while on the other it remained an environment where women's relationships were at best tolerated, but rarely openly validated or valued.

Conclusions

Drawing on the notion of the home as a locus of social relations, this chapter has shown how sexuality affects family relations within the parental home, as well as the ties created between the parental home and the home of choice. Negotiating one's sexuality within the parental home emerged as a particularly sensitive issue, especially for younger women, who were exposed to the regulatory gaze of other family members, particularly parents. Young women were not necessarily dependents, as resources and responsibilities were often shared within the parental home. Nonetheless, they occupied a subordinate position and experienced the parental home as a site of gender socialisation where they were potentially vulnerable to repercussions, both emotional and material, if their sexuality was disclosed. Thus, within the parental home sexuality was experienced as a family matter, both because it was subjected to the surveillance and potential censorship of other family members, and because the whole family could be subjected to homophobic prejudice by the wider community (for example, in the case of parents ridiculed or held responsible for young women's homosexuality). Moreover, the parental home was experienced as a space which allowed little privacy, and where disclosure was not necessarily a deliberate and empowering choice, but often resulted from family scrutiny and unwanted exposure. Young women often preferred to conceal their sexual identity within the parental home: 'coming out' was not always perceived as a safe or worthwhile option, for reasons ranging from fear of compromising family relations, to concern about withdrawal of material and emotional support, to a sense of responsibility and protection towards other family members. The invisibility of same-sex sexuality within the parental home, however, could also be the result of denial or lack of acknowledgement from family members, a fact which underlines how sexual identities, in order to be made visible, need to be validated by others.

The everyday homophobia women routinely experienced in the parental home was rooted in gendered expectations about 'healthy' patterns of development into adulthood. The belief that the experience of motherhood, ideally within a heterosexual relationship, was central to the achievement of adult womanhood meant that lesbian and bisexual women were perceived as 'incomplete' and immature women because of their perceived inability to have children and start a 'proper' family. By the same token, same-sex relations were considered a passing adolescent phase, or as evidence of women's reluctance to embrace the family responsibilities which 'naturally' come with adulthood.

'Family' continued to matter, even after women had moved out of the parental home: social ties between the parental home and the home of choice were sustained, and women's relationships continued to be subjected to the gaze of the family of origin. Same-sex relations often failed to live up to ideals of family symbolically rooted in heterosexual coupledom and parenthood. Lack of acknowledgement, misrecognition or marginalisation of women's same-sex relations by family members was a common experience, and contributed to their invisibility, reinforced in the public sphere by the lack of legal recognition for same-sex unions.

5
The Global Closet? Negotiating Public Space

Chapter 5 continues the exploration of women's practices and strategies for negotiating everyday space. The focus shifts from the private, intimate sphere of home explored in Chapter 4 to more public settings where social interaction is regulated by more formal conventions about propriety and concerns about safety, namely the workplace and the street.

Richardson (1998, 2000) argues that non-heterosexuals are marginalised in the private and public spheres through different mechanisms. Non-heterosexuals are discursively excluded from the private sphere, which is symbolically conflated with heterosexual kinship and intimacy. At the same time, societal tolerance of non-heterosexual subjects is 'constructed largely on the condition that they remain in the private sphere and do not seek public recognition' (Richardson, 1998, pp. 89–90). As Moran and Skeggs (2004) note, however, the boundaries between 'private' and 'public' are in fact blurred in the everyday experiences and spatial navigations of non-heterosexuals. Indeed, as this chapter will show, the workplace is a setting governed by formal rules, but it is also a location where personal friendships and social networks are formed; the public street can be perceived as potentially dangerous and intimidating, but it can also turn into a familiar and comfortable space when used as the meeting point of informal queer *tusovki*. Social interactions within specific settings, rather than pre-conceived abstract notions of 'private' and 'public', are the focus of the present analysis. Drawing on Goffman (1959/1990a), the chapter explores how women negotiate their sexuality by managing the expression they *give* (verbal cues) and the expression they *give off* (non-verbal cues).

The chapter begins with an exploration of women's negotiation of their sexuality at work and then proceeds to discuss their strategy to navigate the public street, examining issues around comfort, privacy, personal safety and anonymity. The chapter also highlights how location affects spatial norms by exploring different perceptions and strategies to navigate city centre space in metropolitan Moscow and provincial Ul'ianovsk. Drawing on the empirical exploration of women's practices of disclosure developed here and in the previous chapter, the chapter also critically discusses theorisations of the closet/coming out (Sedgwick, 1990; Brown, 2000; Seidman et al., 1999; Seidman, 2004). Two main limitations of this paradigm are highlighted: the closet/coming out narrative as ethnocentric; and as unable to account for women's agency in negotiating their sexuality.

Work performances

The formalised environment of the workplace entails taking up 'appropriate' gender roles and performances, which are informed by the wider gender order (Adkins, 1995; Connell, 1987). Most obviously, the gender order is reflected in the traditional split between 'masculine' and 'feminine' professions, where the latter typically involve caring roles (nurse, teacher etc.), or semi- or de-skilled jobs subordinated to women's roles as mothers, homemakers and carers (Skeggs, 1997; Adkins, 1995). In Soviet Russia, women made up almost half of the labour force; however, in spite of claims to formal equality between men and women, gender remained an organising principle of the labour market, resulting in occupational segregation, unequal pay and uneven career opportunities (Ashwin, 2000; Buckley, 1992, 1989). In post-Soviet Russia, women continued to make up just under half of the workforce, and research shows that work remains important to women's identity and sense of self-worth (Ashwin, 2006). Nonetheless, the transition to a very unregulated labour market where the right to work is no longer guaranteed arguably exacerbated the gendered segregation of labour, reinforcing the notion of women as 'secondary' workers and earners, and making them potentially more vulnerable to discrimination and sexism at work (Bridger et al., 1996; Kay, 2000; Ashwin, 2006). Discrimination on the basis of workers' gender continues to be forbidden by Russian law; however, there is no explicit prohibition against discrimination on the basis of sexual orientation (Ashwin, 2006; Alekseev, 2002). Moreover, despite formal legal provision against gender discrimination, women remain extremely vulnerable to discriminatory treatment and unfair dismissal (Kozina and Zhidkova, 2006, pp. 59–61). Research on perceptions of women's rights in Russia indicates that women have little trust in antidiscriminatory legislation, which is often not enforced, and perceive gender norms to override abstract notions of 'right to work' (Turbine, 2007). Although women may be aware of 'losing out' to male employees, they may not necessarily challenge commonly shared notions of gender-appropriate roles and occupations (Kozina and Zhidkova, 2006). Gender and sexual norms also inform workplaces in more subtle ways, and are reflected, for example, in work regulations and dress codes. In her study of the UK tourist industry, Adkins shows how women working in service sector jobs are under greater pressure than men to comply with very specific criteria relating to their appearances; this includes being attractive and having a feminine appearance. 'Proper' feminine appearance is treated in the industry as a sexual commodity, 'a quality that encourages custom' (Adkins, 1995, p. 91); the fact that women are accorded a 'subordinate sexual status' in the workplace is reflected in male co-workers' and clients' behaviour, and in women's tacit acceptance of unwanted sexual attention (Adkins, 1995, pp. 85–102). Thus, workplaces are gendered and sexualised spaces, where only certain types of femininities may safely be enacted.

The workplace is also an institutionalised 'stage', where interactions are ruled by formal rituals and hierarchies and where individuals constantly work to present a 'front' and to perform appropriate identities (Goffman, 1959/1990a). Although the workplace is a sexualised space, sexuality is largely constructed as belonging to the 'backstage' (private sphere) rather than the 'frontstage' of ritualised public interaction. 'Other' sexualities are usually made invisible by a tacit assumption of heterosexuality as the 'natural' norm: only uncontroversial and 'natural' aspects of sexuality may safely be expressed, while same-sex desire is typically censored (Adkins, 1995, p. 51; see also Taylor, 2007, pp. 88–114; Holliday, 1999). The performance of one's homo- or bisexuality, either verbal ('expression given') or expressed through appearance and demeanour ('expression given off', Goffman, 1956/1990a), may be problematic on two accounts. First, it may challenge the range of feminine performances which are permissible in the workplace and stand out as out of place; secondly, it may be considered inappropriate because references to 'other' sexualities more immediately evoke associations with sexualised behaviour, a sphere that is potentially taboo in the formal work environment. Indeed, Skeggs (1997, p. 131) insightfully points out that 'the homosexual subject has become the very sign of sex', since gay or lesbian identity is signified primarily through sexuality. By contrast, sexual signifiers are not perceived to be as central to heterosexual identities, since they are associated with 'natural' reproduction and therefore concealed. Workplaces are governed by different sets of spoken and unspoken rules; these may vary significantly across different workplaces, influencing the ways in which sexuality can legitimately be signified (Adkins, 1995, 2000; Ward and Winstanley, 2005; McDermott, 2006). The women who took part in this study worked in a range of different jobs and professions: interviewees included professionals, blue- and white-collar workers, service sector employees and civil servants.[1] A detailed analysis of how spatialised sexual norms are enacted in specific workplaces, however, is beyond the scope of my analysis.

Managing sexuality at work

Being open about one's sexuality at work was perceived as unsafe and potentially risky by interviewees, since disclosure may elicit hostile reactions, compromise work relationships and jeopardise career prospects. As a result, women were usually very guarded in talking about their private life, and careful in choosing whether, when and who to come out to. They generally emphasised the importance of taking responsibility by performing appropriate gender and sexual roles at the workplace, and stressed personal agency in avoiding discomforts and situations which may make them vulnerable. For most women, self-presentation at the workplace was not only a matter of assessing the risks and discomforts involved, but also of complying with notions of decorum and respectability:

No, well, in general at work I don't broadcast it. I always thought that work is work, and personal [*lichnye*] relationships are personal relationships. [...] At the moment I work for a small company, where we have a young team, from twenty – twenty-two to thirty years old. We're all young, some people are on friendly terms. I didn't open up to anyone, thinking that work is work and personal [*lichnye*] relationships are personal relationships. [...]. All the rest doesn't count. They see what I am like. They don't point their finger at me, as, perhaps, they may do. But I don't think that I look in your face [*vyzyvaiushche*], in your face in such a way that you could tell from the first glance that I am a lesbian. I don't blame men for anything. I mingle with them too. Perhaps, sometimes I flirt with them, in a purely friendly manner. I flirt with women and men, just for fun, as you do with nice people. But they don't ask me about my private life [*o moei lichnoi zhizni*]. Perhaps because of the way I present myself. I just don't want to, I don't trust these people with my private [*lichnaia*] life.
Did they never ask anything directly?

No. When ... Perhaps they tried to ask me something, and I hinted that I have someone. But I didn't specify who. It is tacitly understood that I have a man. Let them think so. Thank God. They didn't give me a straight question. I didn't give them a straight answer.

(Varvara, Moscow, bookkeeper)

Like many other women who took part in this study, Varvara drew a line between her private life and her work persona, a contrast stressed by the repeated use of the adjective *lichnyi* (private), a nuance partly lost in the English translation.[2] For Varvara, the workplace is a formal environment where appearances and first impressions count, and where disclosing details of one's personal life is potentially unsafe ('I don't trust these people with my private life'). Many women were not open about their sexuality at work, and this often involved keeping one's distance from co-workers. Strategies deployed to maintain a respectable feminine 'front' involved, in Goffman's terminology, controlling expressions 'given' (verbal communication), rather than impressions 'given off' (non-verbal communication) (Goffman, 1959/1990a).[3] 'Impression management' involved hiding behind co-workers' tacit assumption of heterosexuality, as in Varvara's case or, more rarely, actively 'passing' as heterosexual by making up imaginary boyfriends:

If they ask me I say that I have a common law husband, that we're not officially married. A mythical, imaginary husband.

(Alia, Moscow, employee in a publishing house)

However, social interaction at work did not always involve a deliberate disguise, but was more often a case of not spelling things out:

If I was sure that at work they'd be ok with it I would be happy to tell them. They know that I live with Nadia, that we bought a flat together. The whole process of buying the flat was very much in the public eye, I researched on the internet different options and I even borrowed money at work. When I tell them something I say, Nadia, Nadia and I, but I don't tell them what kind of relationship we have. Of course, it would be easier for me to dot the i's and cross the t's, but I don't do it, because I am not sure that the reaction would be adequate. It would even make conversation easier, but as things are you have to check what you say.

(Galia, Moscow, graphic designer)

Galia's demeanour and behaviour at work may not have been as discreet as what she verbally shared with colleagues: she regularly printed material for a local lesbian fanzine at work, an event witnessed by her workmates. Nonetheless, Galia was reluctant to spell things out in order to avoid any awkwardness; both Galia and her colleagues, who may or may not be accepting of her sexuality, may have found more comfortable a 'front' which leaves her sexuality open to interpretation. Thus, as already noted in the case of women's negotiation of the parental home, coming out is a collective process whose outcome can remain ambiguous. At the same time, the secrecy surrounding women's personal life often limited their ability to form meaningful relationships with colleagues (Valentine, 1993b).

Many women were not out at work because they feared that disclosure may jeopardise career prospects or compromise their status at work. Women working as teachers and psychologists were particularly discreet because they were aware that, in their workplace, homosexuality was still considered to have a 'corrupting' influence on young and vulnerable people, despite official demedicalisation. Women in professional jobs were also conscious of how their reputation may be affected should their sexuality become known: Zulia, a lawyer with a prestigious job in the civil service, repeatedly stressed that her job required an 'immaculate reputation', while Ul'iana, a young associate in a law firm, was weary of work colleagues happening on her when she was socialising with other lesbians in central Moscow. Zhanna, the former manager of a trade union branch in Greater Moscow, recalled how her very public coming out compromised her authority, as well as relations with colleagues and subordinates:

At the time I was working as president of a trade union. And the trade union has a lot of power. All the financial documents are signed by the director and by the president [...]. And I dealt especially with social programs. So everyone knew me. Everything concerning flats, plots of land for the *dacha*,[4] I don't know, services and utilities... Several people came to see me when they had complaints. Everyone knew me. And then, [...] after the interview which was broadcast on TV [*in which she publicly came out as a lesbian*], everyone knew, and people fitted into three types. Some continued to treat me as they had done before, they continued to socialise with me. Others showed a new morbid interest, with a specific innuendo. Because many people think that if you are gay or lesbian then you must be some kind of pervert [...]. They even made propositions, of the kind 'my wife also wants to try it, let's have a threesome'. But these are not even the most unpleasant propositions, I heard worse than this. And there were other people who simply stopped associating with me; they didn't even greet me anymore. They stopped noticing me.

(Zhanna, photographer, Moscow)

Although responses to disclosure ranged from loyalty to marginalisation to stereotyping, Zhanna's public coming out entailed a loss of respectability and authority, and brought to the surface commonly held associations between lesbian sexuality, promiscuity and immorality. The dormant danger of prejudice and stereotyping in the workplace was often signalled by scathing or derisive comments about gay people from co-workers. Women whose sexual identity remained ambiguous often felt unable to, or could only feebly attempt to challenge homophobic views and jokes. Latent prejudice could become a very real threat, as Sonia's experience shows. Sonia suddenly found herself unemployed while in between nursing jobs:

[...] I didn't get the job because of this [*because her sexuality became known*], because, as it turned out, when I resigned from my previous job, there was a person who was jealous of me, he just told them at the new workplace and they turned me down on another pretext. I mean, they were ready to hire me [...], but when this transpired they turned me down, and I didn't try again to find work in nursing. Because this is a small city, all the doctors hang out together, they all know each other. When I was looking for a job it was hard, because I wanted to work in medicine, I dreamed about it because I had worked as a nurse for a long time. But I understood that there is no point, because it would be hard to find work, because of the long tail of my reputation, that I am not like everyone else, it would have been difficult for me to live here. So I found a job in another sector, it was difficult, because I only have a nursing qualification.

(Sonia, retail manager, Ul'ianovsk)

Concerned about her tainted reputation, Sonia did not seek employment as a nurse after her dismissal, and eventually found a job as manager in a retail unit after being unemployed for a year. Although she felt powerless to do anything about it, Sonia was positive that her dismissal was linked to gossip circulated after a colleague she had been romantically involved with started to attract undue attention by acting 'demonstratively', in an attempt to win her back. Sonia's experience also highlights the peculiarity of living in a relatively small provincial city, where rumours spread quickly, and 'the long tail of one's reputation' was more likely to jeopardise job opportunities and to affect people's lives outside of the workplace.

Caution in disclosing one's sexuality was dictated not only by fears of repercussions and of being marginalised, but also by concerns of being stereotyped and boxed in under a label. For this reason, women usually verbally disclosed their sexuality only to selected colleagues, if at all, and talked about disclosure as a gradual process requiring a certain amount of negotiation.

> I don't arrive and say 'Hello, I am a lesbian', of course not. If I go to a new workplace, I look at the team, if there are people of old principles, there's no need to tell them, they won't understand. But if there are mostly young people, then yes, because they have a more easy-going attitude. Some understand by themselves, they guess, and I just confirm a fact, – Is it so?, – Yes. With some we strike up good relations, and I say, do you remember I told you about Vasia [*an abbreviation of the male first name Vasilii*]? It is not Vasia, it is Vasilisa. I mean, I usually tell a single person, not a crowd. I mean, I think that if you suddenly tell a big group of people, they will look at each other to see how to react, and as a rule there will be a negative reaction, then jokes, while if you tell each one singularly [. . .] after a while everyone will know, [..] and they're ok with it, and if someone makes a comment in their presence, they won't dare to do anything, because the majority is already in favour. [. . .]This word, lesbian, first of all it sounds rough, and secondly people get scared, what is that, who are they . . .
>
> (Nastia, Moscow, unemployed)

Nastia's view that being upfront about one's sexuality may be counterproductive, because it may be too confronting and direct, and elicit negative associations, was shared by other women, who emphasised the importance of 'not broadcasting it' (*ne afishirovat'*), not putting 'everything on display' and 'being accepted first as a person, rather than as a lesbian'. On the contrary, disclosure can be empowering if it is gradual and is premised on making sexuality unremarkable by finding common ground first and emphasising similarity (dating 'Vasia/Vasilisa') rather than difference ('Hello, I am a lesbian'). Nastia's remark about how generational differences may affect attitudes towards sexuality and expectations about disclosure also resonated in other interviews: it was commonly acknowledged that younger colleagues were more likely to openly discuss sexual matters, and to read non-verbal clues (ranging from demeanour to clothing, jewellery, and rainbow-themed accessories) as signifiers of queerness.

Although the workplace was often experienced as a formal environment, for many women it also provided opportunities for socialising and to strike up friendships which may develop outside of the workplace. Indeed, as Goffman points out, the workplace as a setting may shift from 'frontstage' (in the presence of a superior) to 'backstage' (when, in the absence of superiors, co-workers can subvert rules and interact on a more informal basis); workers' performances have to be adapted accordingly (Goffman, 1956/1990a). While some women deliberately kept their work and personal life completely separate, others were willing to socialise and develop more informal relationships with colleagues. Nonetheless, as other research shows, interacting on the 'backstage' and developing meaningful friendships with co-workers can be difficult precisely because of the pressure non-heterosexual women experience to conceal their sexuality at work (Valentine, 1993b; Adkins, 2000). Some women remarked that appropriate gendered performances, such a flirting with male colleagues or going to the toilet with a group of female co-workers, were expected at work in order to 'fit in'; they feared that coming out would disrupt routine scripts of social interaction with co-workers, and make them look out of place. However, being secretive about one's personal life was an obstacle to forming more meaningful relationships, as Nadia, a Moscow-based psychologist, points out.

> At work I didn't tell anyone for a long time, the problem is also that I am a psychologist, and, since here this [*homosexuality*] is still considered a disease, it is common wisdom that, how can you, being ill, cure other people? In general, in Russia it is considered a deviance [...]. Then I began to understand that the relationship with my colleagues stopped at my private life. They tell me everything about their private lives, and I don't tell them anything. I didn't want this, I didn't want to only hang out with lesbians. I wanted to have as close friends people that I like, and not necessarily people with the same sexual orientation. At some point I had to tell two of my closest colleagues about myself.
>
> (Nadia, Moscow, psychologist)

For Nadia, disclosure helped her to forge closer relations with selected co-workers. In some women's experiences, gradual disclosure still caused surprise and negative reactions among co-workers; however, it was more congruent with the unspoken rules of 'backstage' performance, where there was an expectation that co-workers will share aspects of their personal and intimate lives. Gradual disclosure was perceived as safer when women felt that co-workers valued them first of all for their personal qualities and professional skills, and were better able to see past labels and stereotypes. A friendly work environment seemed more conducive to disclosure: the minority of women who felt completely comfortable talking about their private life at work all had particularly informal and relaxed work relations.

How to be streetwise

This section examines how considerations about safety, privacy and personal comfort are reflected in women's strategies to negotiate public urban space, particularly the street. As Moran and Skeggs (2004) point out, urban space is associated with personal vulnerability and with the possibility of violence and danger, but this potential vulnerability has particular connotations for non-heterosexuals. Public space is largely constructed, imagined and experienced as heteronormative: thus, the visible display of non-heterosexuality/queerness is likely to stand out as out of place, and it may elicit intimidation and violence (Skeggs, 1999).

In relation to Goffman's useful framework, negotiating one's sexuality on the street involved managing non-verbal expressions 'given off', rather than verbal expressions 'given' (Goffman, 1959/1990a). Much has been written on the aesthetisation of the lesbian/queer body, a process intertwined with the commoditisation of sexuality (Adkins, 2000) which has produced new 'homonormativities' regarding body image within queer communities as well as bodies widely recognised as 'queer' by mainstream audiences (Clark, 1993). Nonetheless, as Dyer (2002) notes, unlike gender or race, sexuality is not 'written on the body', as it is not obviously marked or visible to others. Signifiers of queerness are part of a cultural code 'designed to make visible the invisible' (Dyer, 2002, p. 19). Thus, while not everyone is necessarily acquainted with this cultural code, specific bodies and embodied performances are more likely to be recognisable and read as 'lesbian/queer'. Women who look butch, or androgynous, and whose embodied performances do not conform to expected notions of femininity are more likely to stand out as 'out of place' in public settings (Skeggs, 2001). By contrast, as

Skeggs (2001, p. 209) notes, the femme ('the lesbian embodiment of femininity') may remain invisible as a lesbian in the absence of the 'masculine' butch who, by transgressing gender norms, foregrounds the femme as a 'feminine' lesbian. Common turns of phrase such as 'I look like a lesbian' (Ania, Ul'ianovsk), or 'you would not say I am a lesbian' (Sveta, Ul'ianovsk) indicate that 'looking like a lesbian' was also understood in the Russian context as involving non-conformity to conventional notions of femininity by looking masculine or androgynous, for example, by wearing unisex or sporty clothes, avoiding make-up and wearing short haircuts.[5]

'Looking like a lesbian'

Embodiment, visibility and appearance were routinely negotiated by women across different everyday spaces and routes across them. Maia, a woman in her early 20s who was part of the Ul'ianovsk queer *tusovka*, minimised the potential for confrontation and aggression from strangers by avoiding certain places:

> *Have you ever had any unpleasant experience because of your sexual orientation?*
> No. Not so far. Not from strangers [*s postoronnymi liud'mi*]. The only thing is, sometimes they say, is that a boy or a girl. This puts them on guard, but I avoid this. I try not to mix with these people and not hang out in these places.
> *What places, for example?*
> Bars. There are bars that are hangouts for arty [*tvorcheskie*] people, we have some of those. And there are those where they stare, and if you're not the same as them, then they have to beat you up, just so. And I don't go there.
>
> (Maia, Ul'ianovsk)

Maia's androgynous looks ('is that a boy or a girl?') made her immediately stand out from the crowd, making the threat of aggression a very real possibility in some bars. Issues of personal safety and comfort influenced her navigation through urban space: this involved avoiding establishments where she looked out of place and choosing arty bars where she blended in. Another visual clue that may 'give off' a woman's sexuality to outsiders is the company of other lesbians, particularly the unmistakeable act of being affectionate with a girlfriend in public.

> *Have you ever had any unpleasant experience because of your sexual orientation?*

Not major ones. You know, if I can't remember any it means no. If I had had any, I would tell you straight away [*laughs*]. No. [*She pauses to think*]. Perhaps there were some jokes, that kind of thing, but I wasn't particularly bothered. Sometimes I was hurt that I could not go to some places, or behave the way I wanted to. [...] For example, I walk down the street and if, say, I start kissing a girl, this is a bit out of the ordinary [*nenormal'no*]. I mean, people... But if I kissed a man, no one would say anything.

(Ul'iana, Moscow)

Ul'iana instinctively knows that she has to watch the expression she 'gives off' in public spaces, particularly in the company of a girlfriend. As she perceptively noted, while a kiss between a man and woman is unremarkable, the same behaviour between two women would stand out and cause a reaction. It could be verbally sanctioned by outsiders as 'improper' and 'rude' behaviour (*dikost'*, Elizaveta, Ul'ianovsk). Negotiating public space involved considering not only personal risk and safety, but also feelings of dis/comfort. Indeed, one of the main reasons for socialising in lesbian/queer *tusovki* was that women were not made to feel out of place because of their sexuality.[6] Ira, a woman in her mid-20s who had grown up in a provincial city in the South of Russia, explained that during her teenage years she had escaped hostile and derisive comments from outsiders in a gay-friendly bar:

And after this you started hanging out with gay people . . .
Yes. Because people stared. Because you stand out from the crowd. And I was more comfortable sitting in that bar [*a bar unofficially known to have a queer clientele*] and drinking a coffee, a beer, rather than in an ordinary bar. Because at that time hanging out with men already bothered me. You know what our men are like? Like, in your face [*chut' li v glaz*]. And I was also feisty [*boevaia*], and I was afraid that I would go around with bruises and lumps. [...] I was never beaten up because of my sexual orientation. They threatened me, laughed at me. But I wasn't particularly bothered, because I already knew where I stood. [...] I love physical contact. If I am with my girlfriend, I want to hold her by the hand, so we held hands and kissed, and walked in an embrace. Of course, people saw the way we looked at each other. And it was a great laugh: look at those lesbians! As if, I don't know, we had an elephant on leash.

(Ira, Moscow)

Ira's experience of socialising in a gay-friendly bar with a mixed clientele is an important reminder that the boundaries between queer and heterosexualised space were often experienced as porous. While Moscow hosted relatively well-established community and commercial venues which were clearly signposted as 'queer' space, these did not exist in Ul'ianovsk. Moreover, public and semi-public places were sometimes only temporarily used and appropriated as 'lesbian/queer', particularly in Ul'ianovsk, which, unlike Moscow, did not have a gay scene: a gay and lesbian night was hosted in a mainstream club and a couple of bars in the city centre were unofficially known as hangouts for the local queer *tusovka*. Moreover, in both cities queer space did not comprise only enclosed locations, such as bars, clubs and the premises of LGBT organisations, but also the public street. At the time when the research took place, a specific stretch of Tver'skoi Boulevard in central Moscow and of a thoroughfare in central Ul'ianovsk were popular hangouts for lesbian/queer *tusovki*, a theme which will be further explored in Chapter 6. The appropriation of these street locations as queer space, however, seemed mostly lost to the unattentive or untrained eye of passers-by. Neither in Moscow or Ul'ianovsk was this space visibly marked as 'lesbian/queer': it blended in the urban landscape, particularly since it was located in busy city centre locations commonly used as meeting places by all sorts of youth *tusovki*. Moreover, socialising on the street also involved 'front' and 'backstage' performances, as behaviour was constrained by the awareness to be in the public eye. Thus, the street was perceived at once as harbouring potential risks and as a place evoking feelings of comfort and belonging, when appropriated as 'lesbian/queer' leisure space.

Safety, anonymity and gendered space in Moscow and Ul'ianovsk

Perceptions of safety, comfort and privacy in public leisure space were different in Moscow and in Ul'ianovsk, as illustrated by Kristina, a student and call centre worker in her early 20s who had moved to Moscow two years earlier with her partner Sveta. On her periodic visits to her hometown, Kristina felt under intense scrutiny, an experience she contrasted with being inconspicuous on the streets of Moscow:

> I've been to Ul'ianovsk not long ago, and it was such a shock, really, I walked down the street and I caught everyone staring, especially *gopniki*.[7] I walked, and I felt physically sick, I withered and twisted from the sheer number of prying eyes. They were hostile stares, and it is hard to understand what they are trying to demonstrate,

whether it's their stupidity or what, what they are trying to express. I felt physically sick from this, and I understood that when I walk through Moscow I feel like a grey mouse, because I don't try to stand out, I just wear what I want, I don't try to impress. But when I come back to Ul'ianovsk I understand that I attract too much attention.

Did you change your style [since moving to Moscow]?

I wear what I want to wear and I feel comfortable with this style, and my behaviour doesn't change, it's just that in Moscow ... [...] I feel I can allow myself more in Moscow, but I restrain myself because it's a habit, a form of defence.

(Kristina, Ul'ianovsk)

Like Kristina, women talked about their experiences of provincial and metropolitan cities very differently. Moscow was seen as offering the advantage of anonymity and of passers-by's general indifference, while androgynous, butch or otherwise unconventional looks were more conspicuous in Ul'ianovsk. Kristina makes clear that her appearance (short haircut, jeans, sporty top, no make-up) did not seem to raise eyebrows in Moscow. Particularly in the city centre, the traditional meeting place of youth *tusovki*, the capital's more cosmopolitan atmosphere was apparent in the range of different styles, looks and clothing displayed by young people, and it was common for young women to wear casual or sporty, rather than conventionally girlish clothes. In central Ul'ianovsk, however, where young women usually exhibited the conventional attributes of femininity, such as high heels, skirts, skimpy tops and lots of make-up, Kristina's looks were more likely to stand out. In Ul'ianovsk, women were extremely conscious of the fact that, in a relatively small city where rumours spread quickly, the possibility of being exposed and outed was greater, and this translated in additional pressure to remain invisible as a lesbian or bisexual woman. For example, being overtly affectionate with a partner on the street was avoided, even when women were socialising with the 'lesbian/queer' *tusovka*.

In the episode related by Kristina, the danger of homophobic violence and intimidation is embodied by *gopniki*, whose threatening presence on the streets of Ul'ianovsk was a pervasive narrative; a point I will return to in Chapter 6. By contrast, in Moscow interviewees rarely expressed concerns about safety and personal comfort when socialising on the street in the capital's gentrified city centre, which was habitually patrolled by the police. During my Ul'ianovsk fieldwork, several women expressed the view that their city was particularly unsafe compared to other Russian cities: for example, I was told that while in Moscow or Kazan' it is common practice to stop private cars and be given a lift for an agreed price, in Ul'ianovsk car owners would not stop for fear of crime.[8] Nonetheless, perceptions of safety and violence may have been different in Moscow had fieldwork taken place a few months later, when the run-up to the first Moscow Pride was accompanied by a series of homophobic attacks.[9]

Chapter 6 will explore in more detail how different perceptions and expectations of safety and anonymity affect strategies to carve out lesbian/queer space in public urban places in the different contexts of Ul'ianovsk and Moscow. A final point to make, however, concerns gendered perceptions of violence and safety, and how these may affect how women collectively and individually occupied public space. This is significant in light of the fact that in existing literature the use of the public street by lesbians is virtually undocumented and unexplored. Yet in both Moscow and Ul'ianovsk, specific street locations in the city centre were regularly used as meeting places by lesbian/queer *tusovki*. The virtual absence of any discussion about women's use of the street contrasts sharply with the well-documented use of the street by gay/queer men as cruising ground or as leisure space. The absence of lesbian/queer women on the street is generally explained with heteropatriarchal gendered divisions of space into private and public: the public street is constructed as the domain of men and evokes feelings of fear in lesbian/queer women, who socialise in private, indoor settings such as flats, bars and community centres (Casey, 2004; Valentine, 1995, 1996; Johnston and Valentine, 1995; Adler and Brenner, 1992).[10] Yet the case studies explored here defy these generalisations, and call for more research on women's everyday appropriation and use of street space. They also beg the question as to what makes possible the appropriation of street locations by 'lesbian' or mixed *tusovki* in urban Russia. This appropriation reflects a common pattern of socialising among Russian youths, who habitually meet friends, hang out and consume alcoholic drinks on the street, particularly during the warm summer months. A few factors may explain the perception of street *tusovki* as a relatively safe spaces for women: their city centre location (particularly for the Moscow women-only *tusovka*, which met in a gentrified part of the city centre, with a visible police presence); for the Ul'ianovsk mixed *tusovka*, the presence of gay men, which contributed to make the *tusovka* invisible as a queer group to passers-by; and the deliberate strategies used by members of the *tusovki* to remain discreet and inconspicuous.

Nonetheless, perceptions of safety and comfort and experiences of violence emerged as deeply gendered, particularly in Ul'ianovsk. During my fieldwork, the poor attendance at one of the gay and lesbian club night was partly attributed to rumours that *gopniki* had been tipped off about the event, and might target patrons, particularly gay men. The latter were reportedly more exposed and more concerned than women about episodes of homophobic violence, which had resulted in the death of a male member of the *tusovka*, targeted because of his sexuality. While women were less directly affected by episodes of gay bashing, an episode related by Kristina also highlights how gender informed experiences of street violence. Kristina was the victim of an attempted sexual attack at the hands of an older man:

> I allowed myself the same things in Ul'ianovsk [*as in Moscow, where she had moved to*], until I came across some problems. When a man got out of a *marshrutka* [*a share taxi*] and tried to follow me, with a very clear aim, you understand yourself what, I mean, with the clear suggestion that sooner or later he would have me [*menia poimet*], to put it bluntly. Because before this Sveta [*her girlfriend*] and I had been kissing on the *marshrutka*, and the guy was sitting there and you could see from his eyes, he had a maniacal look. His hands slipped where they shouldn't have, and when I got out at my stop he followed me, and I just ran away from him as fast as I could. Well, until then, I acted freely. As soon as this started, I began to restrain myself.
>
> (Kristina, Ul'ianovsk)

This episode, the only instance of attempted violence reported by women from the Ul'ianovsk *tusovka*, highlights how 'acting gay' in public can make women no less vulnerable than men, although they may be more likely victims of a different kind of violence – sexual victimisation rather than physical aggression. Thus, navigating the street and public leisure spaces involved being mindful of what may elicit aggression, and acting in ways which preserved personal safety and comfort. Women generally emphasised personal responsibility, deploring overt or demonstrative behaviour as inappropriate and 'in your face'. 'Posing' or 'showing off' (*rabota na publiku, pokazukha, risovat'sia*) through overt performances of lesbianism was seen as a deliberate attempt to attract attention, an attention most women tried to avoid. This behaviour was reprimanded and dismissed as typical of the very young, and motivated by teenage rebelliousness, a period of self-searching, or a fascination with the hyped-up media portrayal of lesbianism. In Moscow's lesbian community spaces, such open and conspicuous behaviour was widely considered as typical of the *Pushka* street *tusovka*, which had a reputation for being rough and in your face.

Interrogating the closet/coming out paradigm

Theorisations of queer oppression have centred on the notion of the closet as a space of concealment and silence, and of coming out as the public avowal of a secret identity (Sedgwick, 1990; Seidman et al., 1999, p. 19; Brown, 2000). This final section of Chapter 5 interrogates the closet/coming out paradigm as an analytical tool for interpreting women's everyday negotiation of their sexuality. In so doing, I engage with debates about the need to reassess ethnocentric theorisations of the closet/coming out paradigm (Jolly, 2001; Manalansan, 1997), and to reappraise their centrality to non-heterosexuals' negotiations of everyday space (Seidman et al., 1999).

The use of the term 'closet' as a sexualised metaphor ('being in/coming out of the closet') is thought to have originated in Anglo-American gay slang, probably in the 1950–1960s (Brown, 2000). From the 1970s, the expression was popularised by the gay and lesbian liberation movement, for which 'coming out of the closet' became a political slogan (Brown, 2000). Ever since, the closet has become central to both LGBT politics and to academic theorisations of queer oppression: in Sedwick's definition, the closet is a metaphor for the symbolic erasure and forced concealment of non-heteronormative sexualities (Sedgwick, 1990; Brown, 2000). The closet is inextricably linked to the act of 'coming out' of it, understood as both privately coming to terms with a stigmatised sexuality and as affirming one's identity by making it public (Sedgwick, 1990). Coming out has both private and public connotations, and is imagined as an act of both personal liberation and political significance (Sedgwick, 1990, p. 72; Seidman et al., 1999). At a personal level, the closet is posited as a place of self-denial, concealment, shame and guilt, while disclosure involves asserting oneself by reclaiming a stigmatised identity. At a collective level, the closet is a metaphor for the oppression of same-sex sexualities, which are policed though silence, denial and pathologisation. Therefore, the act of coming out makes visible the existence of 'other' sexualities while challenging heterosexuality as the 'natural' norm. Far from being confined only to politics, the closet/coming out narrative has also become 'the most distinctive form of les-bi-gay life writing' (Jolly, 2001, p. 476) as well as a dominant narrative mainstreamed in Anglo-American and western popular culture

(Brown, 2000, p. 6). Through the globalisation and hybridisation of sexual cultures, this narrative has become influential beyond Anglo-American societies, as the expression 'coming out of the closet' has gained currency in other languages (Manalansan, 1997, p. 498; see also Binnie, 2004; Leap, 2002; Brown, 2000, pp. 116–139; Murray, 1995).

Albeit not undisputed, the notions of invisibility as oppressive and of coming out as an empowering act is commonplace in sexuality/queer studies. Yet there are two main problems with theorisations of the closet/coming out. First of all, both the closet and coming out are value-laden concepts, which originated in the very specific socio-historical contexts of gay liberation. Secondly, the closet/coming out paradigm is of limited use to account for women's agency in the complex negotiations of their sexuality across 'everyday' space.

Coming out as an ethnocentric narrative

It is worth bearing in mind that coming out as an affirmative and empowering narrative emerged within social movements such as feminism and gay liberation in Anglo-American societies, as Plummer points out:

> The most momentous act in the life of any lesbian or gay person is when they proclaim their gayness – to self, to other, to community. [...] [*Since the 1970s*] [t]he full circle of private, personal, public and political tellings has become possible. 'Coming out' [...] becomes the central narrative of positive gay experience.
>
> (Plummer, 1995, pp. 82–83)

The notion that the personal is political on which the 'coming out' narrative is premised, however, found little resonance in Soviet Russia, where the state's ability to interfere with citizens' private lives meant that the intimate sphere was actively sheltered from public scrutiny in everyday life (Oswald and Voronkov, 2004; Kharkhordin, 1995, 1999). As Kharkhordin points out, the notion of privacy for Soviet citizens was associated with dissimulation, rather than authenticity.

> [...] new means of self-fashioning also developed, characteristic of this informal sphere. The first development was the spread of individual dissimulation, the practice protecting the individual from any interference, which resulted in the creation of a secret sphere of intimate life, available to the gaze of the closest friends and family members, but sometimes kept secret even from them. This

proliferation of secret, intimate spheres, created and controlled by the individual, prepared the way to the easy public assertion of the value of privacy after 1991. We must not forget, however, that the sphere of Soviet privacy originated in dissimulation, unlike its Western counterpart.

(Kharkhordin, 1999, p. 357)

As Kharkhordin shows, in contemporary Russia notions of privacy continue to be shaped by the Soviet past. Indeed, interview data discussed in this chapter and in chapters 3 and 4 shows that coming out in order to make visible one's authentic 'self' was rarely experienced by women as empowering; on the contrary, dissimulation was often a pragmatic strategy used to navigate both intimate and public spaces. This is reflected in the language women used to talk about disclosure: although the expression 'coming out' had gained a certain currency in Russian LGBT media at the time when the research took place, women very seldom used it in interviews and in naturally occurring conversation. A variety of other expressions were used to describe the process of self-discovery (*osoznat' sebia, iskat' sebia*; 'to understand oneself', 'to search for oneself') and attitudes towards concealment and disclosure (*otkryvat'sia, skryvats'ia, neotrytaia, otrkrovenno, raskryvat'sia* – 'to open oneself', 'to hide', 'not open', 'openly', 'to open up'). When asked about the way they present themselves, however, a recurring expression used by interviewees was *ne afishiruiu* ('I don't broadcast it'), or similar turns of phrase (*ne idu s plakatami, ne demonstriruem, ne sprovotsiruiu*; 'I don't go around with banners', 'We are not demonstrative', 'I don't provoke').

In this respect, this monograph echoes the findings of other research, which shows that visibility and authenticity in themselves are seldom prized by Russian non-heterosexual women (Omel'chenko, 2002b; Nartova, 2004c; Zelenina, 2006). More importance seems to be placed on managing one's identity appropriately across different social contexts, which is associated with rules of propriety and risk-assessment, rather than on being 'out'. Nartova (2004c) argues that invisibility was seen as enabling by the lesbian women she interviewed in Saint Petersburg. Practices of self-management, however, are not necessarily seen as problematic, and may not always be the evidence of internalised homophobia. The fact that authenticity and visibility are not prominent in women's narratives may reflect their specific understanding of privacy rooted in different configurations of private and public (Nartova, 2004c; Oswald and Voronkov, 2004). This contrasts with findings from research conducted in Anglo-American societies, which indicate that authenticity and visibility emerge as core positive values for LGBT individuals, even for those who have limited access to spaces where it is safe and comfortable to be 'out' (Holt and Griffith, 2003; Dunne, Prendergast and Telford, 2002; Predergast, Dunne, and Telford, 2002; Taylor, 2007). This is a point worth stressing, since the closet has been theorised in 'the west' as a global form of oppression (Brown, 2000). Yet research conducted in non-western societies has critiqued the culturally specific and normative character of the 'coming out' narrative, buttressed by global LGBT politics based on recognition and visibility (Manalansan, 1997, 2002, 2003; Johnson, 1998; Decena, 2011). I argue, therefore, that truly global theorisations of the closet need to be able to account for the contradictory aspects of visibility and how they play out in specific contexts, rather that assuming the sameness of oppression embodied in the closet; I will return to this point in the concluding chapter of the monograph.

Structure, agency and women's negotiations

As shorthand for the regulation of 'deviant' sexuality through invisibility, the closet was a useful theoretical tool to analyse women's navigations of everyday space. Women had learned certain places as heteronormative; successfully navigating everyday space involved avoiding certain places (for example, bars where women may be confronted because their appearance stood out), refraining from behaviour that could make one visible as 'queer' (for example, kissing a girlfriend on the street), or not disclosing details of one's intimate life (for example, not coming out to colleagues at work). Thus, awareness of the spatial norm embodied in the concept of the closet was central to women's navigations of space.

The closet is a useful sensitising concept to analyse the structural constraints, inscribed in cultural norm, which affect women's spatial navigations. However, the closet/coming out paradigm is too blunt a theoretical tool to account for women's agency in negotiating these structural constraints. First, positing the closet as a global form of oppression may obscure how the closet as a spatial norm operates very differently in different locales, as evidenced here through the comparison between metropolitan Moscow and provincial Ul'ianovsk. Secondly, the closet/coming out paradigm implicitly relies on binary, rigid notions of private and public, which are unable to account for the complexities of women's social interactions and performances. The boundaries between 'private' and 'public' were typically experienced as blurred: for example, the private, intimate setting of the parental home was experienced as difficult to negotiate precisely because it afforded little privacy; public settings such as the workplace or the street could also become places where intimate relationships are formed, and where sexuality may be safely expressed. Goffman's notions of 'front' and 'backstage' in the presentation of the self are useful here because they do not imply a neat divide between the private and public spheres (Goffman, 1959/1990a). Emplaced social interaction is a process based on setting boundaries between 'front' and 'backstage' and managing expectations about what can legitimately be disclosed and known. Thirdly, and most importantly, the closet/coming out paradigm is based on the notion of visibility as empowering; yet women emphasised how self-management, or negotiating their sexuality appropriately across different places and social contexts, was a way of taking charge and being in control. Strategies women used to negotiate their sexuality did not necessarily involve 'passing' as heterosexual, but rather exploiting grey areas in order to 'blend in' and remain invisible as a lesbian/bisexual woman. 'Closetedness', or lack of disclosure, therefore, was not always perceived as a negative space of forced concealment, hypocrisy and self-denial; it also symbolised a privacy which was often seen as desirable, but not necessarily accessible.

It has been suggested that practices of self-management and routinised division between 'queer' and 'non-queer' spheres of existence are more prevalent in Russia than in western societies, where LGBT citizens enjoy a greater degree of recognition and protection from the state (Nartova, 2004c; Essig, 1999). However, differences in practices of self-management may be more a matter of semantics than of substance: the 'coming out' narrative mainstreamed in western LGBT politics and popular culture does not necessarily reflect everyday practices. Research conducted in Britain has highlighted that self-management remains a pervasive feature in the lives of LGBT-identified individuals, and that considerations of safety and comfort are often placed ahead of ideals of authenticity, particularly in negotiations of public space (Valentine, 1993a; Corteen, 2002; Moran and Skeggs, 2004; Taylor, 2007). While in the past this happened in the context of state hostility, more recently, practices of self-management are framed within more inclusive policies and discourses of 'responsible citizenship' which still place the onus on LGBT citizens for their personal safety (Moran and Skeggs, 2004). Moreover, visibility and the public avowal of one's sexuality may be more central to the experiences of those who have greater access and entitlement to 'queer' space. In her work on British working-class lesbians, Taylor (2007) argues that lesbian visibility is intertwined with class privilege, since it is easier to be 'out' in places, such as universities or the commercial gay scene, to which working-class lesbians have more limited access. She also argues that supposedly desirable, 'gay-friendly' neighbourhoods and the commercial scene engender dis-identifications in women who are 'othered' because of their class background. Indeed, celebrations of queer visibility tends to erase from the picture exclusions and differences based on class, 'race'/ethnicity, gender, age and able-bodiedness.

Empirical findings and reflections about the limitations of the 'closet/coming out' paradigm feed into calls to 'come out of the "coming out" story' (Jolly, 2001) and to think 'beyond the closet' (Seidman, 2002). Adams (2010) points out that coming out is framed in the literature as a healthy, mature and responsible act, which has the potential to challenge the stigmatisation of same-sex sexualities. However, the extent to which visibility alone can undermine heterosexism and homophobia is disputed (Sedgwick, 1990; Seidman et al., 1999, p. 10; Binnie, 2004). Indeed, as Sedgwick (1990) points out, the paradox embodied by the closet is that disclosure is at once expected and forbidden, and that no one can ever be completely out of the closet, as new encounters generate new closets, requiring fresh decisions about disclosure or secrecy. More importantly, coming out and 'outness' are not necessarily empowering acts, and their subversive potential may be conditional on specific places and contexts. Rather than conceptualising it as a metaphor of oppression and symbolic erasure, Seidman et al. (1999, p. 10) redefine that the closet as 'a site of both accommodation and resistance which both reproduces and contests aspects of a society organised around normative heterosexuality'. This reconceptualisation is productive because it makes room for individual and collective agency and for the contextual meanings of in/visibility, while not forgetting the structural norms which affect and constrain everyday practices.

Conclusions

The chapter has explored women's negotiations of their sexuality at work and on the street. Women were aware of unspoken rules of propriety shaping social interaction in these settings, and of the potential emotional and material risks involved in becoming visible as a lesbian/bisexual woman. While they adopted different strategies in negotiating their sexuality, managing impressions by controlling both verbal and visual signifiers of their sexuality was a key part of their everyday practices of self-presentation. Disclosure was not necessarily seen as empowering or feasible, and women retained a sense of control over everyday social transactions by constantly drifting in and out of public visibility.

As Valentine (1993a) points out, women's identity negotiations are conducted according to complex personal maps of time and space. Negotiating the workplace and the street often involved drawing boundaries between a formal 'front stage', where performances are dictated by set roles, and a more intimate 'backstage', where individuals slip out of set roles and where details of one's personal life may be revealed (Goffman, 1959/1990a). Women's embodied performances were not dictated by abstract binary notions of private/public space. Indeed, the boundaries between private and public were perceived as blurred: for example, risk of exposure may be greater in the private realm of the parental home than in formal social interaction with work colleagues. Similarly, the street may be simultaneously experienced as dangerous, anonymous or a space of belonging, depending on whether it is a site of potential violence and intimidation, a transitional space where one's sexuality remains invisible, or a meeting place for lesbian/queer *tusovki*.

The closet/coming out paradigm offers valuable insights into how socially constructed spatial norms deploy notions of private and public to uphold heteronormativity. However, the closet and coming out are both culturally specific and value-laden terms: the former is conceptualised as a negative space of repression and concealment, while the latter is equated with the empowering act of making public and visible one's sexuality. 'Coming out' itself has acquired a normative status as 'the central narrative of positive gay experience' (Plummer, 1995, p. 83); yet this narrative did not resonate with the experience of Russian women. Uncritical celebrations of coming out as empowering fail to acknowledge that visibility is not equally available to all queer subjects, and that its subversive potential is contingent and conditional on place and time. While the closet/coming out effectively encapsulates structural constraints to expressions of non-normative sexualities, it is unable to account for the role of individual and collective agency in women's complex time/space navigations and identity negotiations.

6
Carving Out Queer Space: In/visibility, Belonging and Resistance

There has been a growing interest within sexualities studies in the construction of queer space, understood a space collectively appropriated by non-heterosexuals as an alternative to heteronormative urban space (Oswin, 2008). Existing research generally focuses on metropolitan, territorialised forms of queer space, such as the gay 'scene' (understood as a territorially concentrated cluster of commercial venues and community organisations), or on inner city neighbourhoods known to have a high concentration of LGBT residents (Binnie and Skeggs, 2004; Moran and Skeggs, 2004; Valentine and Skelton, 2003). As Binnie (2004, p. 4) notes, however, this literature locates queer space in the metropolitan west and 'within major urban centres of gay consumer culture', thus neglecting both the existence of spaces precariously and less overtly claimed as queer, and the experiences of queers who live in locales which lack institutionalised and visible gay scenes.

This chapter explores how 'lesbian/queer' space is carved out in the two different urban contexts of Moscow and Ul'ianovsk. It maps configurations of 'lesbian/queer' space in both Moscow, a global city with a lively gay scene, and Ul'ianovsk, a provincial city with no institutionalised scene, and explores how metropolitan/provincial location shapes the appropriation of urban space as queer, focusing mainly on provincial Ul'ianovsk. While territorial concentration and visibility are themes that feature prominently in the literature on metropolitan queer space, I focus here instead on more transient and precarious appropriations of urban space as queer. The first part of this chapter shows both the similarities and differences between Moscow and Ul'ianosk, exploring the characteristics of lesbian/queer locales and strategies used to appropriate them. The second part focuses entirely on Ul'ianosk, and considers whether the appropriation of urban space by the local lesbian/queer *tusovka* can be seen as subversive and political, even when this appropriation is neither overt nor visible. Thus, the chapter continues to engage with debates about the closet and about the enabling/disabling potential of in/visibility outlined in Chapter 5.

Sexuality, urban space and resistance

Literature on sexuality and space has emphasised the importance of queer space in the lives of non-heterosexuals. In societies where same-sex desire is often devalued, stigmatised and pathologised, queer space provides a safe environment to explore one's sexuality, 'find oneself' and form a positive sexual identity (Valentine and Skelton, 2003; Holt and Griffin, 2003). Research has highlighted the importance of the 'scene' as a space where young people's sexuality is validated and can be freely and safely expressed, unlike other social contexts where it has to be concealed or is misrecognised. Beyond the 'coming out' stage, the personal networks and relations individuals form in queer space often remain an important reference point (Moran and Skeggs, 2004). Queer space is most commonly discussed in the literature with reference to leisure space, and in particular to the gay 'scene', understood as a loose cluster of commercial venues and community organisations catering for non-heterosexuals, usually located in the gentrified centres of big cities (Binnie, 2004; Valentine and Skelton, 2003; Moran and Skeggs, 2004). Even when not expressively focusing on the scene, research has tended to concentrate on the most visible expressions of queer space, for example, on residential areas with a conspicuous concentration of queerly identified residents (Castells, 1983; Adler and Brenner, 1992), or on events such as gay Pride parades, whereby urban space is temporarily but very visibly appropriated as queer (Browne, 2007; Johnston, 2007).

Existing literature has emphasised the link between queer space, leisure, consumerism and cosmopolitanism, for example, by exploring how visible queer enclaves, such as Manchester's gay village, are actively marketed as tourist attractions, and used to promote the cosmopolitan and multicultural image of the host city (Binnie and Skeggs, 2004). Thus, the creation of visible queer space is a phenomenon linked to the gentrification of inner city areas, urban regeneration, and the emergence of policy agendas supporting equal rights, safety and protection from hate crimes for LGBT citizens (Moran and Skeggs, 2004). Insights from this literature can be applied, to some extent, to the Russian context: for example, in Moscow the development of a relatively well established 'scene' was linked to broader processes of post-Soviet urban regeneration, including the gentrification of the city centre and the commercialisation of urban leisure space (Brade and Rudolph, 2004; Rudolph and Brade, 2005). As pointed out in other contexts, far from being an inherently inclusive and 'progressive', queer space can also generate exclusions, as classed, gendered and racialised boundaries regulate access to and consumption of queer space (Taylor, 2007, 2008; Casey, 2004; Manalansan, 2003). Although an in-depth exploration of these boundaries is beyond the scope of the present study, in Moscow their existence was apparent in the near-absence of non-white, non-Slavic women on the scene, and in the market-oriented character of many commercial and community initiatives, which implicitly targeted a relatively affluent, educated and middle-class audience.[1] First of all, the widespread focus on the consumption of queer space often translates in a metropolitan bias in the literature, as Binnie (2004, pp. 4–5) points out:

> The queer cosmopolitan is routinely located within the major centres of gay consumer culture. The other to this cosmopolitan is therefore the rural and the provincial ... Commentaries on queer consumer culture commonly imagine the world ends at the boundaries of the metropolis.

This metropolitan bias is also present in the not extensive literature on queer space and subcultures in Russia, which has thus far focused on Moscow and Saint Petersburg (Nartova, 1999; Essig, 1999; Zelenina, 2006; Sarajeva, 2010, 2011). Yet many non-heterosexuals do not have access to 'major centres of gay consumer culture', but live in peripheral locations lacking any kind of institutionalised and visible queer space, as was the case with the Ul'ianovsk *tusovka*. As Pilkington and Johnson (2003) argue, the prevalent focus on consumption and on 'lifestyle enclaves' in leisure/youth studies reflects a bias towards western consumer societies in the literature. However, consumption is less relevant to account for leisure practices and the construction of subcultural spaces in less affluent societies, although classed exclusions based on access to economic and social capital are still at work. As Pilkington's work on Russian youth shows, lack of access to global cultural commodities and limited mobility shape the experiences of 'peripheral' youth from provincial and rural areas, whereas individualised choice between different consumer 'lifestyles' may have more resonance in metropolitan centres such as Moscow, particularly among more affluent youth

(Pilkington et al., 2002; Pilkington and Johnson, 2003; Pilkington et al., 2010).

Queer space is understood here to encompass both 'the scene' and other public and semi-public urban locations, only temporarily and precariously appropriated as 'lesbian/queer'. This holistic notion of queer space is better able to capture the experiences and patterns of socialising of non-heterosexual women in both Moscow and Ul'ianovsk. The analysis of queer space presented here encompasses both the specific geographic locations appropriated as queer and the social relations that arise within them. I draw on the notion of *tusovka*, a Russian term which refers to an informal and loose social network whose boundaries are relatively fluid and open, and where social interaction is based on shared interest and on the practice of socialising in specific city centre locations (Pilkington, 1994; Zdravomyslova and Voronkov, 2002). *Tusovka* blurs the boundaries between spatiality and social relations, since it refers to a gathering place ('I have been going to the *tusovki* since I was 15') as well as to a group of people linked by common interests and bonds of friendship and solidarity who habitually meet at a certain place ('our *tusovka* is very friendly', Pilkington, 1994, pp. 236–238). In this chapter the focus of analysis is the practices through which the Ul'ianovsk *tusovka* appropriated urban space as queer. By comparing provincial Ul'ianovsk to metropolitan Moscow, the chapter explores the impact of location on the ways in which queer space is produced and experienced. The chapter also highlights similarities, as well as differences, between 'lesbian/queer' *tusovki* in Ul'ianovsk and Moscow, thus fracturing rigid polarisations between metropolitan and provincial queer space.

Mapping queer space in Moscow and Ul'ianovsk

At the time when the fieldwork was conducted, Moscow, Russia's biggest and most affluent city, hosted a lively and well-established queer scene, which had developed since the early 1990s. The scene comprised a range of clubs, cafes and restaurants, several lesbian, gay or LGBT organisations and grassroots initiatives, as well as the most successful Russian LGBT information resources.[2] Queer space was not confined to semi-public commercial and community spaces: well-known meeting places for non-heterosexual men and women were located on the public street in city centre locations. Kitai-Gorod was known to be a cruising area for gay men, while young women met and socialised on a specific stretch of

Tverskoi Boulevard, a place known in the Moscow lesbian community as the *Pushka*.[3] The Moscow scene was very noticeably segregated along gender lines, as both commercial and community events were generally labelled as either 'gay' or 'lesbian'. In commercial establishments, gender segregation was encouraged by the management: with the exception of the club *12 Vol't* (*12 Volts*), which had a mixed clientele, clubs encouraged male patronage by charging women more than men, occasionally reversing the policy for 'women-only' nights. Women-only spaces were more transient than men-only, as they were generally hosted on an ad-hoc basis by mainstream or gay clubs; attempts to set up women-only bars by lesbian entrepreneurs were ongoing at the time when fieldwork took place, but eventually proved unsuccessful (Sarajeva, 2010, 2011). Despite occasionally joining forces on individual projects, community initiatives also tended to be either women- or men-only. Even when this was not the case, a spontaneous divide seemed to emerge: for example, despite its name, the Moscow Lesbian and Gay Archive, based in the private home of a lesbian woman, was predominantly a meeting place for women.

Unlike Moscow, Ul'ianovsk did not have a gay scene, either in the form of commercial venues or community organisations. However, this does not mean that the city lacked any kind of queer space, as specific city centre locations were informally used as meeting places by a local queer *tusovka*. The group was mixed, and included both men and women, predominantly in their late teens to mid-to-late 20s; however, within the broader *tusovka*, men and women formed distinct groups, which interacted only intermittently (for example, during the monthly gay and lesbian club nights organised at a local mainstream club). The *tusovka* had originated in a small group of friends of similar age, and had gradually expanded to include friends of friends, lovers and former lovers; although some heterosexual friends were invited to gatherings and events, their participation was marginal to the life of the *tusovka*. The group had expanded when Kristina and Sveta, a very popular couple and part of the *tusovka*'s original core group, had started to organise club nights for gays and lesbians. However, at the time of fieldwork, the extended *tusovka* had become fragmented, and its diminished vitality was partly attributed to the fact that several core members had moved away from Ul'ianovsk for work or study. Crucial to the life of the *tusovka* was a specific bench located in an alley of one of the city's central thoroughfares; members of the *tusovka* arranged to meet there, or just casually dropped by without previous arrangement, as Lada, a student at the local university in her early twenties, explained:

> We have our favourite alley [...] where there is our favourite bench where everyone gathers. Sometimes you have nothing to do at home and you go there and hang out. This is how everyone met.
>
> (Lada, Ul'ianovsk)

Other popular meeting places in Ul'ianovsk were located nearby, and included two cafes not specifically marketed as 'gay' or 'lesbian', but informally known to be frequented by the *tusovka*; as Marusya, a teacher in her early 40s, explained, 'We also have a café, and it has a certain reputation of being a hangout for queers [*nashi, literally "our people"*]'. Moreover, a closed-doors event for members of the *tusovka* was organised monthly in a local mainstream club.

In/visible queer space in Moscow and Ul'ianovsk

The presence or absence of a relatively visible and established queer scene was the most conspicuous difference between Moscow and Ul'ianovsk. Indeed, in Ul'ianovsk the lack of amenities and leisure space was often contrasted by members of the *tusovka* to the range of opportunities for socialising offered by bigger, more 'civilised' cities, and the Moscow scene often featured in conversation as a yardstick and a term of comparison. Lada and Tamara, both in their mid-20s and in service sector occupations, were critical of the club nights organised by the local *tusovka*, and had discussed opening a commercial gay club in Ul'ianovsk, modelled on the 'classy' Moscow venues, with the support of an investor (a heterosexual man). Liza, a woman in her early 40s working as a janitor, noted that she had limited opportunities to socialise with lesbian women of a similar age in the Ul'ianovsk *tusovka*; for this reason, she maintained links with the Moscow lesbian *tusovki*, occasionally attending the gatherings of the lesbian leisure club *Klub Svonodnogo Poseshcheniia*, and planned to organise a similar grassroots initiative in Ul'ianovsk. Renata, an apprentice lawyer in her early twenties, jokingly commented with another member of the *tusovka* that, now that a new monument to the poet Puskin had been erected in central Ul'ianovsk, the local lesbians could legitimately claim to have their own *Pushka*.[4]

Bigger cities like Moscow were also seen as offering more opportunities to purchase lesbian-themed books and films which were not available in Ul'ianovsk, or to attend gigs of Russian pop and rock bands, such as Zemfira and Butch, which were popular among lesbian and bisexual women but unlikely to perform in peripheral cities like Ul'ianovsk. For the Ul'ianovsk *tusovka*, and for women who had moved to Moscow from small towns and provincial cities, the capital held a special allure as a hub of queer consumer culture and as a city offering greater opportunities to socialise with like-minded women. In this respect, Moscow was perceived as more progressive and cosmopolitan than provincial Russia: the capital was experienced first-hand, or imagined, as a city where non-heterosexual women could find spaces where they belonged, and feel free from the social scrutiny experienced in towns and smaller cities.

Widespread perceptions of Moscow as being exceptional vis-à-vis the rest of Russia reinscribe a narrative pitting 'queer-friendly', cosmopolitan Moscow against deeply conservative provincial and rural areas, where queers were both invisible and isolated. As Weston (1995) notes, the symbolic contrast between the metropolitan and the provincial/rural has long been central to gay imagination, as big cities are imagined as more tolerant of diversity, and as hosting gay enclaves which enable individuals to find a community and fully live a gay lifestyle. However, Weston also points out that the symbolic contrast between the metropolitan and the provincial seems to depend on 'an idealised portrait of the two as separate, self-contained space' (Weston, 1995, p. 257). Indeed, while differences between queer space in Moscow and Ul'ianovsk may be more noticeable, important similarities between the ways in which queer space was carved out in both cities also emerged.

While relatively more visible and established compared to Ul'ianovsk, the Moscow scene did not constitute a recognisable gay enclave like Marais in Paris, Soho in London or the Manchester Village (Collins, 2004; Provencher, 2007; Moran and Skeggs, 2004). Unlike them, the Moscow scene was neither territorially concentrated nor showcased and marketed to promote the city's cosmopolitan image. Indeed, while similarities in the emergence and development of urban gay enclaves in Anglo-American societies have been widely studied, the emergence of queer space in urban Russia does not fit into patterns of 'ghettoisation', gay-led gentrification and integration theorised by Castells (1983), Collins (2004) or Ruting (2008). Commercial and community initiatives were geographically scattered in different districts of Moscow; some of them, such as the gay and lesbian bar *12 Vol't*, the gay-friendly club *Propaganda* and the LGBT organisation *Ia+Ia* were located within the Boulevard Ring in central Moscow, but not in close proximity to each other; others, such as the gay club *Tri Ob'ezyany* and the mainstream club *Udar* (which hosted weekly lesbian nights) and the Gay and Lesbian

Archive were located in more peripheral locations, outside the Boulevard Ring or on the very outskirts of Moscow. Moreover, Moscow's queer commercial and community establishments were not immediately visible and recognisable, a fact that reflects both the chaotic character of post-Soviet Moscow reconstruction and a deliberate strategy to avoid unwanted attention. Although commercial establishments were listed both in the gay and lesbian press and in magazines such as *Time Out Moscow* and *Afisha*, even the most successful were not visibly signposted or recognisable as 'queer' from the outside.[5] Community initiatives also enjoyed low visibility, partly because they did not have their own dedicated premises, and their use of indoor space relied on the goodwill of the local administrators, private businesses or neighbours[6]: keeping a low profile was a way to avoid potential problems. Indeed, for both community and commercial initiatives, 'blending in' rather than standing out seemed a deliberate strategy to avoid unwanted attention or confrontation. For commercial establishments, remaining discrete seemed to be a decision partly dictated by concerns about patrons' safety and anonymity: some clubs advised patrons to stay until closing time (6 am) in order to avoid the risk of petty crime and homophobic violence, and in the club *Baza* my camera was temporarily confiscated when a Russian friend taking pictures of us and of other patrons caused alarm among staff. Thus, even in metropolitan Moscow, which is widely considered one of the most cosmopolitan and outward-looking Russian cities, visibility was not encouraged, either as a symbol of recognition or as a means to encourage custom.

Queer street tusovki in Moscow and Ul'ianovsk

Another important similarity between queer space in Moscow and Ul'ianovsk was the presence of street *tusovki* meeting in relatively safe and gentrified city centre areas. In Moscow, young women in their teens and early 20s met at the Esenin monument on the central Tverskoi Boulevard, a location known as the *Pushka*. The *Pushka* attracted a similar age group to the Ul'ianovsk *tusovka*, although it was a women-only group, rather than a mixed one. Patterns of socialising were very similar, and involved spending time with friends, meeting new acquaintances, chatting, drinking beer or spirits; flirting and meeting potential sexual partners was also an important part of the life of the *tusovki*. Group interaction revolved around practices which marked and constructed the *tusovki* as queer space. For example, the appropriation of a particular kind of music, perceived to have a 'lesbian' sensibility, was common in both Moscow and Ul'ianovsk.

Do you have any cult music in your circle?

Of course. Diana Arbenina, Surganova, Zemfira, among others, I don't know them all, well, Mara and Butch as well. [...] I really like Mara, for example, it's very energetic music, music it's great to get up to, even if you didn't sleep much at night – it's still great to get up to it.

Do you listen to them especially because they are, in a way, temnye [*queer*]*?*

First of all, I like the music, secondly, it's something to talk about, because in the circle of friends I hang out with everyone listens to this music. For example, when a new album is released, we listen to it and then discuss it, whether we liked it or not; when we meet we listen to this music all together. There is music I listen to that is not queer [*tematicheskaia*], but I listen to this more often.

(Nastia, Moscow)

It just turns out that people who are in the *tema* [*v teme*] have some kind of interests, they don't just sit around and drink beer. They don't bother you, with them you can talk about serious things. Of course among straights [*naturalov*] you'll find people like that, but they think a bit differently, they have different aspirations.

What common interests do you have in your circle?

Well, it just happens to be like this. Even music, it matches. What we have in common – it's our [*sexual*] orientation, and secondly we listen to almost the same music, Zemfira, Nochnye Snaipery, Radiohead, Placebo.

(Maia, Ul'ianovsk)

Although many women rejected the notion of 'lesbian' music, pointing out that music has no sexuality and it is largely a matter of personal taste, the names of Zemfira, Nochnye Snaipery, Svetlana Surganova, Mara and Butch kept cropping up both in naturally occurring interactions and in interviews, sometimes in the context of a broader interest in rock music. These popular Russian artists were credited by both mainstream and the gay and lesbian media to have a large following among lesbians (Gurova, 2003; Zelenina, 2006). Thus, listening to their music had a specific relevance and meaning in the *tusovki*: 'lesbian' music was part of a distinctive cultural code that circulated as common currency in both Moscow and Ul'ianovsk – at once a conversation topic, a social glue and a focus of group leisure activity. Listening to 'lesbian' music, alongside with other practices (such as exchanging copies of the lesbian *samizdat* magazine *Ostrov* among members of the Ul'ianovsk *tusovka*), was part of a cultural code which facilitated the production of urban space as lesbian/queer by creating a shared narrative. These shared practices bridge the distance between metropolitan and provincial queer space.

At the same time, these practices should be read in the broader context of youth subcultures in contemporary Russia. Indeed, practices like meeting on the street, chatting, drinking and listening to music reflect common patterns of socialising among young people: youths who share a particular interest (e.g. in punk music) become part of loose social networks (*tusovki*) which meet in specific city centre locations, particularly in the warmer months. As Pilkington points out, the claiming of city centre space is a signifier of social prestige, although not all the *tusovki* members are necessarily from middle-class or privileged backgrounds, or live in the more upmarket inner city areas (Pilkington, 1994; Pilkington et al., 2002, p. 251). *Tusovki* are associated with *neformaly* milieus, or 'alternative' countercultural environments; in this respect, they differ from other youth groups, such as informal groups of friends (*formaly*) and youth gangs (*gopniki*) gathering in more peripheral neighbourhoods. While appropriating city centre locations, both the Ul'ianovsk *tusovka* and the Moscow *tusovka* gathering at the *Pushka* were self-styled 'democratic' spaces, in principle open to all, irrespective of their socio-economic background, education and financial resources.

> Well, it was just interesting to socialise in a *tusovka* where people are so different, and had it not been for the *tema* they would not hang out together. Because some people work, some study, some have just finished school, and they all hang out together, it was very interesting.
>
> (Alisa, Ul'ianovsk)

> Well, first of all, people who hang out there [*at the Pushka*] act defiantly, and imagine some business woman, who has only ever socialised with heterosexuals, and suddenly she understands that she is a lesbian, but even so her material values, her aspirations, have remained the same. What does she have in common with students? Nothing! [...] Although she is a lesbian. But she thinks: I don't want this. Although this is not all, this is just one identity; the rest is all different between them. I think this is just out of pretentiousness, and of feeling self-important. Because I have an acquaintance who is a businesswoman [...], and when their tusovki meet it is in some expensive restaurant. So I say to her: 'Tania, if you want we are going

out, if you want don't feel out of place in your high heels, in your Versace clothes'. She comes, parks her expensive car nearby, and joins us. I mean, she is not a pretentious person.

(Sasha, Moscow)

Both the Ul'ianovsk and the Moscow *tusovki* are presented here as diverse and democratic spaces, where acceptance into the group does not depend on money, education or social class. Indeed, in her work on Moscow lesbian subcultures Sarajeva (2010, 2011) shows that, in the case of the *Pushka*, it is those who do not comply with its egalitarian ethos who struggle to fit in. Despite the *tusovki's* self-professed egalitarian ethos, however, access to them was marked along generational and class lines. With a few exceptions, older women did not socialise in the *tusovki*, both because age difference acted as barrier to socialising, and because in other lesbian circles street *tusovki* (particularly the Moscow *Pushka*) had a reputation for being rough, in your face and full of 'silly' young women, whose main interests revolved around drinking, swearing and casual sex. In Ul'ianovsk, a substantial part of the *tusovka's* regulars were students from local universities and colleges (mostly working students); the high percentage of students is also remarked upon by Sasha and noted by Sarajeva in the case of the Moscow *Pushka* (Sarajeva, 2010, 2011). Nonetheless, both *tusovki* were fairly diverse in terms of their members' socio-economic backgrounds: in Ul'ianovsk women in manual or low-skilled jobs were also regulars in the *tusovka* alongside students and young professionals, and Sarajeva notes the presence of homeless women from other Russian cities at the *Pushka* (*ibid.*). However, in the Ul'ianovsk *tusovka* some of the students, through their background and education, as well as through their personal investment in 'lesbian' subculture, had accrued a 'subcultural capital' (Thornton, 1995), which gave them a more authoritative position within the *tusovka*. Access to personal technology (particularly the internet), personal networks and the relative freedom from the time constraints of student life were important resources for them. Subcultural capital could occasionally be turned into economic capital: for example, an entry ticket was paid at the monthly club nights, which covered expenses but also compensated the organisers from the *tusovka* for their work.

Carving out lesbian/queer space in Ul'ianovsk

The political significance of carving out queer space as a way of claiming a legitimate presence in the public space, and of exercising the 'right to the city' (Purcell, 2003; Hubbard, 2013; Lefebvre, 1996) has been widely debated in the literature. Moran and Skeggs (2004), for example, note that in western cities the presence of visible and territorialised gay villages in gentrified city centres has become invested with political meaning, and read as evidence of hard-won recognition of LGBT communities and of the legitimisation of queer presence in public space. This understanding is premised on the notion of invisibility (the closet) as oppressive, and of visibility (coming out) as enabling and subversive: the visible appropriation of heterosexual city space is understood to challenge implicit heteronorms. I engage with these debates by considering the strategies used by the Ul'ianovsk *tusovka* to appropriate urban space as queer. A focus on Ul'ianovsk allows both an exploration of how provincial location may impact on the *tusovka's* strategies to appropriate urban space, and a consideration of whether non-overt and inconspicuous appropriation of queer space can be seen as challenging gendered and sexualised spatial norm. Resistance is understood in this context not as organised opposition to institutionalised power embodied in social movements, but as encompassing unstructured and quotidian forms of defiance (Scott, 1986). This understanding of resistance is premised on the notion that social actors have the capacity to produce social change by giving collective meanings to their actions (Pile, 1997, pp. 14–15).

Safety, privacy and strategies to carve out queer space

As seen in chapters 4 and 5, different perceptions of safety and anonymity emerged from the Moscow and the Ul'ianovsk case studies. In Ul'ianovsk, women were very conscious that, in a relatively small city where rumours spread quickly, the possibility of being exposed was greater, and this translated into anxieties about being outed and ensuing pressures to blend in and remain invisible as a lesbian or bisexual woman. Contrasting her views to those of young participants in a discussion group for lesbian women, which she attended during a trip to Moscow, Zoia, a teacher in her mid-20s, thus explained different attitudes to 'coming out' in the capital and in her native Ul'ianovsk:

> I had a conversation with the Moscow girls, they tell their colleagues [*about their sexuality*]. Well, if that's what they want, if this makes them freer, God bless [*radi Boga*]. But we [*she and her girlfriend*] don't want to break our neck over this. They began to discuss in detail how they tell their colleagues. I told them, 'Girls, come back to planet Earth, for us in the provinces [*v glubinke*] it is all different'. [...] They are freer in Moscow because there are many of them, and they are all incomers, they don't care about what people say about them. Here, it

is different: as one woman puts it, she knows what her husband has been up to before he gets home, because her acquaintances will tell her. If someone learns anything about me, my parents, my acquaintances, everyone will know. Why make my life more difficult if I live in this city. If no one knew me I would not care.

(Zoia, Ul'ianovsk)

Zoia may be overstating Muscovites' willingness to be open about their sexuality; nonetheless, the perception that freedom stemmed from the greater anonymity afforded by living in a big city resonated in interviews with women from Moscow, particularly those who had moved to Moscow from other parts of Russia (see Stella, 2013b). Ul'ianovsk, on the other hand, was repeatedly described as a small provincial city where not conforming to expectations meant becoming the subject of public scrutiny, which could be an extremely uncomfortable experience, particularly for the many women in the *tusovka* who still lived in the parental home. Perceptions of safety in Ul'ianovsk compared negatively to those of the more affluent and cosmopolitan Moscow: the threatening presence of violent gangs and *gopniki*, and the possibility of intimidation and violence on the street was feared particularly among the men from the Ul'ianovsk *tusovka*. Moreover, youth leisure space in Ul'ianovsk was much less diverse than in central Moscow, where a range of *tusovki* sporting different styles habitually gathered: women (and men) whose bodily performance did not comply with gendered expectations were more likely to look conspicuous and stand out as out of place in Ul'ianovsk.

Homogeneity and heightened levels of surveillance were reflected in the strategies used by the Ul'ianovsk *tusovka* to collectively appropriate and inhabit public and semi-public space as queer. The *tusovka* regularly met at a particular bench on one of the city's central thoroughfares; however, this place was not visibly marked as queer, and passers-by seemed mostly unaware of the nature of the *tusovka*, and oblivious to the meanings its members ascribed to this place. Members of the *tusovka* were generally keen not to disrupt this blissful ignorance, and to remain unmarked as a queer/lesbian group: affectionate behaviour with a partner was avoided on the street and in the cafes even when members were socialising with the *tusovka*, and women often emphasised the importance of responsible and appropriate behaviour, deploring conduct which could be seen as provocative or in your face:

[...] there was an episode when a waitress beat up a gay guy, she wasn't alone to be precise, there was also one of her friends with her boyfriend, he held the guy, and she beat him. I don't know how he was drawn into this. It is a very obscure story, and it is possible that he [*the gay man*] provoked them – it was an assault. The guy was injured, they painted his face with bruises. I think that he was in the wrong and that he provoked them, because we were all hanging out at the same place, and it was one waitress from the club, she was fired. Yes, there were episodes like this, one guy was killed, they slit his throat. Simply because of who he is.

(Kristina, Ul'ianovsk)

Episodes of street violence (*remonty*), including the murder of a gay man mentioned by Kristina, were also reported by other members of the *tusovka*, although they were reluctant to offer details. Kristina, one of the core members of the original *tusovka* and the co-organiser of the first club nights, emphasised the importance of discretion and of avoiding rowdy or provocative behaviour, based on previous episodes of intimidation and violence. Overtly performing queerness was generally imputed to gay men and to 'immature' young women (*maloletniki*), and was sanctioned by members of the *tusovka*, who emphasised instead the importance of avoiding attracting attention and of taking responsibility for one's own safety. The behaviour of *tusovka* members on the street and in the mainstream cafes nearby was constrained by the awareness of social scrutiny and potential risk to a greater extent than that of the Moscow *Pushka*. The *Pushka tusovka*'s appropriation of public space was similarly ambiguous, as passers-by were mostly unaware of it as a 'lesbian' space, and members of the *tusovka* played along with this ambiguity (Sarajeva, 2010). Nonetheless, the Moscow *Pushka* was more overtly visible as a lesbian space, through its members' looks (sporting crew cuts and unisex clothing) and behaviour (kissing or making playful reference to lesbian sex); moreover, the *Pushka* had attracted the attention of the capital's tabloid press (Minorskaia, 2004; Krongauz, 2005; Maksimov, 2006), and thus its existence as a 'lesbian' space was known to outsiders, not just to members of the lesbian community.

While for members of the Ul'ianovsk *tusovka* behaviour on the street and in mixed cafes was constrained by the awareness of inhabiting very public locations, in the more secluded environment of the monthly gay and lesbian club nights members of the *tusovka* could express themselves more freely. Klavdia, an unemployed mother of two with a chronic illness in her mid-30s, was particularly wary of being affectionate with her partner in public. She thus explained the more relaxed atmosphere of the club nights:

Everyone is one of us [*vse svoi*], and no one judges you, and what you can't do on the street you can do there.

(Klavdiia, Ul'ianovsk)

Club nights offered a welcome respite from public scrutiny; the all-queer environment created a comfortable atmosphere where members of the *tusovka* felt free to display affectionate or sexualised behaviour. However, once again carving out a safe and comfortable space was conditional upon sheltering it from public scrutiny, rather than making it visibly queer. The club nights had been organised for the past three years in different mainstream clubs, with the help of sympathetic staff who were acquainted with members of the *tusovka*. However, unlike other events held at the same establishments, they were advertised by word of mouth only, and not promoted in the local media or through fliers and posters. On the night, the organisers stood at the entrance and monitored potential patrons: access was granted to known members of the *tusovka* but other patrons were admitted only on production of a membership card, or through personal introduction by a member of the *tusovka*. This caution was partly dictated by considerations about patrons' safety, since men in particular were concerned about being targeted by *gopniki*, as shown in Chapter 5. However, many women also pointed out that advertising the event more widely could attract the attention of the local media and the general public and turn the event into a 'freak show', disrupting the relaxed atmosphere of the club nights and possibly leading to unwanted disclosure. Valia, a retail manager in her early twenties and a very active member of the *tusovka*, explained that when the local press had tried to infiltrate the club night, most patrons had not enjoyed the prospect of being under the spotlight.

Some journalists showed up unexpectedly at the club, they tried to get in. We hold closed door events, they only admit people who have a membership card, and this sudden interest in us was unexpected. Everyone got a fright. No one wanted their sexuality to be known.

(Valia, Ul'ianovsk)

Thus, considerations about personal safety, comfort and anonymity were paramount in the strategies collectively used by the *tusovka* to carve out queer space.

Solidarity, resistance and the politics of in/visibility

While the *tusovka* inhabited and appropriated public and semi-public locations, this appropriation was not overt or explicit. Visibility was not considered desirable or empowering: on the contrary, a sense of comfort and safety could only be maintained by actively sheltering the *tusovka*'s habitual hangouts from the prying eyes of the wider community. The existence of queer space in the city was, to some extent, an open secret: some women pointed out that one of the cafes where the *tusovka* regularly met was known in the city to attract a queer clientele, or that many young people were aware of the existence of the *tusovka*, either because they were personally acquainted with some of its members or from hearsay. Nonetheless, strategies to carve out queer space in the city were premised on the need to remain unmarked, in order to deflect unwanted attention and avoid potentially uncomfortable or intimidating situations.

The most obvious disadvantage of the deliberate invisibility of queer space in Ul'ianovsk was that they were potentially very difficult to access for isolated individuals. The lack of an established gay scene and the limited availability of personal technology constrained opportunities to access queer space, and access relied more heavily on personal contacts and gatekeepers. Alisa, a university student in her early 20s, noted:

In Moscow they organize gatherings, festivals, concerts, they have cafes where you can meet people. Here even meeting someone is difficult, some people we met on the street, I mean, someone [*in the local tusovka*] approached them and asked them, are you *tema* or not? People still meet through newspapers, through personal ads, I mean, there are no places like in Kazan', Moscow, Piter [*Saint Petersburg*], there you have venues where *temnye* gather, and you can make acquaintances. Not everyone has the possibility to surf the net, even among our *tema* there are people who have no internet and no mobile phone, and how can they meet anyone?

(Alisa, Ul'ianovsk)

As Alisa pointed out, geographical location influenced women's opportunities to access both physical and virtual queer space. For example, internet use was much more widespread in Moscow than in Ul'ianovsk, and in the capital the internet played an important role in facilitating access to queer space by making available information about commercial and community events. Among Moscow respondents, online fora such as the one hosted by the popular website lesbiru.com were commonly used for dating and to make contact with other lesbians; online interaction was not limited to virtual space, and was often a way to access non-virtual lesbian/queer spaces and *tusovki* (Zelenina, 2006; Sarajeva, 2011). The growing role of cyberspace in breaking individual isolation and in brokering virtual LGBT communities has been noted both in western societies and in Russia (Munt et al., 2002; Kon, 1998; Zelenina, 2006). Nonetheless, at the time when the research was conducted, internet usage was very low in Russia, and was mostly concentrated in big cities such as Moscow, with better infrastructure and a more affluent population. By contrast, in Ul'ianovsk the internet played a very small role in facilitating access to the *tusovka*, and personal contacts and newspaper ads were much more crucial, as Sveta, a core member of the original *tusovka* and organiser of the first club nights, explained:

Well, they [*her queer friends and acquaintances*] appeared little by little, I can't say there was a particular pattern to find them. Somehow it all happened by itself. Some people knew each other, with other we just hang out in the same places, and that's how we met. We met through newspapers, through ads. In Ul'ianovsk there is a paper called *Iz ruk v ruki* [*a weekly paper of various classified ads*]. I befriended the girls I met through [*personal*] ads. Nothing much happened with them, but we became friends, hang out.

Sveta and Alisa highlight not only the limited opportunities available in Ul'ianovsk to make inroads into queer space, but also the importance of collective agency and group solidarity in breaking individuals' isolation. Originating in a rather narrow circle of friends, the *tusovka* made a very conscious effort to expand the original network and reach out to isolated individuals. The very organisation of the monthly gay and lesbian party was part of a conscious effort to broaden the local queer network beyond its original core, as Viktoriia, a university student in her early 20s who was in charge of organising the club nights at the time of fieldwork, explained:

I just remember one of our first club nights, it was simply a masterpiece, because before us no one did anything of this kind, and suddenly everyone gathered, got together, and everyone relaxed; because there's no one [*else*], and you don't need to play any role, many people hide it [*their sexual orientation*], but here you didn't need to hide anything. And it was so comfortable, I don't know, it was a good atmosphere, and there was an emotional and energetic upsurge, there was such a union.

(Viktoriia, Ul'ianovsk)

For many patrons, attending the club nights had been a liberating experience: they represented a rare opportunity to meet other non-heterosexuals, while also providing recognition and validation of their sexuality, a recognition that may not be available or sought in other environments. In this respect, the *tusovka's* everyday practices resonated with familiar notions of identity politics: they were grounded in affinity and solidarity, and allowed the collective articulation of shared experiences and identities. Motivations and meanings ascribed to participation in the *tusovka's* activity differed among its members, and some of them clearly saw the *tusovka* chiefly as an 'interest club', or as an opportunity to socialise and meet potential sexual partners. However, the most active members of the *tusovka* also saw it as a form of mobilisation around a common identity, and clearly considered the organisation of the club nights as an attempt to unite in order to change the status quo.

Claiming certain public and semi-public locations as queer can be seen as conscious resistance to pressures to conform to heteronorm, which ranged from being publicly humiliated for looking 'odd' or 'queer' to being pressurised to get married and start a 'normal' family. Queer space was perceived as empowering as it allowed members of the *tusovka* to freely explore and express their sexuality. At the same time, the collective creation of queer space subtly challenged the heterosexualised landscape: as Viktoriia jokingly remarked, in its early days the *tusovka* originally met 'under Lenin's nose', as she put it, or in the central Lenin Square, dominated by a bronze statue of Lenin. In this joke, Lenin symbolises the repressive and homophobic Soviet sexual morals.

Unlike the sexual identity politics embodied in Pride parades, the *tusovka's* practices are not premised on the notion of coming out as an empowering act, or based on the strategic occupation of public space through the visible display of stigmatised sexual identities. On the contrary, the *tusovka's* occupation of public space was based on the understanding of invisibility as enabling: carving out queer space in the city landscape involved discreetly and unobtrusively inhabiting certain public locations, while at the same time actively sheltering this space from public view. The *tusovka's* practices not only constructed public space as queer, but actively preserved the boundaries between queer and non-queer space, although these remained porous and precarious.

Indeed, as Rushbrook (2002, p. 203) remarks, 'the term *gay space* or *queer space* implies coherence and homogeneity which do not exist': queer space can also be appropriated or given different meanings by heterosexuals, in the same way that putatively heteronormative space can be inhabited by queers (Skeggs, 1999, 2001; Casey, 2004).

At first glance, the idea of invisibility as resistance may seem counterintuitive, since the choice to remain invisible may collude with, rather than challenge, the marginalisation of non-heteronormative sexualities, and leave the heterosexual majority unmoved or unaware. However, as pointed out in the previous chapters, invisibility (rather than visibility) was perceived as enabling and as subversive, since by sheltering the *tusovka* from societal scrutiny it allowed the emergence of forms of solidarity among marginalised queers, and their collective appropriation of urban space. Accommodation and resistance to heteronorm are here intertwined in complex ways: while the *tusovka*'s collective performance on the 'frontstage' may indicate acquiescence to heteronorm, on the 'backstage' the very same performance may be perceived as defiant and empowering (Goffman, 1959/1990a). Indeed, if the power of heteronorm is understood in a Foucauldian sense as pervasive and multifocal, it is not only oppressive but also productive (Ortner, 1995). In Foucault's words, 'where there is power there is resistance, and yet, or rather consequently, this resistance is never in a position of exteriority in relation to power' (Foucault, 1978/1998, p. 95). Moreover, the boundaries between visibility and invisibility, and between heterosexualised and queer space, are porous and fluid, and this allows the *tusovka*'s appropriation of public space to subtly challenge the status quo. Consider, for example, this episode of verbal confrontation related by Zulia, a lawyer in her mid-20s who, earlier in the interview, observed that her extremely feminine looks sheltered her from prying eyes, as she was assumed to be heterosexual:

> Well, it happened, that we were sitting somewhere with our group of friends, strictly *temnye* girls only, and it happened, that some bloke said, look at those lesbians sitting there [*lesbiianki sidiat*]. I had a verbal skirmish with those blokes, because we were passing by and they said, 'oh, the lesbians have come', I turned around and I told them what I thought of them.
> *What did you say?*
> I can't remember what I said, it was very emotional and those poor lads could not talk back. I also howled like a cat. There were shocked by the fact that I approached them and sorted them out.
> (Zulia, Ul'ianovsk)

On the one hand, the public street is learned and perceived as a hetero-sexual space, where 'other' sexualities stand out as being out of place and unsightly; for this reason, it can be intimidating, as it harbours risks of violence (physical and verbal) and exposure. On the other hand, it turns into a familiar and relatively comfortable space when used as a meeting point and hangout by the local *tusovka*. Numbers guarantee a certain safety, and the very presence of a queer *tusovka* in public space challenges the heterosexualised landscape. However, in this instance, the challenge is also verbal, defying heterosexism and claiming a legitimate presence in public space.

Conclusions

This chapter engages with, and contributes to critical debates on the construction and meaning of queer space by exploring how city space is appropriated as queer in two Russian cities. By focusing on Ul'ianovsk, a postsocialist provincial city with no scene space, the chapter inter-rogated unspoken absences in existing literature on queer space. The latter focuses predominantly on visible and territorialised forms of queer space, with the consequence of overexposing some sexual subjects, typically based in (western) metropolitan areas, while making those located in more peripheral regions even more invisible. This narrow focus, however, betrays ethnocentric assumptions about the emancipatory potential of 'outness' and about what counts as effective sexual politics, while overlooking forms of resistance to heteronormativity which are not overt or explicitly political.

The chapter has adopted a holistic definition of queer space, which is able to account for transient and precarious appropriations of urban space as queer. This approach is useful in avoiding rigid polarisations between metropolitan queer space, usually equated with territorialised hubs of queer consumer culture, and provincial queer space, assumed to be lacking or non-existent. By comparing Moscow and Ul'ianovsk, the article has highlighted striking similarities between queer space in the two cities, particularly with regards to similar patterns of socialising in the Moscow *Pushka* and the Ul'ianovsk queer *tusovka*. Similar practices were also deployed to produce urban space as queer/lesbian, such as listening to 'lesbian' rock.

The comparison between Ul'ianovsk and Moscow throws into relief important differences between the experiences of metropolitan and provincial queers, particularly in terms of ease of access to queer space, perceptions of safety and comfort, and degree of scrutiny from the wider community. In Ul'ianovsk greater concern about intimidation and violence (particularly at the hands of *gopniki*), and awareness of intense scrutiny meant that members of the *tusovka* were particularly careful to protect their privacy, which was not sheltered by the anonymity granted by living in a big city. The general unwillingness to be publicly open about one's sexuality was reflected in individual practices to negotiate city space, but also in the collective practices used to carve out queer space. Thus, the *tusovka*'s presence in public and semi-public places was not obvious to outsiders, and it was deliberately camouflaged for fear of exposure and repercussions. Carving out queer space in the city landscape involved striking a difficult balance between the protective shadow of invisibility and the desire to lay claims to public space.

The *tusovka*'s unwillingness to be visibly queer in public, however, should not be equated to a passive acquiescence to existing social norms. Equating reluctance to be 'out and proud' with the internalisation of homophobic social norms would mean denying the *tusovka* any forms of agency to defy such norms. Instead, this chapter has emphasised the importance of understanding the *tusovka*'s practices within the context in which they are produced, and has argued that, in the context of provincial Ul'ianovsk, invisibility is an expression of both accommodation and resistance to existing social norms. Resistance was expressed not through visibility, which is rarely considered empowering or desirable, but through collective action, which produced fluid boundaries between the *tusovka* and the outside world, and allowed the articulation of solidarity grounded in a shared sexuality within these boundaries. The boundaries between non-queer and queer space remained porous, and thus the very presence of the *tusovka* in public space challenged its heteronormative character, although this challenge was not overt.

7
Conclusions: From Russian to (Post)Socialist Sexualities

In this final chapter, I summarise the key empirical and conceptual contributions of this research monograph, while also engaging with current debates in queer and sexuality studies about theoretical ethnocentrism, the value of situated knowledge and queer geotemporalities. These debates have been particularly prominent in work on non-western sexualities and 'global queering', and reflect pressing conceptual, epistemological and methodological issues that are widely struggled with. A key strand of these debates has focused on critical approaches to regions, understood both as subnational and supranational territorial units (Binnie, 2013). For example, work on South Asian sexualities has pointed out that essentialism, the reproduction of western-centric, hegemonic queer temporalities, and the perpetuation of symbolic violence against the non-western 'Other' are potential pitfalls often found in regional approaches to territorially bounded areas (Johnson, Jackson and Herdt, 2000; Boelstorff, 2005; Wilson, 2006; Jackson, 2009a, 2009b). Nonetheless, a critical, post-Orientalist and transnational regionalism has also been invoked as a potentially productive counterweight to hegemonic western-centric theorising, and the widespread assumption that 'legible queer sexualities derive from US-inflicted Western modes of sexuality or from Western-based systems of modernity, such as capitalism' (Wilson, 2006).

I subscribe to the idea that a critical engagement with region and spatial scales can make an important contribution to provincialising 'western' and metropolitan sexualities within global queer studies. Through its focus on Russia, this monograph has hopefully offered new empirical and conceptual insights to global sexualities studies. However, the contribution regional approaches can make is not limited to the production of new 'case studies' and the exploration of underresearched empirical and conceptual worlds. Regional perspectives and comparisons can also offer new opportunities to theorise 'from the periphery', and to rethink epistemological and methodological issues involved in researching global and local sexualities. Beyond the usual summary of the monograph's key findings and arguments, I engage with the notion of postsocialism as an antiessentialist notion of region and as a critical standpoint, and attempt to imagine what a conceptual leap from Russian to (post)socialist sexualities might mean.

'Postsocialism' is not used here as a descriptive category to define a fixed, bounded region, but rather as a historically constructed geopolitical entity whose boundaries are constantly disputed and in flux. 'Postsocialist region' is here used to refer to the geographical area occupied by former socialist states and comprising the former Soviet Union, Central and Eastern Europe and the Balkans. The label '(post)socialist', however, can be and has been applied more broadly to countries such as China, Cuba or Mongolia, which adopted forms of state socialism not necessarily fashioned after the Soviet blueprint, and which, having moved to hybrid socio-economic systems, still retain elements of state socialism (Rofel, 1999). I refer to postsocialism as a critical standpoint emerging from empirical, micro-level and often ethnographic studies exploring how the deep socio-political and economic transformations which followed the demise of state socialism were experienced by ordinary citizens in former communist states (see e.g. Burawoy and Verdery, 1999; Hann, 2002; Kandiyoti, 2002; Hörschelmann and Stenning, 2008; Flynn et al., 2008; Silova, 2010). This body of work draws upon empirical fieldwork 'to show the fallacies of mainstream transitology, a perspective that continued to organize the world in flat Cold War binaries of capitalist West and communist East and to ignore specific relations of work, property, kinship, and other organizational forms' (Chari and Verdery, 2009, p. 9). Unlike mainstream 'transitology', critical postsocialism aimed to shed light on historical continuities and changes in former socialist countries, in terms of institutions, everyday practices and the meanings attached to deep socio-political transformations by the very people who have lived through them (Burawoy and Verdery, 1999; Hann, 2002; Hörschelmann and Stenning, 2008). 'Postsocialism' is thus an open-ended concept, and very much 'part of a larger group of "post" philosophies reflecting the uncertainties of our age' (Sakwa, 1999, p. 125). At the same time, postsocialism allows a productive engagement with different geographical scales, ranging from the body, the local, the regional/provincial, to the national, the regional/supranational and the global. Indeed, the concept of postsocialism as a productive lens to interpret deep socio-economic transformations in Eastern Europe and the former Soviet Union emerged very much from empirical studies privileging a 'local' perspective, qualitative methodologies and micro-level analysis (Burawoy and Verdery, 1999; Hörschelmann and Stenning, 2008). It is my contention that a more sustained engagement with postsocialism among scholars of Eastern European and Eurasian sexualities can make important contributions to critical, post-Orientalist global sexualities studies, which consciously aim to challenge ethnocentric perspectives and to avoid the reproduction of essentialist notions of 'modern' and 'pre-modern' sexualities which map on to 'the west' and 'the rest'.

Time: Generational sexualities and (post)socialist modernities

The monograph has situated non-heterosexual women's lived experiences, everyday practices and subjectivities within the specific socio-historical context of Soviet/post-Soviet Russia. The book engages with, and contributes to, literature on generational sexualities and queer geotemporalities, and attempts to bring together these two perspectives. The generational approach adopted here sheds light on the materialities of women's lived experiences under state socialism, and on how the momentous changes which led to and followed the demise of state socialism affected the lives of non-heterosexual women. The monograph has also shown how the social regulation of same-sex sexualities maps on to different Soviet/post-Soviet gender orders, linked by historical continuity but grounded in different models of socialist and capitalist/postsocialist modernity.

Narratives of Soviet Russia as a traditional, pre-modern, or even an 'anti-modern' society vis-à-vis the 'properly' modern capitalist west abound in area studies literature shaped by Cold War ideology and the bipolar world order. Both 'Sovietology' (the macro-level study of Soviet-type societies, often conducted from afar owing to restrictions to travel beyond the Iron Curtain) and 'transitology' (the study of the region's 'transition' to a capitalist political economy) tended to see socialism as a bankrupt totalitarian ideology hindering 'proper' modernisation, and socialist societies as ruled with an iron fist by the Party-state. Postsocialist perspectives pointed out that 'transitology' was underpinned by teleological, normative assumption about the desired outcomes of social change: privatisation, western-style market capitalism, liberal democracy and civil society (Hann, Humphrey and Verdery, 2002). Moreover, in its insistence on the need to break with the socialist past, the 'transition' narrative perpetuated the east/west dichotomy inherited from the Cold War, and tended to see the region's socialist heritage as a negative factor that hindered progress towards economic stability and political pluralism. Postsocialist perspectives offered an important corrective to transition narratives by privileging local, micro-level perspectives, and by being 'driven less by the overwhelming metanarratives of transition than the complex, diverse and everyday transformations of people's lives' (Stenning, 2005, p. 998). While the shared experience of state socialism was understood as a regional framework for comparison ('postsocialism'), socialism was explored not as a totalitarian ideology, but as 'real existing' state socialism, which could be analysed in terms of institutions, collective memories, everyday practices and lived experiences. Critical of both socialism and capitalism as modernising projects, postsocialist approaches problematised the universality of taken-for-granted theoretical concepts such as 'civil society' and 'democracy', and emphasised the importance of interpreting the present in terms of *both* change and continuity with the socialist past.

Debates on postsocialism inspired and informed this monograph, and are reflected in the generational approach adopted here to explore non-heterosexual women's lived experiences of state socialism, and the continuities between the experiences of women from different generations. The exploration of the socialist past throws into relief 'everyday' mechanisms of surveillance, stigmatisation and shaming of same-sex desire, and situates them within the distinctive gender order generated by the political economy of Soviet state socialism. The monograph teases out the complex interplay between structure and agency in women's lived experiences, rather than assuming Russian women to be the oppressed, powerless victims of the totalitarian Soviet state first and of homophobic institutions and attitudes after the demise of state socialism. Thus, I foregrounded women's agency in building intimate and family relationships and in negotiating their sexuality in everyday settings, and undertook a holistic exploration of women's lived experiences and the everyday practices through which they negotiate their sexuality, rather than focusing more narrowly on identity and subjectivities.

The monograph draws on, and contributes to, existing literature on Soviet same-sex sexualities, which has most often focused on state surveillance and control of 'deviant' sexuality through the 'expert gaze' of medicine and the law, while engaging more tangentially with the perspectives and lived experiences of Soviet queers. Empirical explorations of sexualities in socialist societies, including my own, raise new questions to be addressed in future research (Healey, 2001; Nedbálková, 2007, 2013; Liśkova, 2013). For example, how were institutions such as the *Komsomol* and the Comrades' Courts involved in the surveillance of sexual behaviour, and to what extent did they contribute to uphold officially sanctioned sexual morals? What kind of solidarities did informal queer *tusovki* produce in socialist cities? And finally, echoing Liśkova (2013, pp. 14–15), to what extent did 'disciplinary drives' shaped by the materialities of state socialism allow 'for agency, reflexivity and change' in socialist societies?

A generational approach is also useful in softening unhelpful polarisations between reified notions of 'modern' western sexualities and 'pre-modern' Russian ones. In some of the existing literature, Russian same-sex sexualities have been characterised as peculiarly fluid and 'queer' and pitted against binary understandings of sexuality and gender in the 'west' (Essig, 1999; Tuller, 1996; Baer, 2009). Chapter 3 has shown how women's 'identity careers' (Rosenfeld, 2002) map on to shifting discourses on sex and sexuality in late Soviet/post-Soviet Russia, and to Russia's two-tiered 'sexual revolutions' (Rotkirch, 2004), including new opportunities for representation, association and consumption which only became available from the late 1980s. I have also argued that the difference between 'Russian' and 'western' same-sex sexualities has often been overstated or unhelpfully portrayed in very stark terms, unwittingly reinforcing Orientalist representations of Russia as the 'west's uncivilised, underdeveloped and exotic 'Other'. This approach obscures real differences within Russia, for example, between queer lives in different (urban, rural, regional) locales and between differently gendered, classed and racialised queer bodies. Importantly, however, it also reifies a generic 'west', implicitly taken as a given and as a paradigm rather than as a socio-historical construct to be unpacked and critically examined (Bonnett, 2004). An unreflexive use of 'the west' as the taken-for-granted, normative paradigm of sameness and difference allows little scope to consider how states and regions are differently positioned within socio-historical constructions of the 'west', and how diverse sexual cultures and sexual citizenship landscapes emerged within them (Stychin, 2003). At the same time, in positing 'the west' as one, the diverse ontological and epistemological stances that inform dominant (and admittedly ethocentric) theorisations of sexuality are bracketed (Jackson and Scott, 2010b).

I argue that the elephant in the room in existing work on Russian and (post)socialist same-sex sexualities, and the key framework that needs to be unpacked and rethought, is the concept of *modernity*, which often underpins theories of 'transition' as well as discussions of queer geotemporalities in the postsocialist regions. As Baer (2002) perceptively notes, in much of the literature on Russian same-sex sexualities produced in the 1990s, differences between Russia and 'the west' are explained with reference to modernity or tradition.

When Russia was situated on the periphery of Western Europe, with its modern, egalitarian sexuality (the global gay), the Russian gay community would appear as either in transition or underdeveloped. But when Russia was situated in the East, where sexuality was imagined as premodern and had not yet been institutionalised into gay or straight, (homo)sexual desire there appeared to be radically different, polymorphous, a potential erotic alternative to the Western model of desire.

(Baer, 2002, p. 502)

Existing genealogies of the 'modern homosexual' (or the 'modern lesbian', for that matter) posit a strong link between 'western' capitalist modernity and the emergence of distinctive identities associated with same-sex sexual practices (Foucault, 1978/1998; D'Emilio, 1983; Vicinus, 1992; Weeks, 1996). Foucault famously argued that the very idea of sexuality as a discursive practice was the product of (capitalist) modernity, and emerged as a result of a broader process characterised by the demise of feudalism, the rise of the nation-state, secularisation, bureaucratisation and the rise of biopower in western Europe. Work on 'the modern homosexual' traces its origins to biopower and to eighteenth- and nineteenth-century western medical and legal discourses about sexual deviance (Greenberg and Bystryn, 1996; Weeks, 1996; Thornstad, 1995; Vicinus, 2004); it also suggests an intimate link between capitalism and the emergence of widely recognisable, distinctive gay and lesbian identities in the twentieth century (Hennessy, 2000; Chasin, 2000; D'Emilio, 1983), a phenomenon linked to urbanisation, bureaucratisation, individualism and the commercialisation of sex and sexual lifestyles. Foucault's genealogical approach has been productively applied to non-western contexts, including Russia (Engelstein, 1992; Healey, 2001); however, the unquestioned assumption of sexual modernity as uniquely 'western' have elevated the western 'modern homosexual' and its reincarnation as the 'global McGay' to a master narrative underpinned by linear notions of time and by normative assumptions about progress and development. Work on non-western sexualities and queer geotemporalities has problematised linear notions of time as deeply implicated with normative ideals of modernisation and development (Halberstam, 2005; Jackson, 2009a, 2009b; Mizielińska and Kulpa, 2011). In the postsocialist context, Mizielińska and Kulpa (2011, pp. 14–17) discuss the 'temporal disjunction' between 'western' and Eastern European activism, noting that the 'progression' between homophile, gay liberation and queer activism constructs the 'western present' as a future to be achieved in Central and Eastern Europe. Others have argued that the development of 'western-style' sexual identity politics and achievements in the field of sexual citizenship rights are often taken as a measure of a country's successful 'transition' and modernisation in postsocialist Eastern Europe (Stychin, 2003; Binnie, 2004; Binnie and Klesse, 2013). This implies that western-style gay liberation 'represents the high point of modernity' (Binnie, 2004, p. 85), a modernity postsocialist countries can only strive catch up with. After Ong (1999), Binnie (2004, p. 72) suggests that the notion of 'alternative modernities', rather than postcolonialism, may be a productive theoretical framework for debasing hegemonic, western-centric paradigm of development and progress in analysing global sexual politics. Yet an in-depth engagement with the notion of multiple modernities has thus far been absent in literature on Russian or Eastern European sexualities.

While the term 'modernity' is mostly associated with western capitalism and neoliberal globalisation, it is entirely possible and appropriate to talk about socialist (and perhaps postsocialist) modernities (in the plural). Indeed, the concept of multiple modernities, or varieties of modernity, has gained ground in current sociological debates. Against a tendency to equate a particular variant of (western, capitalist) modernity with modernity itself, and elevating it 'to the status of a world historical yardstick' (Wittrock, 2000, p. 52, quoted in Schmidt, 2006, pp. 77–78), proponents of multiple modernities have highlighted the diversity of paths to modernity, particularly outside the 'west' (Featherstone, Lash and Robertson, 1995; Ong, 1999; Rofel, 1999; Dingsdale, 2002), contrasting them to the prescriptive recipes for modernisation advanced in modernisation theory (Rostow, 1971). They have also noted the inadequacy of categories developed to make sense of modernity in the 'west' to fully account for non-western modernities. Indeed, modernity is not a condition and set of social transformations concerning 'the west' alone, nor is modernisation simply spreading from the 'west' to the 'rest', although 'western' ideologies and models of development may have been an influence or a reference point (Suny, 1999). Some area studies scholars have argued that the Soviet Union developed its own model of socialist modernity, whose key features were economic modernisation, collective ownership of the means of production, social interventionism and mass politics (Hoffmann, 2003; Suny, 1999; David-Fox, 2006). This paradigm was imposed as a blueprint on the 'Soviet bloc', and was highly influential as an 'alternative' model of modernity in vast parts of the non-western world. Both in the 'east' and in the 'west', state socialism is frequently conceptualised as an instance of 'failed' modernity and as the ideological antithesis of western modernity (Huntington, 1996; for a critique see Suny, 1999), particularly after the demise of state socialism. Beyond value judgements about socialist ideology and the ways in which it translated into various historical incarnations of real existing socialism, it is fair to say that state socialism was a quintessentially modernising project (Rofel, 1999; Dingsdale, 2002). The very legitimacy of state socialism rested on its promise of economic modernisation, secularism, mass politics and better living standards for the masses.

Echoing some of the arguments put forward by proponents of multiple modernities, postsocialist approaches, as described in the previous section, have also been critical of normative ideals of development embodied in the teleological concept of 'transition'. Theorisations of postsocialism have generally been more attuned to regional variation within the postsocialist region than 'transitology'; importantly, they have also emphasised the importance of interpreting the present and future of the region in terms of both change and continuity with a historically situated socialist past. Postsocialist perspectives show that the present needs to be brought into conversation with the socialist past in order to be understood in its own terms, and argue against measuring the present against the yardstick of a globalised 'western' modernity.

This last point is important because transformations in non-western sexual cultures have often been explained away simplistically as a result of western-driven cultural globalisation. Narratives of authenticity, tradition and modernity are also central to early theorisations of 'global queering', a term coined by Denis Altman (1996a, 1996b, 1997) to capture the proliferation of transnational same-sex and transgender identities and cultures. Altman's work was in many ways agenda-setting (Oswin, 2006), and it remains valuable as an early attempt to conceptualise a trend noted by many other sexualities scholars (Jackson, 2009a); however, it has rightly been critiqued for relying on a simplistic notion of queer globalisation as homogenisation resulting from the diffusion of the global 'McGay' (Boellstorff, 2005; see also Binnie, 2004). Altman presents global queering as a phenomenon spreading from the metropolitan west to the rest of the world, to the detriment of local (and supposedly more authentic) identities and cultures; this reinforces essentialist notions of 'the west' and 'the rest', while neglecting the importance of local agency in negotiating change and precluding the possibility that this encounter may engender hybridisation on both sides (Binnie, 2004; see also Oswin, 2006; Jackson, 2009a). Moreover, as the first part of this monograph has shown, shifting sexual subjectivities map on to endogenous socio-political and cultural change, and are not merely the result of cultural globalisation. In contemporary Russia, global queering can be detected in the appropriation of Anglo-American terms such as *buch* (butch), *fem*, and *daik* (dyke) (see also Zelenina, 2006); yet these terms have replaced, or are used in parallel with, the 'Soviet' terms *byk* (a 'masculine', sexually active lesbian) and *kovyrial'ka* (a 'feminine', sexually passive woman in a lesbian relationship). There is no direct equivalence between *buch* and *byk*, or *fem* and *kovyrial'ka*, as the Soviet terms originated in Soviet prison culture; however, the relatively new use of Anglicisms maps on to pre-existing notion of gendered same-sex subjectivities. This foregrounds hybridisation and appropriation, not merely homogenisation, as a result of western-centric processes of cultural globalisation. These observations echo similar points in empirically grounded work on South Asian sexualities, which has shown how Anglicisms are often appropriated with slightly different meanings to signify new local forms of sexual identity rather than being merely western 'imports' (Boellstorff, 2005), and that these new terms often appear to coexist in rather intricate patterns with other 'local' terms (Manalansan, 2002, 2003; Johnson, 1998; Jackson, 2009a). In foregrounding the global hegemony of western sexualities, theories of global queering often bracket local histories and downplay the agency of local actors as mediators of change.

This stance assumes that globalisation of sexual cultures fills a void, or completely replaces 'traditional' local understandings of sexuality and sexual subjectivities. New research agendas focused on the empirical exploration of sexualities under state socialism, and more explicitly engaging with theories of multiple/socialist modernities, can go a long way towards challenging ethnocentric assumptions which often inform theorisations of global queering, and indeed towards decentering queer globalisations (Oswin, 2006). In the existing literature, the experiences of queers under state socialism have often been portrayed in terms of lack (e.g. lack of opportunities for consumption and political association, lack of positive and well-defined narratives of sexual identity). This monograph is perhaps no exception: despite its effort to start from lived experiences of state socialism rather than from normative assumptions about what 'should' have been there, 'the west' resurfaces as an implicit term of comparison. Bracketing 'the west' as a normative paradigm will no doubt remain a challenge for future researchers; however, real advances can be made by starting from the realities and lived experiences of state socialism rather than from pre-existing notions of sexual communities, politics and identities modelled on the 'western' experience. New theoretical work grounded in empirical research can also go a long way towards debunking western-centric biases in existing theory.

Space: Critical regionalisms and the 'global closet'

The monograph has shown how the intersection of different geographical scales (the body, the 'lesbian/queer' *tusovka*, the urban provincial/regional, the metropolitan, the national, the postsocialist region) can simultaneously make the analysis of Russian sexualities more nuanced and less reifying, and contribute to provincialise western-centric perspectives within sexuality studies. Recent interventions within queer geographies have emphasised the potential of critical regionalism to 'unravel[s] and defuse[s] the power of the national and the global, by showing how narratives of the region "rub against" the triumphant teleologies of nation-making and globalisation in general, and the creation of sexual/gendered subjects in particular' (Manalansan et al., 2014, p. 3). In the previous section I have argued that empirical and theoretical work on post-Soviet and East European same-sex sexualities can provincialise western-centric theorisations by engaging more actively with conceptual frameworks such as multiple modernities and postsocialism, understood as a critical standpoint and critical regionality. Postsocialism refers to a supranational notion of region; however, critical regionality can be explored through different, subnational spatial scales (the urban, the rural, the metropolitan, the provincial/regional, the body), thereby fracturing the nation as a dominant scale and key unit of analysis. As stated in the introductory chapter, the research designs and methodologies underpinning the research presented here were specifically intended to problematise notions of 'Russian exceptionalism', and to fracture essentialising notions of Russia as the 'Other' of western sexual modernity. Indeed, chapters 4–6 have explored women's individual and collective negotiation of their sexuality through different geographical scales: specific settings (the home, the street, the workplace, the meeting places of 'lesbian/queer' *tusovki*) and multiple locations (metropolitan Moscow and provincial Ul'ianovsk). Multisited fieldwork was conducted in two very different urban locations: Moscow, a prosperous, post-industrial, global city hosting a relatively well-established gay scene and several grassroots and community organisations, and Ul'ianovsk, the administrative centre of the Ul'ianovsk province and a city with a sizeable population (650,000) which nonetheless lacked a gay scene. The comparison between queer life in Moscow and Ul'ianovsk problematises the hegemony of urban metropolitan perspectives within sexuality/queer studies, and queries the notion of 'metronormativity', or 'the conflation of "urban" and "visible" in many normalising narratives of gay/lesbian subjectivities' (Habelstram, 2005, p. 36). Indeed, Chapter 6 shows that visibility is not key to the construction of 'lesbian/queer' space, particularly in provincial Ul'ianovsk. In Ul'ianovsk, the collective appropriation of city centre space by the local *tusovka* was based on the premise that this appropriation should remain hidden to outsiders. Among members of the Ul'ianovsk *tusovka* visibility was deliberately avoided because it was not perceived as empowering. On the one hand, it was linked to increased vulnerability and the lingering danger of gay bashing and random violence at the hands of local gangs; on the other hand, in a relatively small city where rumours spread quickly, it was associated with fear of unwanted exposure to family members, workmates and acquaintances and its potential consequences. Although in Moscow queer space was relatively more visible and easy to locate, it was not territorially concentrated and conspicuous, and a degree of secrecy also characterised the ways in which queer space was carved out and inhabited in the capital. The Moscow case study therefore also problematises the taken-for-granted conflation of 'urban' and 'visible' inscribed in narratives of the queer cosmopolitan (Phillips, Watt and Shuttleton, 2000; Binnie, 2004; Habelstram, 2005).

To some extent the in/visibility of queer space in Russian cities reflects the broader national, post-Soviet context, where the LGBT community was never legitimised as a political subject, as the decriminalisation and demedicalisation of same-sex sexualities were premised on the notion that same-sex desire should only be expressed in the private sphere. The recent political backlash against the new visibility of same-sex sexualities culminated in a series of regional laws banning the 'propaganda of homosexuality' to minors, later extended to the whole of the Russian Federation in June 2013. This highlights the paradoxes of queer visibility in post-Soviet Russia. In a recent interview, Masha Gessen, a Russia-born journalist who grew up in the US and returned to Russia in the early 1990s, where she has lived and was actively involved in

LGBT activism for over 20 years, summed up the implications of the new homophobic policies and of the current socio-political climate for non-heterosexual Russians. In the late 1990s and early 2000s, 'people were living in what they thought was a normal country – not Western Europe, but not the Soviet Union, either'; however, as homophobic prejudice began to be explicitly endorsed in policy and legislation, those who had come out found themselves exposed and vulnerable. 'Their friends knew, their neighbours knew, their paediatrician knew. Now we have nowhere to go, not even the closet.' (Remnick, 2013). Evidence suggests that, despite criminalisation and medicalisation, the invisibility of same-sex desire translated into low awareness of same-sex relations during the Soviet period, and this sheltered individuals involved in same-sex practices from public scrutiny (Clark, 1997; Kon, 1998). Remaining invisible and unnamed had costs, as seen in Chapter 3; however, staying under the radar also provided a degree of freedom. By contrast, in recent years the backlash against the visibility of homosexuality, endorsed by the state, has gone hand in hand with a general crack-down on civil liberties and political pluralism, and the scapegoating of so-called 'sexual minorities' (among others) has been justified in the name of the protection of national values and the reproduction of a 'healthy' Russian nation (Stella, 2013b; Wilkinson, 2013; Kondakov, 2014). The context of the current moral panic, where the 'new' visibility of same-sex sexualities is problematised as 'non-traditional' and 'non-Russian', has incited ordinary Russian citizens, particularly self-appointed patriots, to out and publicly humiliate non-heterosexuals, or to report LGBT activists and their supporters to the relevant authorities as unfit parents, teachers or role-models for young people.[1] As Gessen notes, in the current climate queer visibility, and the ensuing recognis-ability of individuals as (potentially) queer, makes non-heterosexuals, their supporters, and anyone who could be mistaken as queer easier tar-gets of symbolic and physical violence, which has been documented not only in provincial areas, but also in metropolitan Moscow and Saint Petersburg (Human Rights Watch, 2014). This problematises any facile, linear narrative of progress, hailing the demise of state social-ism, decriminalisation and visibility as ways out of the Soviet closet, and as stepping stones towards 'western-style' liberation and recogni-tion. It also signals a more fundamental problems with the notion of visibility as empowering, and with the notion of the closet as a global form of oppression, which have been examined in some detail in previ-ous chapters, and which I explore here with specific reference to Brown's monograph *Closet Space: Geographies of Metaphor from the Body to the Globe*.

Brown's theorisation of the closet as a global form of oppression acknowledges to some extent the contradictory aspects of visibility highlighted by queer theory (Brown, 2000). However, its main limitation lies, in my view, in its reliance on ethnocentric, binary notions of private v. public, 'the west' v. 'the rest', and metropolitan v. peripheral. Brown largely draws on an analysis of gay travel writing by an American journalist in his attempt to 'globalise' the closet. However, in doing so, he seems to equate peripheral with closeted, and to understand 'peripheral' as rural, small-town America, but also as a range of 'global' locations (variously named as Japan, Buenos Aires, Thailand and Egypt) assumed to be peripheral to global centres of queer consumer culture. Brown's monograph offers valuable insights as a pioneering attempt to spatialise and materialise abstract notions of the closet. However, this attempt, which is by Brown's own admission tentative, ends up reinforcing already-known notions of the liberated, metropolitan 'west' v. the repressed and closeted peripheral 'rest', rather than opening up meaningful ways to explore how the closet works in 'peripheral', often underresearched locations. In her well-known *Epistemology of the Closet*, on which Brown draws, Sedgwick attempts to understand the closet as *epistemology* (i.e. the ways in which someone knows oneself, or is known by others, as gay, mediated by power/knowledge). Brown, more ambitiously, attempts to spatialise the closet not only as a metaphor but as 'a manifestation of heteronormative and homophobic power in time-space', and as a materiality which 'mediates a power-knowledge of oppression' (Brown, 2000, p. 3). In doing so, however, he falls into the trap of theoretical universalism described by Mohanty (1991) with reference to First World feminism and the plight of Third World women: he assumes the *sameness of the oppression*[2] borne by all queers, regardless of their geographic and socio-historical location, and of their differently classed, gendered and racialised subjectivities. In so doing, paraphrasing Mohanty (1991, pp. 56–57) 'the focus is not on uncovering the material and ideological specificities that constitute a particular group of women' (*read: a particular group of queers*) 'as "powerless" in a particular context'. It is, rather, on finding a variety of cases of '"powerless" groups of women' (*read: 'powerless' groups of queers*[3]) 'to prove the general point that women as a group are powerless'. Not only is this type of theory tautological (we set out to find what we already assume, that women/queers are powerless); it also assumes that some groups of women/queers in so-called 'developing' countries are *especially* powerless victims of patriarchy/homophobia vis-à-vis (relatively) liberated women/queers from the metropole.

This may seem like an unnecessarily harsh judgement on Brown's work. I don't mean to berate him or to belittle the significant contribution his work has made to queer geographies: in *Closet Space* (Brown, 2000), his exploration of the spatial and material dimension of the closet was indeed innovative and pioneering. Moreover, he reflects on and acknowledges the potential limitations of his approach, particularly the fact that exporting the concept of the closet itself 'may be a form of colonisation' (Brown, 2000, p. 137), and the fact that his conceptualisation of the closet relies on binary categories which may 'imply a static fixity' (*ibid.*, p. 146). Brown's work is used here as an example of a widespread reliance in much empirical and theoretical work within sexuality/queer studies on the binaries 'the closet' and 'coming out' as a shorthand for oppression and liberation. It is the latter I take issue with.

I have argued that, while the forced invisibility embodied in the metaphor of the closet is an important structural mechanism deployed to regulate and stigmatise non-normative sexuality, the concept of 'coming out of the closet' is unsuitable to account for women's agency in negotiating their sexuality. Since the expression 'coming out of the closet' was popularised by gay liberation, 'the closet' and 'coming out' are value-laden terms: the former is imagined as negative space of internalised homophobia, repression and concealment; the latter as an empowering and liberating act, bringing visibility and recognition. Yet binary constructs of 'in/out', 'private/public', 'repression/liberation' are unable to account for women's everyday negotiations of their sexuality (Fuss, 1991). Valentine's concept of 'time/space' strategies, and Goffman's presentation of the self (1990a) and stigma management (1990b) offer more useful theoretical insights to make sense of women's everyday negotiations. Goffman highlights how the presentation of the self is dependent on situated interaction, and indeed previous chapters have shown that context-specific notions of propriety and privacy play a significant role in women's negotiations of their sexuality in the context of the home, the workplace and the street. Moreover, disclosure is not always an individual 'speech act', as implied in the notion of 'coming out': it can be performed by others through discovery, exposure or recognition (Plummer, 1975). Indeed, spaces which allowed little privacy, such as the parental home, were considered particularly difficult to negotiate because women's sexuality could not be concealed or played down, and therefore could not be negotiated on women's own terms. On the other hand, the compartmentalisation between one's private and public life was assumed in many workplaces, and was accepted by many women as unproblematic, even as they were aware of sexual double standards. These were reflected in their experiences and expectations that the disclosure of same-sex desire would be seen as particularly inappropriate and may have unpleasant consequences. Previous chapters have shown that the strategies to negotiate 'closet space' were rooted in local materialities, as were the ways in which 'everyday' homophobia was expressed. Many women experienced homophobia as anchored in normative femininity and underpinned by motherhood as a fundamental rite of passage to adult womanhood, which can be traced back to the strong emphasis on motherhood as a duty to the state in the Soviet 'working mother' gender contract.

The key point made in the previous chapters is that disclosure was not necessarily perceived as empowering, and in some contexts it was deliberately avoided because of the possible risks and discomforts that may ensue. Indeed, women retained control over their everyday interactions by constantly drifting in and out of public visibility, and often emphasised their agency and personal responsibility in avoiding unpleasant situations. Remaining unmarked, playing down one's sexuality, or going along with interlocutors' expectations of heterosexuality, were some of the strategies women used to cope with stigma and to negotiate certain spaces. Without glamorising the closet, these strategies did not necessarily imply acquiescence, internalised homophobia or an unwillingness to challenge the status quo. Indeed, if power always generates the conditions of resistance to it, as Foucault has it, invisibility can be both a form of accommodation and resistance to the status quo (Foucault, 1978/1998, p. 95; Seidman et al., 1999). Remaining unmarked and unnamed may be a passive strategy; however, it also creates the conditions for the emergence of spaces and informal networks, such as the *tusovki*, where queer solidarities can be forged. Conversely, 'coming out' may more deliberately challenge heteronormativity; however, as Fuss (1991, p. 4) points out, the 'in/out' dichotomy is unhelpful, both because most queers are simultaneously in and out of the closet, and because 'coming out' paradoxically reconstructs the closet it purports to destroy: 'to be out is really to be in – inside the realm of the visible, the speakable, the culturally intelligible'.

Alternative epistemologies: Postsocialism and global sexualities

In the concluding remarks of this final chapter, I would like to return to a conceptual problem flagged up earlier in the book and widely struggled with, namely the pervasive 'east/west' dichotomy (or rather 'west/east', given that global geopolitics translate in the relative power of the 'west' over the 'east') within which virtually all discussions of Eastern European/postsocialist sexualities are framed. Orientalising discourses portraying Eastern Europe as the 'west's constitutive other can be traced back not only to the Cold War, but further back to the Enlightenment, when the region was symbolically located not in the 'civilised' western Europe, but somewhere in between 'the developmental scale that measured the distance between civilisation and barbarism' (Wolff, 1994, p. 13). Unpacking this Orientalist 'east/west' binary and thinking through epistemologies and methodologies that can productively contribute to undoing this dichotomy has been an important debate in critical area studies, which have often drawn on postcolonialism and/or postsocialism as potentially productive critical standpoints (Chari and Verdery, 2009; Owcarzak, 2009; Mizielińska and Kulpa, 2011). The dichotomy 'east' v. 'west' is pervasive in work on postsocialist sexualities produced both within the region and outside of it (typically in 'the west'), and it informs both spatial and theoretical imaginations. The uncritical use of the 'east/west' binary presupposes and perpetuates a geopolitical and socio-historical division between Eastern and Western Europe, while also raising questions about the deeply ethnocentric character of dominant, universalising theoretical perspectives within sexuality/queer studies, which are based on a hidden western-centric geography.

In earlier chapters I have taken issue with some work produced by western scholars in the 1990s which portrays Russian sexualities as exceptional and radically different form 'western' ones. I have argued that this work unhelpfully (and perhaps unwittingly) reifies both Russian and western sexualities by portraying Russia as the west's pre-modern or post-modern exotic 'Other'. These representations sometimes smack of Orientalism, a western-centric perspective where knowledge about the peripheral 'east' is mostly produced in the metropolitan centre situated in the west, and therefore reflects an ethnocentric perspective (Said, 1978). This knowledge, according to Said, is not generated from a careful consideration and interpretation of empirical realities, but largely produced 'at a distance' and based on pre-conceived notions and prejudices. Said argues that Orientalism's production of the 'east' as the west's 'Other' is not politically innocent, as Orientalising representations of 'the east' were also used as an instrument of colonial rule to subjugate the 'Other' through power/knowledge.

While Said mainly defines Orientalism as a case of western misrepresentation of the 'east', escaping the 'western gaze' (as a spatial and theoretical perspective) sometimes proves difficult for scholars from the Eastern European region too. Indeed, as Navickaite (2013) perceptively points out in her critical reading of Eastern European sexuality scholarship, some work produced by scholars from the region too relies of fixed notions of 'east' and 'west', and often falls into the Orientalist trap of taking the 'west' as a paradigm for sexual liberation and progress. For example, in the introduction to their edited volume on gender and sexuality on post-communist Eastern Europe, which includes a majority of contributions by scholars from the region, the co-editors Štulhofer (a Croatian scholar) and Sandfort (a Dutch scholar) ponder:

> In conclusion, it seems that in many respects postcommunist Europe is following the sexual trajectory of the West, probably with a delay of some two to three decades. Should we assume that in time sexual landscapes of the postcommunist East will become the mirror image of the West? If so, will it be the triumph of social and economic development, the outcome of the successful modernisation of the East?
>
> (Štulhofer and Sandfort, 2005, p. 16)

As Mohanty (1991) argues, the dominance of the 'western gaze' is not entirely reducible to issues of authenticity (being a native of the region/an outsider); the possibility to challenge and go beyond the 'western gaze' is bound up in more complex ways with positionality (which involves various degrees of insider/in-betweener/outsider positions) and related epistemological, methodological and ethical issues (how knowledge is produced and for whom).

Unlike Štulhofer and Sandfort, other interventions by scholars from the region have explicitly tried to problematise the notion of 'western' sexualities as the assumed paradigm and reference model for homegrown activism and academic research. The boldest of these not numerous interventions is the edited volume curated by Kulpa and Mizielińska (2011), which explicitly problematises the dichotomy 'the west' v. 'the rest'. They show how Central and Eastern Europe, a region ambiguously positioned between 'east' and 'west', problematises the notion of 'Europe-as-the-west', and invite a reconsideration of regionalism and ethnocentrism in sexuality studies. Constructed as Europe's unruly and backwards borderland since the Enlightenment, the region was reconceptualised as 'non-west' during the Cold War, when it was separated from western Europe by the Iron Curtain; the demise of state socialism was widely hailed in the region as a symbolic 'return to Europe', more so in Central and Eastern Europe than in most of the former Soviet Union (Wolff, 1994; Malia, 1999). Mizielińska and Kulpa's contribution productively draws on postcolonialism in its attempt to illuminate the relationship between Central and Eastern Europe and 'the west' proper:

> Is it possible to establish a relationship between 'West' and 'CEE' as between (respectively) 'metropolis/centre' and 'colony/periphery' (popular in post-colonial writings)? And considering that CEE is not (so far) a region of much interest to post-colonial theorists, what would be the implication of such a juxtaposition of geographical regions and academic theories?
>
> (Mizielińska and Kulpa, 2011, p. 12)

Mizielińska and Kulpa's borrowing of 'centre' and 'periphery' from postcolonial theory is a productive contribution to current debates, as it foregrounds unequal power relations which operate within the 'new Europe', a geopolitical space emerging from the demise state socialism, the breakup of the Soviet Union and of the Soviet bloc, and the incorporation of the region into broader global flows of capital and cultural exchange. Given postcolonialism's emphasis on epistemological issues, the centre/periphery metaphor also allows a critical engagement with theoretical constructions emanating from the (western) metropole. As Connell (2007, p. 46) writes, echoing critiques of postcolonial feminist theorists such as Mohanty (1991), social theory (and sociological theory in particular) has a hidden geography which goes unacknowledged under its pretence of universality.

> [S]ocial theory is built in a dialogue with empirical knowledge [. . .]. When that empirical knowledge derives wholly or mainly from the metropole, and where the theorist's concerns arise from the problems of metropolitan society, the effect is the erasure of the experience of the majority of human kind from the foundations of social thought.

Connell argues that, in order to be truly 'global', social theory needs to take seriously, and engage with, ideas, intellectual traditions, concepts and empirical knowledge coming from the postcolonial global South. A similar point can be made about the postsocialist region, which, while not fitting into the category of 'postcolonial', remains peripheral to the metropolitan 'west', and can produce empirical and theoretical work that is able to 'de-centre' western perspectives. In this respect, Mizielińska and Kulpa's claim that Central and Eastern Europe is a 'a contemporary periphery' is productive. It opens up new ways to think about how empirical work on the postsocialist region and theorisations emerging from it may contribute to 'provincialise' ethnocentric theory and to make room for the kind of situated, grounded theory advocated by Connell, a theorising that does not seek to produce abstractions transcending context.

> The goal of dirty theory is not to subsume, but to clarify; not to classify from outside, but to illuminate a situation in its concreteness. And for that purpose – to change the metaphor – all is grist to the mill. Our interest as researchers is to maximise the wealth of materials that are drawn into the analysis and explanation. It is also our interest to multiply, rather than slim down, the theoretical ideas that we have to work with. That includes multiplying the local sources of our thinking, as this book attempts to do.
>
> (Connell, 2007, p. 207)

However, there are, in my view, two main problems in Mizielińska and Kulpa's attempt to present 'Central and East European Perspectives' as a way to 'decentre' hegemonic, western-centric theorisations: their wholesale adoption of a postcolonial framework and their lack of sustained engagement with critical regionality through the prism of postsocialism. The descriptive 'Central and Eastern Europe', which is used throughout the book, refers to a fixed, bounded region, and is juxtaposed to 'the west', thus creating a rather rigid, potentially essentialising dichotomy. By contrast, the term 'postsocialist' clearly designates the region as a cultural and geopolitical construct. Mizielińska and Kulpa briefly dismiss the term 'postsocialist' as fixing the region in a perpetual 'transition' from the (communist, Second World) past to the (capitalist, 'European') present; however, in my view, 'postsocialist' encapsulates precisely the ambiguities of the geopolitical boundaries and of the contested histories that they describe (Central and Eastern Europe as geographically 'European' but temporally 'not quite European yet'; Europeanisation, global capitalism and 'global queering' as simultaneously embraced as a marker of progress and resisted as colonising, homogenising forces). As shown earlier, (post)socialism also grounds the region's present in its recent past, and shows how past and present coexist and shape everyday practices and aspirations about the future; it also allows an engagement with the notion of multiple, hybrid modernities, thus displacing the notion of 'linear time' and of 'the west' as the pinnacle of (sexual) modernity and as a normative model of 'development'.

Secondly, and more importantly, assimilating the postsocialist into the postcolonial is problematic: it risks eliding the shared history of state socialism and postsocialist transformations, while a wholesale adoption of postcolonialism potentially collapses different histories and geotemporalities. Importantly, the racial dimension of (post)colonial analysis may have limited purchase for the region (Owczarzak, 2009, p. 5). Postcolonial perspectives have clear analytical value in the exploration of the regional transformations which occurred after the demise of state socialism, when modes of 'transition' and 'modernisation' were largely dictated by 'global' or 'western' institutions such as the International Monetary Fund (IMF), the World Bank, the European Union and the Council of Europe. In this respect, postcolonialism and postsocialism converge in their critical reflections on the failures of modernisation projects (Chari and Verdery, 2009, p. 10, n. 1). However, when considering the socialist past, it is more difficult to coherently apply the label 'postcolonial' to the region. Whether the entire region was colonised by the Soviet Union after WWII, and whether Russia can be seen as the metropole of a Soviet overland empire is open to debate: the diverse history of state socialism in different countries should caution us against wide-sweeping generalisations (Owczarzak, 2009, p. 5). 'Postsocialism', a critical standpoint which explicitly builds on insights from postcolonial thinking, has the clear advantage of being more directly and clearly rooted in the region's shared past.[4]

Although the concept of postsocialism was originally articulated by (mostly) 'western' ethnographers working in the region, such as Burawoy and Verdery, I don't believe that postsocialism should be dismissed as yet another example of ethnocentric theorising. 'Postsocialism' has been enthusiastically taken up and developed by scholars from, and working in and on the postsocialist region precisely as a way to reclaim the value of micro-level, locally grounded perspectives on the deep transformations that accompanied the demise of state socialism, and of challenging prescriptive and teleological notions of transition and modernisation (Novikova and Kambourov, 2003; Svašek, 2005; Berdahl, 2010; Silova, 2010). While, unlike postcolonialism, postsocialism is yet to be mainstreamed in the internationally recognised canon of gender and queer/sexualities studies, it has been productively used in recent work on gender and sexuality in Eastern Europe (Novikova and Kambourov, 2003; Ghodsee, 2005; Berdahl, 2010). Indeed, it is in their shared critiques of ethnocentric modernisation and power/knowledge that postsocialist and postcolonial perspectives converge, as Chari and Verdery (2009, p. 11) perceptively note,

Over time, 'postsocialism' too came to signify a critical standpoint, in several senses: critical of the socialist past and of possible socialist futures; critical of the present as neoliberal verities about transition, markets, and democracy were being imposed upon former socialist spaces; and critical of the possibilities for knowledge shaped by Cold War institutions. Here, post-socialist studies began to converge somewhat with the agenda of postsolonial studies as Chari and Verdery (2009, p. 11) perceptively note, just as postcoloniality has become a critical perspective on the colonial present, postsocialism could become a similarly critical standpoint on the continuing social and spatial effects of Cold War power and knowledge (such as in the remaking of markets, property rights, democratic institutions, workplaces, consumption, families, gender/sexual relations, or communities).

Chari and Verdery (2009) invite us to 'think through the posts' by considering how postsocialist and postcolonial perspectives may be productively and creatively combined in order to imagine a different world. This could challenge the nesting Orientalism of Cold War-era 'Three Worlds' ideology which still informs how we look at the world today. For Chari and Verdery (2009, p. 12), 'thinking through the posts' means going beyond regional imaginaries which associate 'postcoloniality with a bounded space called the Third World and postsocialism with the Second World'. 'Thinking through the posts' also involves considering how postsocialism and postcolonialism can be applied to the study of 'western' societies. Indeed, in the 1990s, amidst narratives that proclaimed socialism a bankrupt ideology, and portrayed the demise of 'real existing' state socialism in Eastern Europe and the former Soviet Union as the 'end of history' and the triumph of neoliberal global capitalism (Fukuyama, 1992), it was argued that the 'postsocialist condition' concerned not only the 'east', but also the crisis of the Left in the capitalist 'west'. Amidst a widespread perception that Marxist-inspired alternatives had become discredited, the political Left veered towards an indistinct centre, and debates about social justice became stilted and ruled out radical alternatives (Fraser, 1997). This, to my mind, is yet another reason why postsocialism is a potentially productive framework to explore sexualities and gender, both within the so-called postsocialist region and beyond. A lack of engagement with the materialities of sex is widely recognised as a limit of queer perspectives, which (like postcolonial theory) have their roots in literary theory and text-based research (Browne and Nash, 2011b). By contrast, as a critical standpoint emerging from micro-level ethnographic explorations on everyday practices and lived experiences, postsocialism allows a greater engagement with the materiality of everyday life. This is important, because, as Buchowski (2006) has eloquently argued, in postsocialist Eastern Europe orientalist thinking is often applied to domestic 'Others', typically the 'losers' of capitalist transition, portrayed as unable and unwilling to adapt to the new conditions and therefore in need of being re-educated. This results in a societal 'orientalisation' prompted by the logic of neoliberal capitalism, which (re)produces class distinctions between elites and a post-industrial 'lumpenproletariat' unable to cope with the new world. Against discourses which position the 'global gay' as the ultimate neoliberal subject, rescued from its abjection by its ability to consume, and 'global queering' as the end-point of queer history, using postsocialism as a tool to imagine ways to integrate the politics of recognition and the politics of redistribution can hopefully point to routes out of neoliberal queer dystopias. This involves, of necessity, thinking of postsocialism not as an end-point but as an alternative which 'incorporates, rather than repudiates, the best of socialism' (Fraser, 1997, p. 5).

Appendix 1: Interviewees' demographic and socio-economic profiles

Projects:

LIS: Lesbian Identities and Spaces in Contemporary Urban Russia

OH: Female homosexuality and actually existing socialism: an oral history project of lesbian relations in Soviet Russia

Name	Project	Place of residence	Education	Occupation	Official marital status	Cohabiting female partner	Date of birth
Lara	Pilot, LIS (2004)	Moscow	Higher	Lawyer	Divorced	No	1981
Nadia	Pilot, LIS (2004)	Greater Moscow	Higher	Psychologist	Not married	Yes	1972
Galia	Pilot, LIS (2004) OH (2010)	Greater Moscow	Higher	Graphic designer	Not married	Yes	1959
Zhanna	Pilot, LIS (2004) OH (2010)	Greater Moscow	Higher	Photographer	Divorced, 1 child	No	1961
Ul'iana	Pilot, LIS (2004)	Greater Moscow	Higher	Lawyer	Not married	No	1978
Aglaia	Pilot, LIS (2004)	Moscow	Higher	Student	Not married	No	1980
Alia	LIS main fieldwork (2005)	Greater Moscow	Higher	Employee in a publishing house	Not married	No	1972
Natasha	LIS main fieldwork (2005)	Moscow	Higher	Graphic designer	Not married	No	1978
Dasha	LIS main fieldwork (2005)	Greater Moscow	Higher	Bookkeeper	Not married	No	1973

Name	Source	Location	Education	Occupation	Marital status		Year
Aleksandra	LIS main fieldwork (2005)	Moscow	Higher	Teacher and translator	Divorced	No	1946
Lena	LIS main fieldwork (2005)	Moscow	Incomplete higher	Programmist	Married	No	1978
Iana	LIS main fieldwork (2005)	Moscow	Higher	Physiotherapist	Not married	Yes	1966
Oksana	LIS main fieldwork (2005)	Moscow	Secondary	Employee in an online shop	Not married	Yes	1969
Kseniia	LIS main fieldwork (2005)	Moscow	Higher	Manager in a commercial business	Not married	Yes	1978
Liuba	LIS main fieldwork (2005)	Greater Moscow	Higher	Engineer	Not married	No	1962
Veronika	LIS main fieldwork (2005)	Moscow	Higher	Manager in a commercial business	Widowed	Yes	1963
Valentina	LIS main fieldwork (2005)	Moscow	Higher	Real estate agent	Divorced	Yes	1969
Varvara	LIS main fieldwork (2005)	Moscow	Incomplete higher	Bookkeeper	Not married	No	1978
Masha	LIS main fieldwork (2005)	Moscow	Higher	System analyst	Not married	No	1982
Vera	LIS main fieldwork (2005)	Moscow	Incomplete higher	Employee in an advertisement firm	Not married	No	1980
Nastia	LIS main fieldwork (2005)	Moscow	Incomplete higher	Unemployed	Not married	No	1981
Ira	LIS main fieldwork (2005)	Moscow	Secondary specialised	Theatre worker	Not married	Yes	1979

(Continued)

Name	Project	Place of residence	Education	Occupation	Official marital status	Cohabiting female partner	Date of birth
Tania	LIS main fieldwork (2005)	Moscow	Higher	Language teacher	Divorced	Yes	1969
Sasha	LIS main fieldwork (2005)	Greater Moscow	Higher	Assistant in an architect firm	Not married	No	1982
Zinaida	LIS main fieldwork (2005)	Greater Moscow	Higher	Secretary	Not married	No	1979
Raissa	LIS main fieldwork (2005) OH (2010) Withdrawn	Moscow	Higher	Employee in a publishing house	Divorced, 1 child	No	1963
Liudmila	LIS main fieldwork (2005)	Moscow	Higher	Real estate agent	Not married	Yes	1967
Aniuta	LIS main fieldwork (2005)	Moscow	Higher	Museum worker	Engaged to be married	No	1978
Katia	LIS main fieldwork (2005)	Moscow	Higher	Translator	Married, 1 child	No	1956
Marina	LIS main fieldwork (2005)	Moscow	Higher	Employee in a publishing house	Divorced	No	1956
Ol'ga	LIS main fieldwork (2005)	Moscow	Incomplete higher	Employee in a publishing house	Not married	No	1975
Sveta	LIS main fieldwork (2005)	Ul'ianovsk	Higher	Doctor	Not married	Yes	1978

Name	Project	Place	Education	Occupation	Marital status		Year
Kristina	LIS main fieldwork (2005)	Ul'ianovsk	Incomplete higher	Call centre worker	Not married	Yes	1982
Renata	LIS main fieldwork (2005)	Ul'ianovsk	Incomplete higher	Lawyer apprentice	Not married	No	1984
Viktoriia	LIS main fieldwork (2005)	Ul'ianovsk	Incomplete higher	University student	Divorced	No	1983
Marusia	LIS main fieldwork (2005)	Ul'ianovsk	Higher	Lecturer	Not married	No	1964
Zulia	LIS main fieldwork (2005)	Ul'ianovsk	Higher	Lawyer	Not married	No	1980
Sonia	LIS main fieldwork (2005)	Ul'ianovsk	Secondary specialised	Manager in a commercial business	Not married	No	1973
Zheniia	LIS main fieldwork (2005)	Ul'ianovsk	Secondary specialised	Nurse	Not married	No	1977
Mania	LIS main fieldwork (2005)	Ul'ianovsk	Incomplete higher	Unemployed	Not married	No	1983
Asia	LIS main fieldwork (2005)	Ul'ianovsk	Incomplete higher	Student	Not married	No	1988
Zoia	LIS main fieldwork (2005)	Ul'ianovsk	Higher	Teacher	Engaged to be married	No	1978
Elizaveta	LIS main fieldwork (2005)	Ul'ianovsk	Secondary	Tram driver	Married	No	1978
Valia	LIS main fieldwork (2005)	Ul'ianovsk	Higher	Manager in a commercial business	Not married	No	1982

(Continued)

Name	Project	Place of residence	Education	Occupation	Official marital status	Cohabiting female partner	Date of birth
Maia	LIS main fieldwork (2005)	Ul'ianovsk	Secondary specialised	Factory worker	Not married	No	1984
Liza	LIS main fieldwork (2005)	Ul'ianovsk	Incomplete higher	Janitor	Divorced	No	Not recorded (1960s)
Alisa	LIS main fieldwork (2005)	Ul'ianovsk	Incomplete higher	Student	Not married	No	1984
Alina	LIS main fieldwork (2005)	Ul'ianovsk	Incomplete higher	Student	Not married	No	1984
Al'bina	LIS main fieldwork (2005)	Ul'ianovsk	Incomplete secondary	Lap dancer	Not married	No	1984
Klavdiia	LIS main fieldwork (2005)	Ul'ianovsk	Secondary specialised	Unemployed, in receipt of disability benefits	Widowed	No	1971
Lada	LIS main fieldwork (2005)	Ul'ianovsk	Secondary	Shop assistant	Not married	Yes	1978
Tamara	LIS main fieldwork (2005)	Ul'ianovsk	Secondary	Bar worker	Not married	Yes	1980
Avdotiia	LIS main fieldwork (2005)	Ul'ianovsk	Incomplete secondary	Builder	Not married	Yes	1972
Eva	LIS main fieldwork (2005)	Ul'ianovsk	Higher	University administrator	Not married	No	1965

Ania	LIS main fieldwork (2005)	Ul'ianovsk	Secondary specialised	Security guard	Not married	Yes	1978
Bella	LIS main fieldwork (2005)	Ul'ianovsk	Secondary	Security guard	Not married	Yes	1982
Lidiia	LIS main fieldwork (2005)	Ul'ianovsk	Higher	Teacher	Not married	No	1973
Margarita	LIS main fieldwork (2005)	Ul'ianovsk	Higher	Teacher	Widowed	No	1962
Olesia	LIS main fieldwork (2005)	Moscow	Incomplete higher	Student	Not married	No	1988
Roza	LIS main fieldwork (2005)	Moscow	Incomplete higher	Student	Not married	No	1984
Evdokiia	LIS main fieldwork (2005)	Moscow	Incomplete higher	Student	Not married	No	1983
Tamara	OH (2010)	Moscow	Higher	Language teacher	Not married, 4 children	No	1952
Anna	OH (2010)	Moscow region	Higher	Entrepreneur	Married, 1 child	No	1963
Alena	OH (2010)	Moscow region	Higher	Manager	Divorced	Yes	1963
Grusha	OH (2010)	Moscow	Higher	Manager	*Not recorded*	Yes	1964
Kira	OH (2010)	Saint Petersburg	Higher	*Current not recorded*	Widowed, 2 children	Yes	1955

(Continued)

Name	Project	Place of residence	Education	Occupation	Official marital status	Cohabiting female partner	Date of birth
Iulia	OH (2010)	Saint Petersburg	Secondary	Construction worker	Not married, 1 child	Yes	1966
Sofiia	OH (2010)	Saint Petersburg	Higher	Social worker	Not married	Yes	1953
Aglaia	OH (2010)	Saint Petersburg	Secondary	*Current not recorded*	Not married	No	1957
Larisa	(OH (2010)	Saint Petersburg	Secondary	Arts practitioner	Divorced, 2 children	No	1951
Tasha	OH (2010)	Saint Petersburg	Secondary	*Current not recorded*	Divorced	No	1968

Notes

1 Introduction: Locating Russian Sexualities

1. Lesbian, Gay, Bisexual, Transgender, Intersex, Questioning and Asexual.
2. Essig substantiates her argument by referring to the high incidence of bisexual and transgender practices in the community she studied, and to the use of colloquial terms , such as *goluboi*, *rozovaia* and *tema*, rather than clearcut terms of identification such as 'gay' and 'lesbian'. She refers to her Russian informants as 'queer' to mark their difference from western binary constructs of sexual identities, although the term queer was not used among her informants.
3. All Russian terms have been transliterated from the Cyrillic into the Latin alphabet using the ALA-LC Romanisation system (American Library Association and Library of Congress). The system is widely used in North America and Britain; diacritics and two-letter tie characters have been omitted. For more information see http://www.loc.gov/catdir/cpso/roman.html.
4. The research projects the monograph draws on were explicitly presented to potential participants as being about sexuality, rather than gender identity. Trans women were present in the 'lesbian' social networks explored in Moscow and Ul'ianovsk, and were encouraged to take part in the study; two interviewees openly talked about the discrepancy they felt about their bodies and their gender identity. Nonetheless, an element of self-selection operated: two male-identified women declined the invitation to take part in the study, as they felt that their experiences would not be captured by the notion of 'lesbian' or same-sex desire.
5. During the first period of fieldwork conducted in Russia (2004–2005) the term *kvir* was beginning to appear in commercial contexts (e.g. as the title of the eponymous glossy gay magazine first published in 2004), and in academic parlance (Sozaev, 2010), but it was not used as a term of self-identification. Most recently, a member of feminist punk rock band Pussy Riot came out as *kvir* (Stroganova, 2012); this may indicate that the term is becoming more widely used and politicised, although its use seems to be so far restricted to educated and self-consciously counter-cultural urban circles.
6. During fieldwork, I have strived to avoid pre-conceived sexual categories and sought to empirically ground my analysis by taking detailed notes of women's language usage. Moreover, women were explicitly asked about their preferred terms of self-identification during interviews, and invited to articulate the meanings they attached to specific labels.
7. Pilot study: Moscow, May-July 2004; main fieldwork: Moscow and Ul'ianovsk, April–October 2005.
8. One woman who took part in both the original ethnography and the follow-up project withdrew from both studies in 2010, when some material from the ethnographic study had already been published. For consistency, she is

included in the list of participants (Appendix 1), although the interviews have since been deleted and have not been used in the book.

9. Fieldwork May 2010.

10. Three of these were repeat interviews with women who had participated in the previous ethnographic study. One woman later withdrew from the study (the same referred to in note 7).

11. McCall (2005) distinguishes between two contiguous, but different approaches to the complexity of lived experience: anticategorical approaches, associated with poststructuralism and postmodernism (including queer theory), and chiefly concerned with deconstructing and making suspect identity categories as they are founded in language and discourse rather than in social reality; and intercategorical approaches, which, while wary of the homogenising potential of analytical categories, do not 'deny the importance – both material and discursive – of categories', but rather 'focus on the process by which they are produced, experienced, reproduced, and resisted in everyday life' (*ibid.*, p. 1783). The third approach identified by McCall (intracategorical) is less immediately relevant to the above discussion.

2 Same-Sex Sexualities and the Soviet/Post-Soviet Gender Orders

1. The term 'Party-state' refers to the fact that, in the Soviet Union and in many communist countries, the Communist party was the only legal party, and was constitutionally recognised as the leading and guiding force of society.

2. Citizenship is here defined as 'both a set of practices (cultural, symbolic and economic) and a bundle of rights and duties (civil, political and social) that define an individual's member in a polity' (Isin and Wood, 1999, p. 4).

3. In this respect, the Soviet Union pioneered rights to welfare which were not at the time universally recognised in capitalist societies. The 1936 Soviet constitution guaranteed 'the right to work, the right to vacation time, the right to material support in old age and following illness or disability, and the right to a free education' (Alexopoulos, 2006, p. 516).

4. For example, officially sanctioned women's organisations, such as the *zhensovety* (women's councils), which were instituted in the 1960s to allow the articulation of women's collective interests and concerns, were only formally independent, but in reality were strongly embedded into the state apparatus. Their activities were not based on women's initiatives but on agendas set from on high (Racioppi and O'Sullivan, 1997), preventing the articulation of any meaningful sexual politics or the emergence of second wave feminism as a broad-based social movement in Soviet Russia.

5. The first grassroots group to articulate political demands on behalf of 'gays and lesbians' and mobilise for the repeal of antisodomy legislation was *Gai Laboratoriia* (Gay Laboratory), a Leningrad-based group created in 1984. The group disbanded in 1986, after sustained surveillance and harassment by the KGB, which was concerned about the formation of a gay and lesbian group and its contact with a foreign LGBT group (Essig, 1999, pp. 58–59). Other mixed (male and female) grassroots groups, however, formed in the following

years, such as the Moscow Association for Sexual Minorities (1989) and the Tchaikovskii Fund (1989). These were not only tolerated by law enforcement agencies in spite of the continued criminalisation and pathologisation of homosexuality, but also managed to achieve a degree of media visibility (Essig, 1999, pp. 62–64).

6. These include gay.ru, which originally went online in 1997, and its twin site lesbi.ru; they are among the most established and long-running Russian internet resources. Another extremely popular lesbian website is lesbiru.com, created in 2002.

7. In 2004–2005, glossy magazines included the Saint Petersburg based *BF* (http://www.bfmg.ru/) and the Moscow-produced Kvir (first issued in 2004), which in a 2006 survey of commercial sales was rated the second most popular lad glossy magazine in Russia after *Playboy* Available at: http://www.gay.ru/news/rainbow/2006/10/17-8522.htm; lesbian magazines included *VolgaVolga* (first issued in 2004, but discontinued after only three issues) and *Pinx* (2006, Available at: http://lesbi.ru/talk/lgbt/pinx/. Both Pinx and Kvir are part of a broader gay-owned commercial enterprise, which also produces the websites http://www.gay.ru and lesbi.ru.

8. The differentiation between the 'last Soviet generation' and the 'generation of transition' is common in work on post-Soviet Russia based on oral history and biographical methods (Yurchak, 2006; Byford, 2009; Rotkirch, 2004). My use of 'last Soviet generation' and 'generation of transition' roughly corresponds to Rotkirch's 'generation of learned ignorance' and 'generation of articulation', respectively. Rotkirch devised this periodisation in her work on the sexual experiences and sources of sexual knowledge of three generations of Soviet citizens. Rotkirch shows how the ways in which people acquired sexual knowledge reflected changing state-driven policies and legislation on sexual and reproductive rights, and related shifting discourses on sex and sexuality in Soviet society. According to Rotkirch, a two-phased 'sexual revolution' took place in Russia: whilst sexual behaviour among Soviet citizens started to change after WWII along patters similar to those of other industrialised countries, the public articulation of these changes did not occur until the mid-1980s, with the emergence of new discourses linking sex not only to reproduction but also to pleasure and self-expression. Rotkirch calls the cohort born between the early 1950s and 1972, who came of age during the late Soviet period, the 'generation of learned ignorance', and names the successive cohort (born after 1972, and whose formative years coincide with the onset of Russia's second 'sexual revolution' in the late 1980s and the demise of state socialism) the 'generation of articulation'.

3 Lesbian Relationships in Late Soviet Russia

1. For an exception see Rotkirch, 2002.
2. According to Essig and other sources, 'masculine' women, who performed the 'active' role in sexual relations with other women, were often diagnosed as transgender by Soviet psychiatrists (Essig, 1999; Riordan, 1996; Zhuk, 1998): These women were allowed to change their gender identity on official documents (*ibid.*) and, from the 1960s onwards, gender reassignment surgery

was available to those 'properly' diagnosed and willing to undergo the operation (Riordan, 1996, p. 164; Essig, 1999; see also Franeta, 2004). Transgender and transsexual practices are not explored in this monograph, since none of the older women who took part in the study was formally diagnosed or underwent surgery, and only one interviewee identified as transgender. Nonetheless, this is an important topic that deserves to be further explored in future research, not least because in extant literature the availability of gender reassignment during the Soviet period is often interpreted as a repressive mechanism aimed at normalising the sexual practices and subjectivities of individuals whose practices do not conform with their 'natural' birth gender (Essig, 1999). The perspective of individuals who underwent gender reassignment surgery, or expressed a desire to do so, is not explored in the literature.

3. Emphasis in the original.
4. The *Komsomol* (Kommunisticheskii Soiuz Molodezhi), or Communist Youth League, was a state-sponsored youth organisation whose membership numbered tens of millions.
5. A residence permit was required in order to settle in the major Soviet cities (Stephenson, 2006).
6. A pragmatic, utilitarian approach towards marriage among Soviet citizens is also documented in other literature on Soviet housing policies and living conditions (Di Maio, 1974; Attwood, 2010).
7. The names have been changed to preserve anonymity.
8. Today's Almaty, the capital of Kazakhstan, renamed since the breakup of the Soviet Union. At the time of the events described by Liza Alma-Ata was the capital of the Kazakh Soviet Socialist Republic.
9. The term can be roughly translated as 'cruising areas'.
10. Research on queer/lesbian spaces in other geographical contexts has also highlighted its classed connotations: for example, Kennedy-Lapovski and Davis (1993) show how white working-class lesbian women predominantly socialised in bars in 1950s and 1960s Buffalo, while middle-class women socialised in informal networks, meeting in private houses. The Buffalo 'scene' was also very much segregated along racial lines, with women from Black and minority ethnic backgrounds socialising separately from white women.

4   Family Matters: Negotiating 'Home'

1. Unlike Chapter 3, chapters 4, 5 and 6 draw exclusively on ethnographic data (interviews and participant observation) collected during fieldwork conducted in 2004–2005.
2. In the early Soviet period, virtually all urban housing was socialised, but the high speed of industrialisation and rural-urban migration resulted in a severe shortage of housing. Housing construction programmes received a major boost under Khrushchev, with the aim of providing a private flat for every Soviet family. The housing stock was increased, but the supply never caught up with the demand (Attwood, 2010). It was not uncommon for newly married couples to wait for several years before being allocated a flat, and to

continue living in the parental home after their marriage (Shaw, 1999, p. 167; Di Maio, 1974). In post-Soviet Russia, the gradual privatisation of the state-owned housing stock and the construction of new private flats, largely for the benefit of the more affluent, has resulted in the shortage of both social housing and affordable private properties.

3. While the average floor space per person in British urban households was 38 square metres in 1991 and 44 in 2001 (Boardman et al., 2005, p. 29), the average for Muscovites in 2004 was 19.1 square metres pro capita. Figures were similar for the city of Ul'ianovsk (18.8 square metres in 2000), and only slightly higher for the Ul'ianovsk region and the Moscow region (respectively, 21.1 square metres and 24.0 square metres in 2004) (Goskomstat Rossii, 2005, pp. 233–234; Galitskii, 2001, p. 398). Although new housing facilities are being built, statistics registered only a very slight improvement in the average floor space per person (in Moscow the average living space was 16.3 square metres in 1980 and 17.8 in 1990, Goskomstat Rossii, 2005, p. 233).

4. Nonetheless, as alternative ways of 'doing' family are becoming normalised in Britain (for example, through the legal recognition of same-sex unions, and the increasing use of assisted reproductive technology), stigma may have shifted from LGBT people (formet sexual outcasts) to single childless women as 'contemporary spinsters' (unwilling or unable to form couple relations and become mothers)) (Simpson, 2009).

5. A considerable number of research participants came from single-parent households headed by women; they had either been born in single-parent households or their parents had split up. This may explain the emphasis on motherhood not necessarily attached to heterosexual coupledom.

6. In the Russian original: 'Podrugi, podrugi ... a chto podrugi?' Like the English 'girlfriend', the Russian *podruga* is potentially ambiguous, as it indicates both a friend of the female sex as well as a lover in a lesbian relationship.

5 The Global Closet? Negotiating Public Space

1. A few women in my sample did not work, being full-time university students, temporarily out of work, or depending on other sources of income, such as occupational or invalidity pension, or unearned income from rented properties. Among the women in paid employment, most were hired employees, only a handful were self-employed or working freelance, and none managed their own business. For a more detailed profile of participants' occupations see Appendix 1.

2. In Russian, the adjective *lichnyi*, repeatedly used by Varvara, means both 'personal' and 'private', and the two English terms have alternatively been used in the translated quote as appropriate. I would like to draw attention to the way the interviewee, through the repeated use of the word *lichnyi*, draws a very firm boundary between her private life, from which her colleagues are excluded, and the workplace, understood as a public, formal space.

3. UK-based research on how lesbian sexuality is negotiated at the workplace has often focused on non-verbal signifiers (dress, hairstyle, etc.) in workers' embodied performances (Dunne, 1997; Holliday, 1999; Adkins, 2000;

Taylor, 2007), thus emphasising the importance of impressions given off. Non-verbal clues which could be interpreted by co-workers as sigs of 'queerness' were rarely discussed in any detail by the women involved in my research, who tended to focus on verbal negotiations. For this reason, non-verbal communication is not part of my analysis.

4. A second home (small country house or cottage) typically used as a holiday home during the summer, and located in the exurbs of Russian cities.

5. Notions of 'butch/kobel' and 'fem/kovyrial'ka' as embodiments of femininity and masculinity in lesbian relationships have a certain currency in Russian lesbian subcultures (Zhuk, 1998; Sarajeva, 2011), although binary divisions are inadequate to account for the range of identifications and embodied performances among the women who participated in the research.

6. Not all women were equally invested in socialising in lesbian/queer space: some felt they did not quite belong in the *tusovki*, and for others interest in them faded over time. Nonetheless, for most women, socialising in lesbian/queer space was a rite of passage of sorts, and was particularly important for those who were beginning to explore or were coming to terms with their sexuality. The *tusovki* provided an alternative framework of reference to other leisure spaces where same-sex sexualities were typically devalued or stigmatised.

7. A pejorative label that can be roughly translated as 'yobs', the term *gopniki* refers to gangs of young people from deprived or working-class neighbourhoods who were feared because of their association with petty crime and aggressive, threatening or violent behaviour. *Gopniki* are known to target members of youth *tusovki*, and violence seems to be triggered by visible difference (e.g. unusual and conspicuous clothing and make-up blurring traditional markers of femininity and masculinity, see Pilkington et al., 2002; Omel'chenko, 2006). Omel'chenko also notes that the term *gopniki* has class connotations: *gopninki* are portrayed in the media as a grey mass of uneducated working-class 'louts' who display irrational violence towards *tusovki*, groups of young people who are characterised as cosmopolitan and upwardly mobile (Omel'chenko, 2006).

8. Perceptions of violence and safety should be related to Ul'ianovsk's struggling economy and growing social inequalities, as Liza suggested when recounting the assault of a gay friend. While leaving the premises of a city centre club, where a monthly gay and lesbian night was being held, her gay friend was assaulted in her presence; according to Liza, however, the attack was a mugging attempt, not necessarily a hate crime. Unlike in Ul'ianovsk, in Moscow the city centre was visibly gentrified and securitised: it had been given a makeover through significant investment from the city administration and private businesses, and there was a visible presence of police and private security.

9. Fieldwork was conducted in Moscow a few months before plans to hold the first ever Moscow Pride were announced in summer 2005. The plans caused controversy and triggered a very damning media campaign against Moscow Pride. Several homophobic incidents preceded, accompanied and followed Pride, which was held in May 2006; these included violent attacks by far-right and religious groups on two gay clubs and on the Pride march itself, as well as episodes of random gay bashings in various parts of the city

(Stella, 2007; Sarajeva, 2010). Perceptions of personal safety may have been different, had the interviews taken place closer to these events.

10. Literature on urban queer space generally focuses on territorially concentrated community and commercial venues. The prevailing focus has been on gay men's appropriation of city space through gentrification and on women's marginalisation within the scene. The dearth of distinctively 'lesbian' spaces within gay urban enclaves has been explained with reference to either women's restricted access to economic and cultural capital or lack of territorial ambitions (Adler and Brenner, 1992; Valentine, 1995, 1996; Casey, 2004; for a rare exploration of a lesbian/queer neighbourhood see Gieseking, 2013).

6 Carving Out Queer Space: In/visibility, Belonging and Resistance

1. In Moscow, classed inclusions and exclusions were apparent in both community and commercial spaces. The boundaries between the two were often blurred, as exemplified by the activities of Labrys, an organisation run as a cooperative by a small collective but funded by an investor on a commercial basis. Labrys' activities ranged from the publication of a lesbian almanac to the organisation of gigs and events for lesbian women; these activities were similar in format and content to community-driven projects such as the samizdat journal *Ostrov* and the Festival of Lesbian Art. However, Labrys launched on a commercial basis products and events which had previously been produced on a non-for-profit basis, and targeted a selected audience of comparatively affluent women, as openly stated both on their website and in an interview with members of the collective.

> As any other commercial organisation, one of Labrys' aims is to make a profit. But this aim cannot be the foundation of our business activities, Labrys has a mission. It is the creation of positive representations of lesbianism in literature [...]. Labrys has an additional aim: the development of a networked structure of management and the creation of a model lesbian cooperative. It has another purpose: the education of queer [*temnye*] audiences. Labrys caters for a 'progressive audience'. [...] We set a rather high price for the first issue of the almanac, so that only those who recognise the value of culture and are ready to pay for it will read it.
>
> (Labrys, 2006)

2. These include the portal gay.ru, and the glossy magazines *Kvir* (established in 2004, for men) and *Pinx* (established in 2006, for women).

3. The colloquial term *Pushka* has different meanings within and outside the Moscow lesbian community. Outside this specific context, *Pushka* refers to a broader area near Pushkin Square, comprising parts of Tverskoi and Strastnoi Boulevards, which is a popular outdoor hangout for all sorts of youth *tusovki* and for Muscovites in general (Pilkington, 1994). In lesbian circles, the term is used to refer to a specific stretch of Tverskoi Boulevard where a young lesbian *tusovka* regularly meets.

4. The Moscow *Pushka* takes its name from a nearby underground station named after the poet Aleksandr Sergeevich Pushkin.
5. For example, the club *12 Vol't*, one of the oldest in the city, was located on Tverskaya street, in the very centre of the city. The main entrance to the club was from a courtyard at the back, where only a tiny rainbow-coloured plaque gave it away as a gay and lesbian club; on the intercom on Tverskaya street (the other entrance) it was simply listed as 'Club 12 Volts'.
6. They either shared premises with other civil society organisations or commercial businesses, (in the case of the lesbian recreational club *Klub Svobodnogo Poseshcheniia* or the support group for lesbian and gay men organised by the LGBT organisation *Ia+Ia*), or were hosted in private flats, like the Moscow Gay and Lesbian Archive.

7 Conclusions: From Russian to (Post)Socialist Sexualities

1. The public humiliation and outing of young gay men, including teenagers, at the hands of nationalist groups such as Occupy Paedophilia and Occupy Gerontophilia, has been documented by Russian LGBT groups and international human rights organisations such as Human Rights Watch (Human Rights Watch, 2014). Gay youths are lured to fake dates via the internet and then filmed as they are bullied, harassed and sometimes beaten or tortured by nationalist gangs; the films are then posted online, thus outing gay youths to unknowing friends and family. Law enforcement agencies have thus far been complacent, as the authors of these attacks, often clearly recognisable in the videos, have never been prosecuted. Violations of the law banning the 'propaganda' of homosexuality to minors are often reported by ordinary citizens to the relevant authorities. Documented cases of individuals reported for violating the 'anti-gay propaganda' law have involved LGBT activists and their supporters, including two teachers (one gay man and one heterosexual woman) who were eventually fired, despite the fact that they engaged in activism outside of their workplace and enjoyed the support of their pupils (Bigg, 2013; Nechupurenko, 2013). Documented cases also include journalists who have spoken out against the 'gay propaganda' law and have actively supported LGBT teenagers, such as Elena Klimova. Klimova was prosecuted, convicted and fined under the 'gay propaganda' law, although the decision was overturned on appeal. (Amnesty International UK, 2014).
2. The emphasis is mine.
3. The text in bracket is my commentary.
4. Colonial frameworks have indeed been widely applied to analyse power relations within the Russian Empire and the Soviet Union, as well as between the Soviet Union and the so-called 'Soviet Bloc' in Central and Eastern Europe, the geopolitical area under its immediate control, largely comprising 'satellite' states (Suny and Martin, 2002; Hirsch, 2005). However, the relationship between the Soviet Union and its 'satellites', and between Russia as the core nation of the Soviet Union and the other Soviet republics, are not so straightforwardly captured by the notion of metropole and colonies. State socialism was not always forcibly imposed from Moscow: in some areas, communist revolutions and national emancipation went hand in hand, and enjoyed

genuine mass support locally. The presence of a regional power (the Russian empire/the Soviet Union) whose metropolitan centre (Russia) was not territorially separated from the 'colonies' further complicates any parallels with other colonial empires such as the British or French ones (Suny and Martin, 2002; Hirsch, 2005). Finally, and most importantly, postcolonial theory has wildly disparate relevance and uses for Russia, the Soviet Union, the former Soviet Republics and the former 'satellite' states of Central and Eastern Europe. Postcolonial notions of subalternity and periphery are least of all applicable to Russia, as the former metropole of the Russian empire and the Soviet Union. There are also significant limitations in assimilating the postsocialist into the postcolonial in the context of Central and Eastern Europe. Lazarus (2012), for example, highlights the uses of postcolonial frameworks among Central and East European scholars to sever links with the former colonial power (the Soviet Union) and to claim a place in the 'new Europe' and the 'west'. This foregrounds 'a tendency to insist precisely on that narrative of "the west" that postcolonial studies, in its indispensable critique of Eurocentrism, has managed to dislodge' (Lazarus, 2012, p. 117).

Bibliography

Adams, T. (2010) 'Paradoxes of Sexuality, Gay Identity and the Closet', *Symbolic Interaction*, 33(2), 234–256.

Adkins, L. (1995) *Gendered Work: Sexuality, Family and the Labour Market* (Buckingham: Open University Press).

Adkins, L. (2000) 'Mobile Desire: Aesthetics, Sexuality and the "Lesbian" at Work', *Sexualities*, 3(2), 201–218.

Adler, S. and Brenner, J. (1992) 'Gender and Space: Lesbians and Gay Men in the City', *International Journal of Urban and Regional Research*, 16(1), 24–34.

Alekseev, N. A. (2002) *Pravovoe Regulirovanie Polozheniia Seksualnykh Menshinstv: Rossia v Svete Praktiki Mezhdunarodnykh Organizatsii i Natsional'nogo Zakonodatel'stva Stran Mira* (Moscow: BEK).

Alexopoulos, G. (2006) 'Soviet Citizenship, More or Less: Rights, Emotions and States of Civic Belonging', *Kritika: Explorations in Russian and Eurasian History*, 7(3), 487–528.

Altman, D. (1996a) 'On Global Queering', *Australian Humanities Review*, July. Available at: http://www.lib.latrobe.edu.au/AHR/archive/Issue-July-1996/altman.html#1, last accessed 7 March 2014.

Altman, D. (1996b) 'Rupture or Continuity? The Internationalization of Gay Identities', *Social Text*, 48, 77–94.

Altman, D. (1997) 'Global Gaze/Global Gays', *GLQ*, 3(4), 417–436.

Amelina, A., Nergiz, D., Faist, T. and Glick Schiller, N. (eds.) (2012) *Beyond Methodological Nationalism: Research Methodologies for Cross-Border Studies* (Abingdon, Oxon: Routledge).

Amnesty International UK (2014) 'Russian Journalist Accused of Anti-Gay "Propaganda" Defeats Charges', 21 February 2014. Available at: http://www.amnesty.org.uk/russia-journalist-elena-klimova-lgbt-gay-propaganda#.UyFmtFKPP4g, last accessed 7 March 2014.

Arnett, J. J. (1997) 'Young People's Conceptions of the Transition to Adulthood', *Youth and Society*, 29(1), 3–21.

Ashwin, S. (ed.) (2000) *Gender, State and Society in Soviet and Post-Soviet Russia* (London: Routledge).

Ashwin, S. (ed.) (2006) *Adapting to Russia's New Labour Market: Gender and Employment Behaviour* (London: Routledge).

Attwood, L. (2010) *Gender and Housing in Soviet Russia* (Manchester: Manchester University Press).

Baer, B. J. (2002) 'Russian Gays/Western Gaze', *GLQ*, 8(4), 499–521.

Baer, B. J. (2009) *Other Russias: Homosexuality and the Crisis of Post-Soviet Identity* (Basingstoke: Palgrave Macmillan).

Baraulina, T. (2002) 'Moral'noe Materinstvo i Vosproizvodstvo Zhenskogo Opyta', in Temkina, A. and Zdravomyslova, E. (eds.) *V Poiskakh Seksual'nosti: Sbornik Stat'ei* (Saint Petersburg: Dmitrii Bulanin), 366–405.

Beck, U. and Szainer, N. (2006) 'Unpacking Cosmopolitanism for the Social Sciences: a Research Agenda', *Journal of British Sociology*, 57(1), 1–23.

Bell, D. and Binnie, J. (2000) *The Sexual Citizen: Queer Politics and Beyond* (Cambridge: Polity).

Berdahl, D. (2010) *On the Social Life of Postsocialism: Memory, Consumption, Germany* (Bloomington: Indiana University Press).

Berman, H. J. and Spindler, J. W. (1963) 'Soviet Comrades' Courts', *Washington Law Review*, 38, 842–910.

Bertone, C. and Pallotta-Chiarolli, M. (2014) 'Intruduction. Putting Families of Origin into the Queer Picture: Introducing This Special Issue', *Journal of GLBT Family Studies*, 10, 1–14.

Besemeres, M. and Wierzbicka, A. (eds.) (2007) *Translating Lives. Living with Two Languages and Cultures* (St. Lucia: University of Queensland Press).

Bigg, C. (2013) 'Russia's Gay-Friendly Schoolteachers in the Crosshairs', Radio Free Europe, 11 November 2013. Available at: http://www.rferl.org/content/russia-gay-teachers-pressure/25164580.html, last accessed 7 March 2014.

Binnie, J. (2004) *The Globalization of Sexuality* (London: Sage).

Binnie, J. (2013) In What Sense Is There a Regional Problem in Transnational Queer Studies? Unpublished paper presented at the symposium 'Queer/ing Regions', Nottingham Trent University, 7 February 2013.

Binnie, J. and Klesse, C. (2013) 'The Politics of Age, Temporality and Intergenerationality in Transnational Lesbian, Gay, Bisexual, Transgender and Queer Activist Networks', *Sociology*, 47(3), 580–595.

Binnie, J. and Skeggs, B. (2004) 'Cosmopolitan Knowledge and the Production and Consumption of Sexualized Space: Manchester's Gay Village', *Sociological Review*, 52(1), 39–61.

Boardman, B., Darby, S., Killip, D., Hinnells, M., Jardine, C., Palmer, J. and Sinden, G. (2005) '40% House'. *Environmental Change Institute Report N. 31* (Oxford: University of Oxford).

Boellstorff, T. (2005) *The Gay Archipelago: Sexuality and Nation in Indonesia* (Princeton: Princeton University Press).

Boellstorff, T. (2011) 'Queer Techne: Two Theses on Methodology and Queer Studies', in Browne, K. and Nash, C. (eds.) *Queer Methods and Methodologies: Intersecting Queer Theories and Social Science Research* (Farnham: Ashgate), 215–230.

Bogdanova, L. P. and Shchukina, A. S. (2003) 'Grazhdanskii Brak v Sovremennoi Demograficheskoi Situatsii', *Sotsiologicheskiie Issledovaniia*, 7, 31–40.

Bonnett, A. (2004) *The Idea of the West: Culture, Politics, and History* (Basingstoke: Palgrave Macmillan).

Borodzina, E., Zdravomyslova, E. and Temkina, A. (2011) 'Materinskii Kapital: Sotisial'naia Politika i Strategii Sem'ei'. Available at: http://genderpage.ru/?p=481, last accessed 7 March 2014.

Borodzina, E., Zdravomyslova, E. and Temkina, A. (2013) 'Materinskii Kapital: Strategii Sem'ei'. Available at: http://polit.ru/article/2013/06/27/family_capital/, last accessed 7 March 2014.

Brade, I. and Rudolph, R. (2004) 'Moscow, the Global City? The Position of the Russian Capital within the European System of Metropolitan Areas', *Area*, 36(1), 69–80.

Brickell, C. (2003) 'Performativity or Performance? Clarifications in the Sociology of Gender', *New Zealand Sociology*, 18(2), 158–178.

Brickell, C. (2005) 'Masculinities, Performativity, and Subversion: A Sociological Reappraisal', *Men and Masculinities*, 8(1), 24–43.

Bridger, S., Kay, R. and Pinnick, K. (1996) *No More Heroines? Russia, Women and the Market* (London: Routledge).

Brown, G. and Browne, K. (2011) 'Sedgwick's Geographies: Touching Space', *Progress in Human Geography*, 35(1), 121–131.

Brown, M. P. (2000) *Closet Space: Geographies of Metaphor from the Body to the Globe* (London: Routledge).

Browne, K. (2007) 'A Party with Politics? (Re)making LGBTQ Pride Spaces in Dublin and Brighton', *Social and Cultural Geography*, 18(1), 63–87.

Browne, K. and Nash, C. (2011a) 'Queer Methods and Methodologies: An Introduction', in Browne, K. and Nash, C. (eds.) *Queer Methods and Methodologies: Intersecting Queer Theories and Social Science Research* (Farnham: Ashgate), 1–23.

Browne, K. and Nash, C. (eds.) (2011b) *Queer Methods and Methodologies: Intersecting Queer Theories and Social Science Research* (Farnham: Ashgate).

Brubaker, R. and Cooper, F. (2000) 'Beyond "Identity"', *Theory and Society*, 29, 1–47.

Buchowski, M. (2006) 'The Specter of Orientalism in Europe: From Exotic Other to Stigmatised Brother', *Anthropological Quarterly*, 79(3), 463–482.

Buck, N. and Scott, J. (1993) 'She's Leaving Home: But Why? An Analysis of Young People Leaving the Parental Home', *Journal of Marriage and the Family*, 55(4), 863–874.

Buckley, M. (1989) *Women and Ideology in the Soviet Union* (Hemel Hempstead: Harvester Wheatsheaf).

Buckley, M. (1992) *Perestroika and Soviet Women* (Cambridge: Cambridge University Press).

Burawoy, M. and Verdery, K. (eds.) (1999) *Uncertain Transition: Ethnographies of Change in the Postsocialist World* (Oxford: Rowman & Littlefield).

Butler, J. (1990/1999) *Gender Trouble: Feminism and the Subversion of Identity* (New York: Routledge).

Butler, J. (1993) *Bodies that Matter: On the Discursive Limits of 'Sex'* (London: Routledge).

Butler, J. (1997) 'Merely Cultural', *Social Text*, 52/53, 265–277.

Byford, A. (2009) '"Poslednee Sovetskoe Pokolenie" v Velikobritanii', *Neprikosnovennyi Zapas*, 64, 96–116.

Casey, M. (2004) 'De-Dyking Queer Space(s): Heterosexual Female Visibility in Gay and Lesbian Spaces', *Sexualities*, 7(4), 446–461.

Casey, M., Hines, S., Richardson, D. and Taylor, Y. (eds.) (2010) Special Issue on Theorizing Sexuality, *Sociology*, 44(5).

Castells, M. (1983) *The City and the Grassroots: A Cross-Cultural Theory of Urban Social Movements* (Berkeley, CA: University of California Press).

Chamberlayne, P., Bornat, J. and Wengraf, T. (2000) 'Introduction: The Biographical Turn', in Chamberlayne, P., Bornat, J. and Wengraf, T. (eds.) *The Turn to Biographical Methods in Social Science: Comparative Issues and Examples* (London: Routledge), 1–30.

Chari, S. and Verdery, K. (2009) 'Thinking Between the Posts: Postcolonialism, Postsocialism, and Ethnography After the Cold War', *Comparative Studies in Society and History*, 51(1), 6–34.

Chasin, A. (2000) *Selling Out: The Gay and Lesbian Movement Goes to Market* (Basingstoke: Palgrave Macmillan).

Chauncey, G. (1994) *Gay New York: Gender, Urban Culture, and the Making of the Gay Male World, 1890–1940* (New York: Basic Books).

Chernilo, D. (2011) 'The Critique of Methodological Nationalism: Theory and History', *Thesis Eleven*, 106(1), 98–117.

Clark, D. (1993) 'Commodity Lesbianism', in Abelove, H., Aina Barale, M. and Halperin, D. M. (eds.) *The Lesbian and Gay Studies Reader* (London: Routledge).

Clark, H. (1997) 'Low Awareness Shelters Russia's Lesbian Moms', *The Moscow Times*, 15 October, 9.

Coffey, A. and Atkinson, P. (1996) *Making Sense of Qualitative Data: Complementary Research Strategies* (London: Sage).

Collins, A. (2004) 'Sexual Dissidence, Enterprise and Assimilation: Bedfellows in Urban Regeneration', *Urban Studies*, 41(9), 1789–1806.

Connell, R. (1987) *Gender and Power: Society, the Person and Sexual Politics* (Stanford, CA: Stanford University Press).

Connell, R. (2006) 'Glass Ceilings or Gendered Institutions? Mapping the Gender Regimes of Public Sector Worksites', *Public Administration Review*, 66(6), 837–849.

Connell, R. (2007) *Southern Theory: The Global Dynamics of Knowledge in Social Science* (Cambridge: Polity).

Corteen, K. (2002) 'Lesbian Safety Talk: Problematising Definitions and Experiences of Violence, Sexuality and Space', *Sexualities* 5(3), 259–280.

Cronin, A. and King, A. (2010) 'Power, Inequality and Identification: Exploring Diversity and Intersectionality Amongst Older LGB Adults', *Sociology*, 44(5), 876–892.

David-Fox, M. (2006) 'Multiple Modernities vs. Neo-Traditionalism: On Recent Debates in Russian and Soviet History', *Jahrbücher für Geschichte Osteuropas*, 55(4).

Decena, C. U. (2011) *Tacit Subjects: Belonging, Same-Sex Desire, and Daily Life Among Dominican Immigrant Men* (Durham: Duke University Press).

D'Emilio, J. (1983) 'Capitalism and Gay Identity', in Snitow, A., Stansell, C. and Thompson, S. (eds.) *Powers of Desire: The Politics of Sexuality* (New York: Monthly Review Press).

Denzin, N. and Lincoln, Y. S. (2005) 'Introduction. The Discipline and Practice of Qualitative Research', in Denzin, N. and Lincoln, Y. S. (eds.) *The Sage Handbook of Qualitative Research, Vol. 1* (London: Sage), 1–40.

Di Maio, J. (1974) *Soviet Urban Housing: Problems and Policies* (London: Praeger).

Dingsdale, A. (2002) *Mapping Modernities: Geographies of Central and Eastern Europe, 1920–2000* (London: Routledge).

Duggan, L. (2002) 'The New Homonormativity: The Sexual Politics of Neoliberalism', in Castronovo, R. and Nelson, D. D. (eds.) *Materializing Democracy: Toward a Revitalized Cultural Politics* (Durham, NC: Duke University Press), 175–194.

Duncan, N. (ed.) (1996) *Bodyspace: Destabilizing Geographies of Gender and Sexuality* (London: Routledge).

Dunne, G. A. (1997) *Lesbian Lifestyles: Women's Work and the Politics of Sexuality* (Basingstoke: Macmillan).

Dunne, G. A., Predergast, S. and Telford, D. (2002) 'Young, Gay, Homeless and Invisible: A Growing Population?' *Culture, Health and Sexuality*, 4(1), 103–115.

Dyer, R. (2002) *The Matter of Images. Essays on Representation* (London: Routledge).

Einhorn, B. (1993) *Cinderella Goes to Market: Citizenship, Gender and Women's Movements in East Central Europe* (London: Verso).

Engebretsen, E. L. (2009) 'Intimate Practices, Conjugal Ideals: Affective Ties and Relationship Strategies Among *Lala* (Lesbian) Women in Contemporary Beijing', *Sexuality Research and Social Policy*, 6(3), 3–14.

Engelstein, L. (1992) *The Keys to Happiness: Sex and the Search for Modernity in Fin-de-Siècle Russia* (Ithaca: Cornell University Press).

Engelstein, L. (1993) 'Combined Underdevelopment: Discipline and the Law in Imperial and Soviet Russia', *The American Historical Review*, 98(2), 338–353.

Engelstein, L. (1995) 'Soviet Policy Towards Male Homosexuality: Its Origins and Historical Roots', in Hekma, G., Oosterhuis, H. and Steakley, J. (eds.) *Gay Men and the Sexual History of the Political Left* (Binghamton, NY: Harrington Park Press).

Erel, U., Haritaworn, J., Gutierrez-Rodriguez, E. and Klesse, C. (2010) 'On the Depoliticisation of Intersectionality Talk. Conceptualising Multiple Oppressions in Critical Sexuality Studies', in Taylor, Y., Hines, S. and Casey, M. (eds.) *Theorizing Intersectionality and Sexuality* (Basingstoke: Palgrave Macmillan), 56–77.

Essig, L. (1999) *Queer in Russia: A Story of Sex, Self, and the Other* (Durham, NC: Duke University Press).

Evans, D. T. (1993) *Sexual Citizenship: The Material Construction of Sexualities* (London: Routledge).

Featherstone, M., Lash, S. and Robertson, R. (eds.) (1995) *Global Modernities* (London: Sage).

Field, M. G. (2000) 'The Health and Demographic Crisis in Post-Soviet Russia: A Two-Phase Development', in Field, M. G. and Twigg, J. L. (eds.) *Russia's Torn Safety Nets: Health and Social Welfare During the Transition* (Basingstoke: Macmillan), 11–42.

Flynn, M., Kay, R. and Oldfield, J. (eds.) (2008) *Trans-National Issues, Local Concerns and Meanings of Post-Socialism: Insights from Russia, Central Eastern Europe and Beyond* (Lanham, MD: University Press of America).

Fotopoulou, A. (2012) 'Intersectionality, Queer Studies and Hybridity: Methodological Frameworks for Social Research', *Journal of International Women's Studies*, 13(2), pp. 19–32.

Foucault, M. (1978/1998) *The History of Sexuality. Vol. I: The Will to Knowledge* (London: Penguin).

Franeta, S. (2004) *Rozovye Flamingo: 10 Sibirskikh Interv'iu* (Tver': GanimedA).

Fraser, N. (1997) *Justice Interruptus: Critical Reflections on the 'Postsocialist' Condition* (London: Routledge).

Fukuyama, F. (1992) *The End of History and the Last Man* (London: Penguin).

Fuss, D. (ed.) (1991) *Inside/Out: Lesbian Theories, Gay Theories* (London: Routledge).

Galitskii, V. I. (2001) *Regiony Rossii: Statisticheskii Sbornik* (Moscow: Goskomstat Rossii).

Garber, L. (2003) 'One Step Global, Two Steps Back? Race, Gender, and Queer Studies', *GLQ*, 10(1), 125–128.

Gessen, M. (1994) *The Rights of Lesbians and Gay Men in the Russian Federation* (San Francisco: IGLHRC).

Gessen, M. (1997) 'Russia', in Griffin, K. and Mulholland, L. A. (eds.) *Lesbian Motherhood in Europe* (London: Cassell).

Ghodsee, K. (2005) *The Red Riviera: Gender, Tourism, and Postsocialism on the Black Sea* (Durham, NC: Duke University Press).

Giddens, A. (1992) *The Transformation of Intimacy: Sexuality, Love, and Eroticism in Modern Societies* (Cambridge: Polity Press).

Gieseking, J. J. (2013) 'Queering the Meaning of "Neighborhood": Reinterpreting the Lesbian-Queer Experience of Park Slope, Brooklyn, 1983–2008', in Taylor, Y. and Addison, M. (eds.) *Queer Presences and Absences* (Basingstoke: Palgrave Macmillan), 178–201.

Goffman, E. (1956/1990a) *The Presentation of Self in Everyday Life* (London: Penguin).

Goffman, E. (1963/1990b) *Stigma: Notes on the Management of Spoiled Identity* (London: Penguin).

Golovin, V. (2003) 'Vtorye posle Dostoevskogo', *Izvestiia*, 17 April, 20.

Gorlizki, Y. (1998) 'Delegalization in Russia: Soviet Comrades' Courts in Retrospect', *American Journal of Comparative Law*, 48(3), 103–125.

Goscilo, H. and Lanoux. A. (eds.) (2006) *Gender and National Identity in Twentieth-Century Russian Culture* (DeKalb, IL: Northern Illinois University Press).

Goskomstat Rossii (2005) *Rossiiskii Statisticheskii Ezhegodnik* (Moscow: Goskomstat Rossii).

Grachev, S. (2002) 'Epidemiia "Tatu" ', *Argumenty i Fakty*, 50(1155), 11 December, 40.

Green, R. J. (2002) ' "Lesbians, Gay Men, and Their Parents": A Critique of LaSala and the Prevailing Clinical Wisdom', *Family Process*, 39(2), 257–266.

Greenberg, D. F. and Bystryn, M. H. (1996) 'Capitalism, Bureaucracy and Male Homosexuality', in Seidman, S. (ed.) *Queer Theory/Sociology* (Oxford: Blackwell).

Gurova, O. 2003 ' "Tatu" (ili Reprezentatsiia Zhenskoi Gomoseksual'nosti v Sovremennoi Rossiiskoi Massovoi Kul'tury)', *Gendernye issledovaniia*, 9, 194–200.

Haavio-Mannila, E., Kontula, O. and Rotkirch, A. (2002) *Sexual Lifestyles in the Twentieth Century: A Research Study* (New York: Palgrave Macmillan).

Halberstam, J. (2005) *In a Queer Time and Place: Transgender Bodies, Subcultural Lives* (New York: New York University Press).

Hall, S. (1996) 'Introduction', in Hall, S. and Du Gay, P. (eds.) *Questions of Cultural Identity* (London: Sage).

Hammack, P. L. and Cohler, B. J. (eds.) (2009) *The Story of Sexual Identity: Narrative Perspectives on the Gay and Lesbian Life Course* (Oxford: Oxford University Press).

Hann, C. (ed.) (2002) *Postsocialism. Ideals, Ideologies and Practices in Eurasia* (London: Routledge).

Hann, C., Humphrey, C. and Verdery, K. (2002) 'Introduction. Postsocialism as a Topic of Anthropological Investigation', in Hann, C. (ed.) *Postsocialism. Ideals, Ideologies and Practices in Eurasia* (London: Routledge), 1–28.

Healey, D. (1993) 'Russian Revolution and the Decriminalisation of Homosexuality', *Revolutionary Russia*, 6(1), 26–54.

Healey, D. (2001) *Homosexual Desire in Revolutionary Russia: The Regulation of Sexual and Gender Dissent* (Chicago: University of Chicago Press).

Healey, D. (2009) *Bolshevik Sexual Forensics: Diagnosing Disorder in the Clinic and Courtroom, 1917–1939* (DeKalb, IL: Northern Illinois University Press).

Heaphy, B. (2007) 'Sexualities, Gender and Ageing: Resources and Social Change', *Current Sociology*, 55(2), 193–210.

Heller, D. (2007) 't.A.T.u. You! Russia, the Global Politics of Eurovision, and Lesbian Pop', *Popular Music*, 26(2), 195–210.

Hennessy, R. (2000) *Profit and Pleasure: Sexual Identities in Late Capitalism* (London: Routledge).

Henrich Böell Foundation Moscow (2012) 'Restriction of Reproductive Rights in Russia, 2011–2012: Populist Politics at the Expense of Women's Health and Welfare'. Available at: http://genderpage.ru/?p=588, last accessed 7 March 2014.

Hermans, T. (2003) 'Cross-Cultural Translation Studies as Thick Translation', *Bulletin of SOAS*, 66(3), 380–389.

Hirsch, F. (2005) *Empire of Nations: Ethnographic Knowledge and the Making of the Soviet Union* (Ithaca: Cornell University Press).

Hoffmann, D. (2003) *Stalinist Values: The Cultural Norms of Soviet Modernity, 1917–1941* (Ithaca: Cornell University Press).

Holliday, R. (1999) 'The Comfort of Identity', *Sexualities*, 2(4), 475–491.

Holliday, R. (2001) 'Fashioning the Queer Self', in Entwistle J. and Wilson, E. (eds.) *Body Dressing: Fashion, Dress and the Embodied Self. Dress, Body, Culture* (Oxford: Berg), 215–232.

Holt, M. and Griffin, C. (2003) 'Being Gay, Being Straight and Being Yourself: Local and Global Reflections on Identity, Authenticity and the Lesbian and Gay Scene', *European Journal of Cultural Studies*, 6(3), 404–425.

Hörschelmann, K. and Stenning, A. (2008) 'Ethnographies of Postsocialist Change', *Progress in Human Geography*, 32(3), 339–361.

Hubbard, P. (2013) 'Kissing Is Not a Universal Right: Sexuality, Law and the Scales of Citizenship', *Geoforum*, 49, 224–232.

Human Rights Watch (2014) 'Russia: Sochi Games Highlight Homophobic Violence. Authorities Turn Blind Eye to Crimes Against LGBT People', 4 February. Available at: http://www.hrw.org/news/2014/02/03/russia-sochi-games-highlight-homophobic-violence, last accessed 7 March 2014.

Huntington, S. (1996) *The Clash of Civilizations and the Remaking of World Order* (New York: Simon & Schuster).

Isin, E. F. and Wood, P. (1999) *Citizenship and Identity* (London: Sage).

Issoupova, O. (2000) 'From Duty to Pleasure? Motherhood in Soviet and Post-Soviet Russia', in Ashwin, S. (ed.) *Gender, State and Society in Soviet Post-Soviet Russia* (London: Routledge), 30–54.

Jackson, P. (2009a) 'Global Queering and [Global] Queer Theory: Thai [trans]Genders and [homo]Sexualities in World History', *Autrepart*, 49(1), 15–30.

Jackson, P. (2009b) 'Capitalism and Global Queering: National Markets, Parallels Among Sexual Cultures, and Multiple Queer Modernities', *GLQ*, 15(3), 357–395.

Jackson, S. (1999) *Heterosexuality in Question* (London: Sage).

Jackson, S. and Scott, S. (2010a) 'Rehabilitating Interactionism for a Feminist Sociology of Sexuality', *Sociology*, 44(5), 811–826.

Jackson, S. and Scott, S. (2010b) *Theorising Sexuality* (Maidenhead: McGraw-Hill/Open University Press).

Jenkins, R. (2004) *Social Identity* (London: Routledge).

Johnson, J. E. and Robinson, J. C. (eds.) (2007) *Living Gender After Communism* (Bloomington, IN: Indiana University Press).

Johnson, M. (1998) 'Global Desirings and Translocal Loves: Transgendering and Same-Sex Sexualities in the Southern Philippines', *American Ethnologist*, 25(4), 695–711.

Johnson, M., Jackson, P. and Herdt, G. (2000) 'Critical Regionalities and the Study of Gender and Sexual Diversity in South East and East Asia', *Culture, Health and Sexuality*, 2(4), 361–375.

Johnston, L. (2007) 'Mobilizing Pride/Shame: Lesbians, Tourism and Parades', *Social and Cultural Geography*, 18(1), 29–45.

Johnston, L. and Valentine, G. (1995) 'Whenever I lay my Girlfriend, That's my Home: The Performance and Surveillance of Lesbian Identities in Domestic Environments', in Bell, D. and Valentine, G. (eds.) *Mapping Desire. Geographies of Sexualities* (London: Routlegde), 88–103.

Jolly, M. (2001) 'Coming Out of the Coming Out Story: Writing Queer Lives', *Sexualities*, 4(4), 474–496.

Kabanova, O. (2003) 'Eshche Raz pro "Tatu" i Dostoevskogo', *Izvestiia*, 20 April, 18.

Kandiyoti, D. (2002) 'How Far Do Analyses of Postsocialism Travel? The Case of Central Asia', in Hann, C. (ed.) *Postsocialism: Ideals, Ideologies and Practices in Eurasia* (London: Routledge), 238–257.

Kay, R. (2000) *Russian Women and Their Organizations: Gender, Discrimination and Grassroots Women's Organizations, 1991–96* (Basingstoke: Macmillan).

Kay, R. (2006) *Men in Contemporary Russia: The Fallen Heroes of Post-Soviet Change?* (Aldershot: Ashgate).

Kaz'mina, O. and Pushkareva, N. (2004) 'Brak v Rossii XX Veka: Traditsionnye Ustanovki i Innovatsionnye Eksperimenty', in Ushakin, S. (ed.) *Semeinye Uzy: Modeli Dlia Sborki. Vol. 1* (Moscow: Novoe Literaturnoe Obozreniie), 185–218.

Kennedy Lapovsky, E. and Davis, M. D. (1993) *Boots of Leather, Slippers of Gold. The History of a Lesbian Community* (London: Routledge).

Kharkhordin, O. (1995) 'The Soviet Individual: Genealogy of a Dissimulating Animal', in Featherstone, M., Lash, S. and Robertson, R. (eds.) *Global Modernities* (London: Sage).

Kharkhordin, O. (1999) *The Collective and the Individual in Russia: A Study of Practices* (Berkeley, CA: University of California Press).

King, A. and Cronin, A. (2010) 'Queer Methods and Queer Practices: Re-Examining the Identities of Older Lesbian, Gay, Bisexual Adults', in Browne, K. and Nash, C. (eds.) *Queer Methods and Methodologies: Intersecting Queer Theories and Social Science Research* (Farnham: Ashgate), 85–96.

Klugman, J. and Motivans, A. (2001) *Single Parents and Child Welfare in the New Russia* (Basingstoke: Palgrave Macmillan).

Kolossov, V. and O'Loughlin, J. (2004) 'How Moscow is Becoming a Capitalist Mega-City', *International Social Science Journal*, 56(3), 413–427.

Kon, I. S. (1995) *The Sexual Revolution in Russia: From the Age of the Czars to Today* (New York: The Free Press).

Kon, I. S. (1997) 'Russia', in West, D. and Green. R. (eds.) *Sociolegal Control of Homosexuality. A Multi-National Comparison* (New York: Plenum Press), 221–242.

Kon, I. S. (1998) *Lunnyi Svet na Zare: Liki i Maski Odnopoloi Liubvi* (Moscow: Izd-vo AST).

Kondakov. A. (2013) 'Resisting the Silence: The Use of Tolerance and Equality Arguments by Gay and Lesbian Activist Groups in Russia', *Canadian Journal of Law and Society*, 28(3), 403–424.

Kondakov, A. (ed.) (2014) *Na Perepute. Metodologiia, Teoriia i Praktika LGBT i Kvir-Issledovaniii. Sbornik Stat'ei* (Saint Petersburg: Tsentr Nezavisimykh Sotsiologicheskikh Issledovanii).

Konitzer-Smirnov, A. (2003) 'Breaching the Soviet Social Contract: Post-Soviet Social Policy Development in Ul'yanovsk and Samara Oblasts', in Twigg, J. L. and Schecter, K. (eds.) *Social Capital and Social Cohesion in post-Soviet Russia* (London: M.E. Sharpe), 189–216.

Kozina, I. and Zhidkova, E. (2006) 'Sex Segregation and Discrimination in the New Russian Labour Market', in Ashwin, S. (ed.) (2006) *Adapting to Russia's New Labour Market: Gender and Employment Strategy* (London: Routledge), 57–86.

Kozlovskii, V. (1986) *Argo Russkoi Gomoseksual'noi Subkul'tury: Materialy k Izucheniiu* (Benson, VT: Chalidze Publications).

Krauze, O. (2009) *Otpetaia Zizn'* (Tver': Novaia Real'nost').

Krongauz, E. (2005) 'Chelovek s Bul'vara', *Bol'shoi Gorod*, 16(142).

Kulick, D. (2000) 'Gay and Lesbian Language', *Annual Review of Anthropology*, 29, 243–285.

Kukhterin, S. (2000) 'Fathers and Patriarchs in Communist and Post-Communist Russia', in Ashwin, S. (ed) *Gender, State and Society in Soviet and post-Soviet Russia* (London: Routledge), 71–89.

Kulpa, R. and Liinason, M. (eds.) (2009) Special Issue 'Queer Studies: Methodological Approaches. Follow-up', *Graduate Journal of Social Sciences*, 6(1).

Kulpa, R. and Mizielińska, J. (eds.) (2011) *De-centring Western Sexualities: Central and Eastern European Perspectives* (Farnham: Ashgate).

Kuntsman, A. (2009) ' "With a Shade of Disgust": Affective Politics of Sexuality and Class in Memoirs of the Stalinist Gulag', *Slavic Review*, 68(2), 308–328.

Kuntsman, A. and Miyake, E. (eds.) (2008) *Out of Place: Interrogating Silences in Queerness/Raciality* (York: Raw Nerve Books).

Kuus, M. (2007) 'Ubiquitous Identities and Elusive Subjects: Puzzles from Central Europe', *Transactions of the Institute of British Geographers*, 32, 30–101.

Labrys (2006) Available at: http://www.labrys.ru, last accessed 29 March 2006 (content no longer on the website).

Lazarus, N. (2012) 'Spectres Haunting: Postcommunism and Postcolonialism', *Journal of Postcolonial Writing*, 48(2), 117–129.

Leap, W. L. (2002) 'Studying Lesbian and Gay Languages: Vocabulary, Text-Making and Beyond', in Lewin, E. and Leap, W. L. (eds.) *Out in Theory* (Chicago: Univerity of Illinois press), 128–154.

Lefebvre, H. (1996) 'The Right to the City', in Lefebvre, H. (ed.) *Writings on Cities* (Oxford: Blackwell), 147–159.

LeGendre, P. (1998) *The Gay and Lesbian Community in Russia* (Kings Hill, Kent: CAF).

Lewin, E. and Leap, W. L. (eds.) (2002) *Out in Theory* (Urbana and Chicago: University of Illinois Press).

Liinason, M. and Kulpa, R. (eds.) (2008) Special Issue on Queer Methodologies, *Graduate Journal of Social Sciences*, 5(2).

Liśkova, K. (2013) '"Against the Dignity of Man": Sexology Constructing Deviance During "Normalisation" in Czechoslovakia', in Taylor, Y, and Addison, M. (eds.) *Queer Presences and Absences* (Basingstoke: Palgrave Macmillan), 13–30.

Long, S. (1999) 'Gay and Lesbian Movements in Eastern Europe', in Adam, B., Duyvendak, J. and Krouwel, A. (eds.) *The Global Emergence of Gay and Lesbian Politics* (Philadelphia: Temple University Press), 242–265.

Lutz, H., Herrera Vivar, M. T. and Supik, L. (eds.) (2011) *Framing Intersectionality: Debates on a Multi-Faceted Concept in Gender Studies* (Farnham: Ashgate).

Maksimov, A. (2006) 'Liubov' Skvoz' Rozovye Ochki', *Superstil'*, 12 May 2006. Available at: http://lesbi.ru/talk/vzgljad/superstyle_lesbi2006.html, last accessed 16 June 2006.

Malia, M. (1999) *Russia Under Western Eyes: from the Bronze Horseman to the Lenin Mausoleum* (Cambridge, MA: Harvard University Press).

Manalansan, M. F. I. (1997) 'In the Shadow of Stonewall: Examining Gay Transnational Politics and the Diasporic Dilemma', in Lowe, L. and Lloyd, D. (eds.) *The Politics of Culture in the Shadow of Capital* (London: Duke University Press), 485–505.

Manalansan, M. F. I. (2002) 'A Queer Itinerary: Deviant Excursions into Modernity', in Lewin, E. and Leap, W. L. (eds.) *Out in Theory* (Urbana and Chicago: Univerity of Illinois Press), 246–263.

Manalansan, M. F. I. (2003) *Global Divas: Filipino Gay Men in the Diaspora* (Durham: Duke University Press).

Manalansan, M. F. I., Nadeau, C., Rodríguez, R. T. and Somerville, S. B. (2014) 'Queering the Middle: Race, Region, and a Queer Midwest', *GLQ*, 20(1–2), 1–12.

Manderson, L. and Jolly, M. (eds.) (1997) *Sites of Desire/Economies of Pleasure. Sexualities in Asia and the Pacific* (Chicago: University of Chicago Press).

Marcus, G. (1995) 'Ethnography in/or the World System: The Emergence of Multi-Sited Ethnography', *Annual Review of Anthropology*, 24, 95–117.

Marshall, T. H. (1977/1992) *Citizenship and Social Class* (London: Pluto Press).

McCall, L. (2005) 'The Complexity of Intersectionality', *Signs: Journal of Women in Culture and Society*, 30(3), 1771–1800.

McDermott, E. (2006) 'Surviving in Dangerous Places: Lesbian Identity Performances in the Workplace, Social Class and Psychological Health', *Feminism and Psychology*, 16(2), 193–211.

McGhee, D. (2004) 'Beyond Toleration: Privacy, Citizenship and Sexual Minorities in England and Wales', *The British Journal of Sociology*, 55(3), 357–375.

McKinnon, C. (1992) 'Sexuality', in Crowley, H. and Himme, S. (eds.) *Knowing Women: Feminism and Knowledge* (Cambridge: Polity Press).

Mills, C. W. (1959/1970) *The Sociological Imagination* (Harmondsworth: Penguin).

Minorskaia, E. (2004) 'Shakh i Mat Patriarkhatu. Otkroveniia Novykh Amazonok', *Medved'*, 3(12). Available at: http://www.lesbiru.com/society/press/medved.html, last accessed 3 September 2005.

Mizielińska, J. and Kulpa, R. (2011) '"Contemporary Peripheries": Queer Studies, Circulation of Knowledge and East/West Divide', in Kulpa, R. and Mizielińska, J. (eds.) *De-Centering Western Sexualities. Central and East European Perspectives* (Farnham: Ashgate), 11–26.

Mohanty, C. (1991) 'Under Western Eyes: Feminist Scholarship and Colonial Discourses', in Mohanty, C., Russo, A. and Torres, L. (eds.) *Third World Women and the Politics of Feminism* (Bloomington: Indiana University Press), 51–80.

Moran, L. J. and Skeggs, B. (2004) *Sexuality and the Politics of Violence and Safety* (London: Routledge).

Morgan, D. H. (2011) *Rethinking Family Practices* (Basingstoke: Palgrave Macmillan).

Morgan, D. H., Patiniotis, J. and Holdsworth, C. (2005) 'Leaving the Home in Comparative Perspective: Negotiating Processes and Meanings', in Pole, C., Pilcher, J. and Williams, J. (eds.) *Young People in Transition: Becoming Citizens?* (Basingstoke: Palgrave Macmillan), 97–115.

Müller, M. (2007) 'What's in a Word? Problematizing Translation Between Languages', *Area*, 39(2), 206–213.

Munt, S. R., Basset, E. H. and O'Riordan, K. (2002) 'Virtually Belonging: Risk, Connectivity, and Coming Out On-Line', *International Journal of Sexuality and Gender Studies*, 7(2/3), 125–137.

Murray, S. (1995) *Latin American Male Homosexualities* (Albuquerque: University of New Mexico Press).

Nartova, N. (1999) 'Molodezhnaia Lesbiiskaia Kul'tura v Sankt-Peterburge', in Kostiusheva, V. V. (ed.) *Molodezhnye Dvizheniia i Subkul'tury Sankt-Peterburga. Sotsiologicheskii i Antropologicheskii Analiz* (Saint Petersburg: Norma), 209–226.

Nartova, N. (2004a) ' "Pro Urodov i Liudei": Geteroseksual'nost' i Lesbiistvo', *Gendernye Issledovaniia*, 10(2), 197–206.

Nartova, N. (2004b) 'Lesbiiskie Sem'i: Real'nost' za Stenoi Mol'chaniia', in Ushakin, S. (ed.) *Semeinye Uzy: Modeli dlia Sborki, Vol. 1* (Moscow: Novoe Literaturnoe Obozreniie), 292–315.

Nartova, N. (2004c) 'Lesbians in Modern Russia: Subjectivity or Soviet Practices of Hypocrisy?', in Frunza, M. and Vacarescu, T.-E. (eds.) *Gender and the (Post) 'East'/'West' Divide* (Cluj-Napoca: Limes), 189–198.

Navickaite, R. (2013) *Sexuality in Eastern European Scholarship. Thinking Backwardness and Difference Through the Lens of Postcolonial Theory*. Unpublished MA thesis, Utrecht University.

Nechupurenko, I. (2013) 'Fallout of Anti-Gay Law Felt in Far East', *The Moscow Times*, 30 October 2013. Available at: http://www.themoscowtimes.com/news/article/fallout-of-anti-gay-law-felt-in-far-east/488716.html, last accessed 7 March 2014.

Nedbálková, K. (2007) 'The Changing Space of Gay and Lesbian Community in the Czech Republic', in Kuhar, R. and Takács, J. (eds.) *Beyond the Pink Curtain. Everyday Life of LGBT in Eastern Europe* (Ljubljana: Peace Institute), 57–71.

Nedbálková, K. (2013) 'Community at the Backstage: Gays and Lesbians in the Czech Republic', in Taylor, Y. and Addison, M. (eds.) *Queer Presences and Absences* (Basingstoke: Palgrave Macmillan), 31–50.

Nelson, L. (1999) 'Bodies (and Spaces) do Matter: The Limits of Performativity', *Gender, Place and Culture*, 6(4), 331–353.

Nemtsev, M. (2007) *The Emergence of a Sexual Minorities Movement in Post-Soviet Russia*. Unpublished MA dissertation (Gender Studies Department, Budapest: Central European University).

Neumann, I. (1996) *Russia and the Idea of Europe: A Study in Identity and International Relations* (London: Routledge).

Neumann, I. (1999) *Uses of the Other: 'The East' in European Identity Formation* (Manchester: Manchester University Press).

Novikova, I. and Kambourov, D. (eds.) (2003) *Men in the Global World: Integrating Postsocialist Perspectives* (Helsinki: Aleksanteri Institute).

Omel'chenko, E. (1999) 'New Dimensions of the Sexual Universe: Sexual Discourses in Russian Youth Magazines', in Corrin, C. (ed.) *Gender and Identity in Central and Eastern Europe* (London: Frank Cass).

Omel'chenko, E. (2000) 'My body, My Friend? Provincial Youth Between the Sexual and Gender Revolutions', in Ashwin, S. (ed.) *Gender, State and Society in Soviet and Post-Soviet Russia* (London: Routledge), 137–167.

Omel'chenko, E. (2002a) 'Izuchaia Gomofobiiu: Mekhanizmy Izkliucheniia "Drugoi" Seksual'nosti v Provintsial'noi Molodezhnoi Srede', in Temkina, A. and Zdravomyslova, E. (eds.) *V Poiskakh Seksual'nosti. Sbornik Statei* (Saint Petersburg: Dmitrii Bulanin), 469–510.

Omel'chenko, E. (2002b) ' "Ne Liubim my Geev ... " Gomofobiia Provintsial'noi Molodezhi', in Ushakin., S. (ed.) *O Muzhe(N)stvennosti. Sbornik Statei* (Moscow: Novoe Literaturnoe Obozrenie).

Omel'chenko, E. (2006) 'Ritual'nye Bitvy na Rossiiskikh Molodezhnykh Stsenakh Nachala Veka, ili Kak Gopniki Vytesniaiut Neformalov', *Polit.ru*, 23 May. Available at: http://www.polit.ru/culture/2006/05/23/gopniki.html, last accessed 18 July 2007.

Ong, A. (1999) *Flexible Citizenship: The Cultural Politics of Transnationality* (Durham, NC: Duke University Press).

Ortner, S. (1995) 'Resistance and the Problem of Ethnographic Refusal', *Comparative Studies in Society and History*, 37(1), 173–193.

Oswald, I. and Voronkov, V. (2004) 'The "Public-Private" Sphere in Soviet and Post-Soviet Society. Perception and Dynamics of "Public" and "Private" in Contemporary Russia', *European Societies*, 6(1), 97–117.

Oswin, N. (2006) 'Decentering Queer Globalization: Diffusion and the "Global Gay" ', *Environment and Planning D: Society and Space*, 24, 777–790.

Oswin, N. (2008) 'Critical Geographies and the Uses of Sexuality: Deconstructing Queer Space', *Progress in Human Geography*, 32(1), 89–103.

Owczarzak, J. (2009) 'Introduction: Postcolonial Studies and Postsocialism in Eastern Europe', *Focaal – European Journal of Anthropology*, 53, 3–19.

Paton-Walsh, N. (2003) 'They're too Risque for Russian MPs but Tatu May Top UK Pops', *The Guardian*, 1 February, 29.

Pavlovskaia, M. (2004) 'Other Transitions: Multiple Economies of Moscow Households in the 1990s', *Annals of the Association of American Geographers*, 94(2), 329–351.

Phillips, R., Watt, D. and Shuttleton, D. (eds.) (2000) *Decentring Sexualities: Politics and Representations Beyond the Metropolis* (London: Routledge).

Pile, S. (1997) 'Opposition, Political Identities and Spaces of Resistance', in Pile, S. and Keith, M. (eds.) *Geographies of Resistance* (London: Routledge), 1–32.

Pilkington, H. (1994) *Russia's Youth and its Culture* (London: Routledge).

Pilkington, H. and Johnson, R. (2003) 'Peripheral Youth: Relations of Identity and Power in Global/Local Context', *European Journal of Cultural Studies*, 6(3), 259–283.

Pilkington, H., Omel'chenko, E. and Garifzianova, A. (2010) *Russia's Skinheads: Exploring and Rethinking Subcultural Lives* (London: Routledge).

Pilkington, H., Omel'chenko, E., Flynn, M., Bliudina, U. and Starkova, E. (2002) *Looking West? Cultural Globalization and Russian Youth Cultures* (University Park, PA: Pennsylvania State University Press).

Plummer, K. (1975) *Sexual Stigma: An Interactionist Account* (London: Routledge and Kegan Paul).

Plummer, K. (1995) *Telling Sexual Stories: Power, Change, and Social Worlds* (New York: Routledge).

Plummer, K. (2005) 'Critical Humanism and Queer Theory: Living with the Tensions', in Denzin, N. and Lincoln, Y. (eds.) *The Sage Handbook of Qualitative Research* (London: Sage), 357–385.

Plummer, K. (2010) 'Generational Sexualities, Subterranean Traditions, and the Hauntings of the Sexual World: Some Preliminary Remarks', *Symbolic Interaction*, 33(2), 163–191.

Popov, A. A. and David, H. P. (1999) 'Russian Federation and USSR Succession States', in David, H. P., Skilogianis, J. and Posadskaya-Vanderbeck, A. (eds.) *From Abortion to Contraception. A Resource to Public Policies and Reproductive Behaviour in Central and Eastern Europe from 1917 to Present* (Westport, CT: Greenwood Publications).

Popov, A. A., Visser, A. P. and Ketting, E. (1993) 'Contraceptive Knowledge, Attitudes, and Practice in Russia During the 1980s', *Studies in Family Planning*, 24(4), 227–235.

Predergast, S., Dunne, G. A. and Telford, D. (2002) 'A Light at the End of the Tunnel? Experiences of Leaving Home of Two Contrasting Groups of Young Lesbian, Gay and Bisexual People', *Youth and Policy*, 75, 42–61.

Provencher, D. (2007) *Queer French. Globalization, Language, and Sexual Citizenship in France* (Aldershot: Ashgate).

Puar, J. K. (2007) *Terrorist Assemblages: Homonationalism in Queer Times* (Durham: Duke University Press).

Purcell, M. (2003) 'Citizenship and the Right to the Global City: Reimagining the Capitalist World Order', *International Journal of Urban and Regional Research*, 27(3), 564–90.

Racioppi, L. and O'Sullivan See, K. (1997) *Women's Activism in Contemporary Russia* (Philadelphia: Temple University Press).

Rahman, M. (2010) 'Queer as Intersectionality: Theorising Gay Muslim Identities', *Sociology*, 44(5), 1–18.

Rapport, N. and Dawson, A. (eds.) (1998) *Migrants of Identity: Perceptions of 'Home' in a World of Movement* (Oxford: Berg).

Remnick, D. (2013) 'Gay Rights and Putin's Olympics', *The New Yorker*, 13 December. Available at: http://www.newyorker.com/online/blogs/comment/2013/12/gay-rights-and-putins-olympics.html, last accessed 7 March 2014.

Rich, A. (1980) 'Compulsory Heterosexuality and Lesbian Existence', *Signs*, 5(4), 631–660.

Richardson, D. (1998) 'Sexuality and Citizenship', *Sociology*, 32(1), 83–100.

Richardson, D. (2000) *Rethinking Sexuality* (London: Sage).

Richardson, D., McLaughlin, J. and Casey, M. (eds.) (2006) *Intersections Between Feminist and Queer Theory* (Basingstoke: Palgrave Macmillan).

Riessman, C. K. (1993) *Narrative Analysis* (Newbury Park, CA: Sage).

Riessman, C. K. (2004) 'Narrative Analysis', in Lewis-Beck, M. S., Bryman, A. and Futing Liao, T. (eds.) *Encyclopaedia of Social Science Research Methods* (London: Sage), 705–709.

Rimashevskaia, N. (2003) 'Family and Children During the Economic Transition', in Twigg, J. L. and Schecter, K. (eds.) *Social Capital and Social Cohesion in Post-Soviet Russia* (London: M. E. Sharpe).

Riordan, J. (1996) 'Sexual Minorities: The Status of Gays and Lesbians in Russian-Soviet-Russian Society', in Marsh, R. (ed.) *Women in Russia and Ukraine* (Cambridge: Cambridge University Press), 156–172.

Rivkin-Fish, M. (1999) 'Sexuality Education in Russia: Defining Pleasure and Danger for a Fledgling Democratic Society', *Social Science and Medicine*, 49(6), 801–814.

Rivkin-Fish, M. (2006) 'From "Demographic Crisis" to "Dying Nation": the Politics of Language and Reproduction in Russia', in Goscilo, H. and Lanoux, A. (eds.) *Gender and National Identity in Twentieth-century Russian Culture* (DeKalb, IL: Northern Illinois University Press), 151–173.

Rivkin-Fish, M. (2010) 'Pronatalism, Gender Politics, and the Renewal of Family Support in Russia: Towards a Feminist Anthropology of "Maternity Capital"', *Slavic Review*, 69(3), 701–724.

Rofel, L. (1999) *Other Modernities: Gendered Yearnings in China After Socialism* (Berkeley, CA: University of California Press).

Rooke, A. (2007) 'Navigating Embodied Lesbian Cultural Space: Towards a Lesbian Habitus', *Space and Culture*, 10, 231–252.

Rosenfeld, D. (2002) 'Identity Careers of Older Gay Men and Lesbians', in Gubrium, J. F. and Holstein, J. (eds.) *Ways of Aging* (Oxford: Blackwell), 160–181.

Rosenfeld, D. (2009) 'From Same-Sex Desire to Homosexual Identity: History, Biography, and the Production of the Sexual Self n Lesbian and Gay Elders' Narratives', in Hammack, P. L. and Cohler, B. J. (eds.) *The Story of Sexual Identity: Narrative Perspectives on the Gay and Lesbian Life Course* (Oxford: Oxford University Press), 425–452.

Rostow, W. W. (1971) *The Stages of Economic Growth: A Non-Communist Manifesto* (London: Cambridge University Press).

Rotkirch, A. (2000) *The Man Question. Loves and Lives in Late 20th Century Russia* (Helsinki: Department of Social Policy, Resarch Reports 1/2000).

Rotkirch, A. (2002) 'Liubov' so Slovami i Bez Slov: Opyt Lesbiiskikh Otnoshenii v Pozdnesovetskom Periode', in Zdravomyslova, E. and Temkina, A. (eds.) *V Poiskakh Seksual'nosti* (Saint Petersburg: Dmitrii Bulanin), 452–468.

Rotkirch, A. (2004) 'What Kind of Sex Can You Talk About? Acquiring Sexual Knowledge in Three Soviet Generations', in Bertaux, D., Thompson, P. and Rotkirch, A. (eds.) *On Living Through Soviet Russia* (London: Routledge), 91–117.

Rotkirch, E. and Temkina, A. (2007) 'Sovetskie Gendernyie Kontrakty i ikh Transformatsiia v Sovremennoi Rossii', in Zdravomyslova, E., Rotkirch, A., Tartakovskaia, I., Temkina, A, Tkach, O. and Chernova, Zh. (eds.) *Rossiiskii Gendernyi Poriadok. Sotsiologicheskii Podkhod* (Saint Petersburg: Izd-vo Evropeiskogo Universiteta v Sankt-Peterburge), 169–200.

Rudolph, R. and Brade, I. (2005) 'Moscow: Processes of Restructuring in the Post-Soviet Metropolitan Periphery', *Cities*, 22(2), 135–150.

Rushbrook, D. (2002) 'Cities, Queer Space and the Cosmopolitan Tourist', *GLQ*, 8(1–2), 183–206.

Rust, P. C. (1993) ' "Coming Out" in the Age of Social Constructionism: Sexual Identity Formation Among Lesbian and Bisexual Women', *Gender and Society*, 7(1), 50–77.

Rust, P. C. (2000) 'Bisexuality: A Contemporary Paradox for Women', *Journal of Social Issues*, 56(2), 205–221.

Ruting, B. (2008) 'Economic Transformations of Gay Spaces: Revisiting Collins' Evolutionary Gay District Model', *Australian Geographer*, 39(3), 259–269.

Said, E. (1978) *Orientalism* (London: Routledge and Kegan Paul).

Sakwa, R. (1999) *Postcommunism* (Oxford: Oxford University Press).

Sarajeva, K. (2010) ' "You Know what Kind of Place this is, don't You?" An Exploration of Lesbian Spaces in Moscow', in Gdaniec, C. (ed.) (2010) *Cultural Diversity in Russian Cities: The Urban Landscape in the Post-Soviet Era* (Oxford and New York: Berghan Books).

Sarajeva, K. (2011) *Lesbian Lives: Sexuality, Space and Subculture in Moscow* (Stockholm: Acta Universitatis Stockholmiensis).

Scherrer, K. (2008) 'Coming to an Asexual Identity: Negotiating Identity, Negotiating Desire', *Sexualities* 11(5), 621–641.

Schmidt, V. (2006) 'Multiple Modernities or Varieties of Modernity?', *Current Sociology*, 54(1), 77–97.

Scott, J. (1986) 'Everyday Forms of Resistance', *Journal of Peasant Studies*, 13(2), 5–35.

Sedgwick, E. (1990) *Epistemology of the Closet* (Berkeley, CA: University of California Press).

Seidman, S. (ed.) (1996) *Queer Theory/Sociology* (Oxford: Blackwell Publishers).

Seidman, S. (2004) *Beyond the Closet. The Transformation of Gay and Lesbian Life* (London: Routledge).

Seidman, S., Meeks, C. and Traschen, F. (1999) 'Beyond the Closet? The Changing Social Meaning of Homosexuality in the United States', *Sexualities*, 2(1), 9–34.

Shaw, D. (1999) *Russia in the Modern World: A New Geography* (Oxford: Blackwell Publishers).

Shlapentokh, V. (1989) *Public and Private Life of the Soviet People: Changing Values in Post-Stalin Russia* (New York: Oxford University Press).

Silova, I. (ed.) (2010) *Post-Socialism Is not Dead: (re)Reading the Global in Comparative Education* (Bingley: Emerald Books).

Simpson, R. (2009) *Contemporary Spinsterhood in Britain: Gender, Partnership Status and Social Change* (Saarbrücken: VDM Verlag).

Skeggs, B. (1997) *Formations of Class and Gender: Becoming Respectable* (London: Sage).

Skeggs, B. (1999) 'Matter out of Place: Visibility and Sexualities in Leisure Spaces', *Leisure Studies*, 18, 213–232.

Skeggs, B. (2001) 'The Toilet Paper: Femininity, Class and Mis-Recognition', *Women's Studies International Forum*, 24(3/4), 295–307.

Sozaev, V. (ed.) (2010) *Vozmozhen Li "Kvir" po-Russki? LGBTK Issledovaniia. Mezhdistsiplinarnyi Sbornik* (Saint Petersburg: Vykhod).

Stanko, E. A. (1985) *Intimate Intrusions: Women's Experience of Male Violence* (London: Routledge and Kegan Paul).

Stein, A. (1997) *Sex and Sensibility: Stories of a Lesbian Generation* (Berkeley, CA: University of California Press).

Stella, F. (2007) 'The Right to be Different? Sexual Citizenship and its Politics in Post-Soviet Russia', in Kay, R. (ed.) *Gender, Equality and Difference During and After State Socialism* (Basingstoke: Palgrave Macmillan), 146–166.

Stella, F. (2008a) *Lesbian Identity and Everyday Space in Contemporary Urban Russia.* Unpublished PhD thesis. Department of Central and East European Studies: University of Glasgow.

Stella, F. (2008b) 'Gomofobiia Nachinaetsia Doma', *Ostrov*, September.

Stella, F. (2008c) 'Homophobia Begins at Home: Lesbian and Bisexual Women's Experiences of the Parental Household in Urban Russia', in Healey, D. (ed.) 'Queer Issue', *Kultura. Online Russian Cultural Review*, June, 12–16. Available at: http://www.kultura-rus.uni-bremen.de/, last accessed 7 March 2014.

Stella, F. (2010) 'The Language of Intersectionality: Researching "Lesbian" Identity in Urban Russia', in Taylor, Y., Hines, S. and Casey, M. (eds.) *Theorizing Intersectionality and Sexuality* (Basingstoke: Palgrave Macmillan), 212–234.

Stella, F. (2012) 'The Politics of in/Visibility: Carving Out Queer Space in Ul'yanovsk', *Europe-Asia Studies*, 64(10), 1822–1846.

Stella, F. (2013a) 'Lesbian Lives and Real Existing Socialism in Late Soviet Russia', in Taylor, Y. and Addison, M. (eds.) *Queer Presences and Absences* (Basingstoke: Palgrave Macmillan), 50–68.

Stella, F. (2013b) 'Queer Space, Pride and Shame in Moscow', *Slavic Review*, 72(3), 458–480.

Stella, F. (2014) 'Issledovaniie Zhizni Lesbiianok v Sovetskoi Rossii: Pokolencheskii Podkhod', in Kondakov, A. (ed.) *Na Perepute. Metodologiia, Teoriia i Praktika LGBT i Kvir-Issledovaniii. Sbornik Stat'ei* (Saint Petersburg: Tsentr Nezavisimykh Sotsiologicheskikh Issledovanii), 231–248.

Stenning, A. (2005) 'Where Is the Post-Socialist Working Class? Working-Class Lives in the Spaces of (Post)Socialism', *Sociology*, 39(5), 983–999.

Stephenson, S. (2006) *Crossing the Line: Vagrancy, Homelessness and Social Displacement in Russia* (Aldershot: Ashgate).

Stroganova, A. (2012) 'Ekaterina Samutsevich: "Nikakikh Gastrolii ne Budet"', *RFI*, 18 October. Available at: http://www.russian.rfi.fr/rossiya/20121018-ekaterina-samutsevich-nikakikh-gastrolei-ne-budet, last accessed 7 March 2014.

Štulhofer, A. and Sandfort, T. (eds.) (2005) *Sexuality and Gender in Postcommunist Eastern Europe and Russia* (New York: Haworth Press).

Stychin, C. F. (2003) *Governing Sexuality: The Changing Politics of Citizenship and Law Reform* (Oxford: Hart).

Suny, R. (1999) 'Socialism, Post-Socialism, and the Appropriately Modern: Thinking About the History of the USSR', *Journal of the International Institute*, 6(2). Available at: http://hdl.handle.net/2027/spo.4750978.0006.207, last accessed 7 March 2014.

Suny, R. and Martin, T. (eds.) (2002) *A State of Nations: Empire and Nation-Making in the Age of Lenin and Stalin* (Oxford: Oxford University Press).

Svašek, M. (2005) *Postsocialism: Politics and Emotions in Central and Eastern Europe* (New York: Berghahn Books).

Takács, J. (2006) *Social Exclusion of Young Lesbian, Gay, Bisexual and Transgender (LGBT) People in Europe* (Brussels: ILGA Europe/IGLYO).

Taylor, J. (2010) 'Queer Temporalities and the Significance of "Music Scene" Participation in the Social Identities of Middle-aged Queers', *Sociology*, 44(5), 893–907.

Taylor, Y. (2007) *Working Class Lesbian Life: Classed Outsiders* (New York: Palgrave Macmillan).

Taylor, Y. (2008) ' "That's Not Really My Scene": Working-Class Lesbians In (and Out of) Place', *Sexualities*, 11(5), 523–546.

Taylor, Y. (2009) *Gay and Lesbian Parenting: Securing Social and Educational Capital* (Basingstoke: Palgrave Macmillan).

Taylor, Y., Hines, S. and Casey, M. (eds.) (2010) *Theorizing Intersectionality and Sexuality* (Basingstoke: Palgrave Macmillan).

Temkina, A. and Zdravomyslova, E. (2002) *V Poiskakh Seksual'nosti* (Saint Petersburg: Dmitrii Bulanin).

Thornstad, D. (1995) 'Homosexuality and the American Left: The Impact of Stonewall', in Hekma, G., Harry, O. and James, S. (eds.) *Gay Men and the Sexual History of the Political Left* (Binghamton, NY: Harrington Park Press).

Thornton, S. (1995) *Club Cultures: Music, Media and Subcultural Capital* (Cambridge: Polity Press).

Titova, V. (2002) 'Also Sprach ZEMFIRA. Lesbiiskii Sindrom v Russkom Roke', *KontrKul'tura*. Available at: http://lesbiru.com/art/music/sindrom.html, last accessed 5 September 2004.

Tuller, D. (1996) *Cracks in the Iron Closet. Travels in Gay and Lesbian Russia* (Chicago: Chicago University Press).

Turbine, V. (2007) 'Russian Women's Perceptions of Human Rights and Rights-Based Approaches in Everyday Life', in Kay, R. (ed.) *Gender, Equality and Difference During and After State Socialism* (Basingstoke: Palgrave Macmillan), 167–186.

Valentine, G. (1993a) 'Negotiating and Managing Multiple Sexual Identities: Lesbian Time-Space Strategies', *Transactions of the Institute of British Geographers*, 18(2), 237–248.

Valentine, G. (1993b) 'Desperately Seeking Susan: A Geography of Lesbian Friendship', *Area*, 25(2), 109–116.

Valentine, G. (1995) 'Out and About: Geographies of Lesbian Landscapes', *International Journal of Urban and Regional Research*, 19(1), 96–111.

Valentine, G. (1996) '(Re)Negotiating the "Heterosexual Street". Lesbians' Production of Space', in Duncan, N. (ed.) *Body Space* (London: Routledge).

Valentine, G. and Skelton, T. (2003) 'Finding Oneself, Losing Oneself: The Lesbian and Gay "Scene" as a Paradoxical Space', *International Journal of Urban and Regional Research*, 27(4), 849–866.

Valentine, G., Skelton, T. and Butler, R. (2003) 'Coming Out and Outcomes: Negotiating Lesbian and Gay Identities with, and in, the Family', *Environment and Planning D: Society and Space*, 21, 479–499.

Valentine, G., Vanderbeck, R., Andersson, J., Sadgrove, J. and Ward, K. (2010) 'Emplacements: The Event as a Prism for Exploring Intersectionality. A Case Study of the Lambeth Conference', *Sociology*, 44(5), 925–943.

Valocchi, S. (2005) 'Not Yet Queer Enough: The Lessons of Queer Theory for the Sociology of Gender and Sexuality', *Gender and Society*, 19(6), 750–770.

Vicinus, M. (1992) ' "They Wonder to Which Sex I Belong": The Historical Roots of Modern Lesbian Identity', *Feminist Studies*, 18(3), 467–497.

Vicinus, M. (2004) *Intimate Friends: Women Who Loved Women, 1778–1928* (Chicago: University of Chicago Press).

Waites, M. and Kollman, K. (eds.) (2009) Special Issue on the Global Politics of Lesbian, Gay, Bisexual and Transgender Human Rights, *Contemporary Politics*, 15(1).

Ward, J. and Winstanley, D. (2005) 'Coming Out at Work: Performativity and the Recognition and Renegotiation of Identity', *Sociological Review*, 53(3), 447–475.

Weeks, J. (1996) 'The Construction of Homosexuality', in Seidman, S. (ed.) *Queer Theory/Sociology* (Oxford: Blackwell Publishers).

Weeks, J., Heaphy, B. and Donovan, C. (2001) *Same-Sex Intimacies: Families of Choice and Other Life Experiments* (London: Routledge).

Weeks, J., Holland, J. and Waites, M. (2003) *Sexualities and Society. A Reader* (Cambridge: Polity Press).

West, D. J. and Green, R. (eds.) (1997) *Sociolegal Control of Homosexuality: A Multi-Nation Comparison* (New York: Plenum Press).

Weston, K. (1991) *Families We Choose: Lesbians, Gays, Kinship* (New York: Columbia University Press).

Weston, K. (1993) 'Lesbian/Gay Studies in the House of Anthropology', *Annual Review of Anthropology*, 22, 339–367.

Weston, K. (1995) 'Get Thee to a Big City: Sexual Imagery and the Great Gay Migration', *GLQ*, 1(2), 253–277.

Widerberg, K. (2010) 'In the Homes of Others: Exploring New Sites and Methods When Investigating the Doings of Gender, Class and Ethnicity', *Sociology*, 44(6), 1181–1196.

Wilkinson, C. (2013) 'Putting Traditional Values into Practice: Russia's Anti-Gay Laws', *Russian Analytical Digest*, 138, 8 November, 5–7.

Wilson, A. (2006) 'Queering Asia', *Intersections: Gender, History and Culture in the Asian Context*, 14. Available at: http://intersections.anu.edu.au/issue14/wilson.html, last accessed 31 January 2012.

Wittrock, B. (2000) 'Modernity: One, None, or Many? European Origins and Modernity as a Global Condition', *Daedalus*, 129(1), 31–60.

Wolff, L. (1994) *Inventing Eastern Europe: The Map of Civilization on the Mind of the Enlightenment* (Stanford: Stanford University Press).

Yurchak, A. (2006) *Everything Was Forever, Until it Was no More. The Last Soviet Generation* (Princeton: Princeton University Press).

Yuval-Davis, N. (1997) *Gender and Nation* (London: Sage).

Zdravomyslova, E. (2001) 'Hypocritical Sexuality of the Late Soviet Period: Sexual Knowledge and Sexual Ignorance', in Webber, S. and Liikanen, I. (eds.) *Education and Civic Culture in Post-Communist Countries* (Basingstoke: Palgrave Macmillan), 151–167.

Zdravomyslova, E. (2003) 'The Café Saigon Tusovka: One Segment of the Informal-Public Sphere in Late-Soviet Society', in Humphrey, R., Miller, R. and Zdravomyslova, E. (eds.) *Biographical Research in Eastern Europe: Altered Lives and Broken Biographies* (Aldershot: Ashgate), 141–180.

Zdravomyslova, E. and Temkina, A. (2007a) 'Sovetskii Etakraticheskii Gendernyi Kontrakt', in Zdravomyslova, E., Rotkirch, A., Tartakovskaia, I., Temkina, A, Tkach, O. and Chernova, Zh. (eds.) (2007) *Rossiiskii Gendernyi Poriadok. Sotsiologicheskii Podkhod* (Saint Petersburg: Izd-vo Evropeiskogo Universiteta v Sankt-Peterburge), 96–137.

Zdravomyslova, E. and Temkina, A. (2007b) 'Neotraditsionalizm(y) – Transformatsiia Gendernogo Grazhdanstva v Sovremennoi Rossii', in Zdravomyslova, E., Rotkirch, A., Tartakovskaia, I., Temkina, A, Tkach, O. and Chernova, Zh. (eds.) *Rossiiskii Gendernyi Poriadok. Sotsiologicheskii Podkhod* (Saint Petersburg: Izd-vo Evropeiskogo Universiteta v Sankt-Peterburge), 201–212.

Zdravomyslova, E. and Temkina, A. (2007c) 'Ot Litsemeriia k Ratsionalizatsii: Transformatsiia Diskursivnogo Rezhima Seksual'nosti', in Zdravomyslova, E., Rotkirch, A., Tartakovskaia, I., Temkina, A, Tkach, O. and Chernova, Zh. (eds.) *Rossiiskii Gendernyi Poriadok. Sotsiologicheskii Podkhod* (Saint Petersburg: Izd-vo Evropeiskogo Universiteta v Sankt-Peterburge), 213–226.

Zdravomyslova, E., Rotkirch, A., Tartakovskaia, I., Temkina, A., Tkach, O. and Chernova, Zh. (2007d) *Rossiiskii Gendernyi Poriadok. Sotsiologicheskii Podkhod* (Saint Petersburg: Izd-vo Evropeiskogo Universiteta v Sankt-Peterburge).

Zdravomyslova, E. and Voronkov, V. (2002) 'The Informal Public in Soviet Society: Double Morality at Work', *Social Research: An International Quarterly*, 69(1), 49–69.

Zelenina, G. (2006) 'Safo, Sufrazhistki, Sem'ianinki? V Poiskakh Lesbiiskoi Obshchiny i Kul'tury v Sovremennoi Rossii', *Russkii Zhurnal*, 15 May. Available at: http://russ.ru/politics/docs/safo_sufrazhistki_sem_yaninki, last accessed 30 September 2006.

Zhuk, O. (1998) *Russkie Amazonki: Istoriia Lesbiiskoi Subkul'tury v Rossii XX-go Veka* (Moscow: Izd-vo Glagol).

Zven'eva, A. (2007) *Golubaia Elita Rossii* (Moscow: Algoritm).

Index

Note: The letter 'n' following locators refers to notes

189

Printed by Printforce, the Netherlands